"Rose?"

"Jake?" I started arou

"Come here."

I hurried to him and he reached for my hand pulling me onto his lap.

"Are you going to be all right?" He searched my face as he pushed back my tousled hair. "You've been from the depths of emotion to the heights. That's a lot to deal with."

I was moved by his concern, this man who refused to love me. Tears pricked my eyes.

"I'll be okay."

He wrapped his arms around me, the first time he'd initiated such a move. I rested my head on his shoulder. We sat there quietly for several minutes. I let out a deep sigh, grateful beyond words for his comfort and presence.

I sat up and looked at him. "Thank you for being my tower of strength these last few days. I don't know how I would have survived without you."

He looked acutely embarrassed but pleased. I leaned over to give him a gentle thank-you peck on the cheek, but he turned his head and suddenly we were kissing. I clutched at him as my head spun and my insides melted as under a summer's desert sun.

Jake pulled back to gasp for air. "There's this woman," he mumbled against my lips.

"I know." I ran my finger down his jaw. "You won't love her."

"I won't." And he kissed me again.

But she'll love you, I thought. *Always and forever.*

♥ *Palisades Pure Romance*

THE DECISION

GAYLE ROPER

Palisades is a division of Multnomah Publishers, Inc.

This is a work of fiction. The characters, incidents, and dialogues are products of the author's imagination and are not to be construed as real. Any resemblance to actual events or persons, living or dead, is entirely coincidental.

THE DECISION
published by Palisades
a division of Multnomah Publishers, Inc.

© 1999 by Gayle Roper
International Standard Book Number: 1-57673-406-4

Design by Andrea Gjeldum
Cover art by Aleta Jenks

Scripture quotations are from *Holy Bible,* New Living Translation (NLT)
© 1996. Used by permission of Tyndale House Publishers, Inc.
All rights reserved.

Palisades is a trademark of Multnomah Publishers, Inc., and is registered in the U.S. Patent and Trademark Office.

Printed in the United States of America

For information:
MULTNOMAH PUBLISHERS, INC.•P.O. BOX 1720•SISTERS, OREGON 97759

Library of Congress Cataloging–in–Publication Data
Roper, Gayle G.   The decision/by Gayle Roper.
p.cm.–(Palisades pure romance)   ISBN 1-57673-406-4
(alk. paper)   I. Title. II. Series.
PS3568.068D44   1999   99-39372   813'.54–dc21   CIP

99 00 01 02 03 04 05—10 9 8 7 6 5 4 3 2 1

To my wonderful friends in the Evening Writers Arena,
Bonnie, Deb, Georgia, Pat, and Rose,
what would I ever do without you?

And with thanks to the kind folks at T. Burke,
who let us plot mayhem and romance
while we hoot and holler at our table
for hours on end.

God saved you by his special favor when you believed.
And you can't take credit for this;
it is a gift from God.
Salvation is not a reward for the good things we have done,
so none of us can boast about it.

EPHESIANS 2:8–9

One

THE FORCE OF THE BLAST KNOCKED ME TO THE GROUND.

I fell into Sophie Hostetter's beautiful red impatiens lining the front walk, breaking off the brittle stems with my legs, torso, even my head. It no longer mattered whether or not the predicted first frost of our warmer than normal autumn struck tonight. The plants were decimated, a fact I grasped much more readily and with more distress than the event that had tossed me willy-nilly into them and had ground expensive licorice bark mulch into my palms and forehead.

Being thrown to the ground by forces too strong to counter was beyond my experience. When the displaced air pushed ahead by the expanding gases of the explosion hit me in the back and sent me sprawling, when the heat of the resulting fire scorched me through my sweater and turtleneck, I couldn't comprehend it. Impatiens I knew; impatiens I could understand. Exploding cars and searing heat were beyond my ken.

Instinctively I raised my hands over my head and pulled my knees to my chest, belatedly protecting myself. I tried to think, to break through the gray fog of shock. After all, I was a nurse and an EMT. I was used to catastrophe. But I usually dealt with the aftermath of other's pain, not participated in it. I was the one who bound up the wounded, not the one who lay flattened, deafened, and blank minded.

I stared at the shattered impatiens and reached out tentatively as if I thought I could repair them. A bruised and bereft crimson flower sat softly on the back of my right hand. I studied it with the intensity of a philosopher, seeking the secrets of the universe in its fragile red petals. Unfortunately, even if I'd discovered some deep truth, I was too fuzzy to comprehend it. My head ached from its encounter with terra firma, and my ears rang from the concussive roar that had filled the air. Even my vision was fuzzy, but I instinctively knew that was because my glasses had fallen off.

Somewhere in the deep recesses of my mind, the part that always responds to personal trauma with denial and trivia, I was thankful that I was wearing my uniform as a home health nurse, navy slacks and cardigan. They wouldn't show the dirt. Then I realized I was lying with my blue-and-white turtleneck nearly buried in soil, mulch, and bleeding flowers.

Rose Martin, RN, EMT, grubby mess.

I sighed and tried to remember if I had any clean uniforms left. If I didn't, did I have any bleach alternative detergent? Or had I used it all up last week? I fretted over the issue like it really mattered and berated myself when I couldn't recall.

I sighed again and slowly my mind began to function rationally. The thought of laundry receded, the least of my problems, and reality hit with the impact of the explosion itself.

I uncurled and pushed myself to my knees. I retrieved my glasses from the mulch and blew them clear. The great roaring continued to fill the air as I forced myself to look at the fire, not a cozy, inviting fire like in a living room hearth, but a conflagration, a pulsing sea of flames, writhing, consuming what had been Ammon Hostetter's car.

And Ammon Hostetter, nice guy and ineffectual CEO of his family's highly successful toy business.

And Sophie Hostetter, his mother and my patient. Sweet Sophie who had suffered so long and so devastatingly. Who had been going on her first outing after several debilitating weeks of chemotherapy. Who had been so excited to finally breathe outside air and watch the bittersweet bloom in the fence rows and cornstalks get collected for silage by silent, industrious Amishmen with flatbed wagons pulled by their horses.

Sophie, who had struggled so to live.

Oh, God, I prayed in terror and distress. *Oh God!* My

mind could form no other words. My eyes shut to block out the devastation of the fire. The Town Car was totally engulfed.

I steeled myself and staggered to my feet. I moved toward the fire, but the intensity of the flames made a close approach impossible.

I circled the car at an awkward run, hand held before my face to protect my eyes from the staggering heat, trying to see if there were someplace the fire wasn't totally overwhelming, someplace I could get near the vehicle, someway I could offer help.

Smoke ascended, twisting and wrapping in on itself like some mythical monster. The flames were undulating arms raised skyward, awful in their red, orange, and white hot glory. The air was acrid with the raw odor of hot metal and burning tires.

My heart fought the realization that there was no life-saving care I could give here. Finally, filled with sorrow, I stumbled toward the house to call 911.

I'd almost reached the front door of the Hostetters' great home on the golf course when a second explosion rocked the early November afternoon and knocked me down again. This time it wasn't brittle impatiens that took the brunt of my fall but my forehead as I struck it against the first riser of the shallow cement front steps.

Pain lanced across my skull, along my neck, and flashed down my spine. Groaning, I rolled on my side and reached up a shaking hand. I found broken skin and blood. The area was tender to the touch, and a swelling had already developed.

I turned back to the blaze, watching it pulse with renewed life, and saw with horror that pools of fiery gasoline were spreading from beneath the car, rivers of flame racing across the drive.

"My car!" I yelled and ran raggedly to the white sedan with Lancaster Home Health Group stenciled on the side along with the agency logo of a blue cross with the outline of a house superimposed over the cross. I threw open the door, wrenched the keys from my slack's pocket, and hit the gas. I drove out onto Route 23 and parked the car as close to the property's privacy hedge as I could. I didn't think the fire would get this far.

"911," I whispered as I rested my aching head on the steering wheel for a minute to ward off vertigo. My eyes were watering from the smoke, and my ears still rang. Even the air here on the far side of the hedge reeked with the odor of burning gasoline. I grabbed the car phone and punched in the emergency numbers.

After I made my report, I called my office to tell them I wouldn't be able to make my last two visits. Madylyn, our whiny office manager, was not pleased.

"Deal with it, Madylyn," I snapped and slammed down the phone. I wasn't up to cajoling or peacemaking right now.

I slid from the car and crept back around the hedge to see whether the fire was still raging so wildly. It was. I looked with a strong sense of unreality at the scene and beyond to the house.

And I froze at what I saw through the pulsing waves of heat and smoke.

Standing at the front door of the mansion, mouth agape, shock in his eyes, was Peter Hostetter watching the conflagration.

"Oh, God!" I prayed inarticulately once again. Tears of sympathy wet my face and a vise gripped my stomach, tightening, tightening until I felt I might implode from the pressure. His mother and his older brother!

I skirted the site of the accident and raced up the front steps.

"Peter!" I laid a hand gently on his arm as I shouted to be heard above the roar of the fire. "Let's wait inside until help comes."

He didn't hear me. He didn't even see me.

I grabbed him and shook. "Peter!"

He looked at me without recognition, confusion struggling with vagueness in his eyes.

"Peter! It's me, Rose! Come inside while we wait for help!"

His eyes slid from me to the car.

"Ammon." His voice was barely audible through the ringing in my head. "Mother."

I swallowed against my tears. "I know." I pushed against him, trying to move him into the house, away from the terrible inferno. He held his place against me for a short minute, then sagged suddenly against the jamb. When I felt his body give, I pushed as hard as I could. We went flying into the vast entry hall, knocking against the pair of antique balloon-back chairs Sophie had found just before her devastating bout with cancer.

We struggled to stay upright, grabbing the curved backs of the chairs for stability.

"Sit here," I ordered when my head stopped spinning. I pushed him down, and disoriented, sweaty, and gray, he folded passively under the pressure, collapsing on a petit-point seat. His breathing was shallow and his pupils were great black circles as he stared out the open front door. I rushed to close it, blocking his view.

In the distance we could already hear sirens, not surprising since the fire company was right down the street. Help was near.

I sank into the twin of the chair Peter sat in and swallowed against tears.

Peter looked at me and shuddered. "I was almost in that car."

I nodded. "I know."

"I was going with them on the ride."

I nodded again.

"I just came in for some sunglasses." He clutched them in his right hand. He looked at me wildly. "That could be me out there!" His voice climbed the scale with every word, his emotional chaos obvious.

"But it isn't." I reached to pat his hand again. "You're fine."

"Right," he said, pulling back from my touch. "I'm fine."

When he pulled back, his elbow cracked against the

chair back, and the pain made him flinch. He swung around to see what he'd bumped, swearing as he rubbed at the ache.

"Your mother loved these chairs." I trailed my fingers over the curving arch of cherry wood that formed the back of my seat.

And she had. In a house filled with valuable antiques and reproductions, Sophie had prized these chairs with their mauve needlepoint seats worked with delicate bouquets of cream, pink, crimson, and green.

"It's the petit point that makes the chairs valuable, so I don't let anyone sit in them," she'd told me once. "They date to the nineteenth century." She grinned. "That's why I keep them in the hall. Everyone gets to see and admire them, but no one uses them because no one sits in the hall."

"Mother loved beautiful things," Peter whispered as he stared at the wedge of seat visible between his legs. He continued to rub his elbow absently.

"She loved you," I whispered back, but if he heard me, he gave no sign.

Rarely had I spoken truer words. Sophie had loved both her boys with a fierceness borne of the unexpected blessing of late-in-life babies. Though these babies were both men now, towering over their mother with strong, hard bodies and equally strong, willful spirits, Sophie's dedication and intense affection had never waned. If anything, it had increased in the three years since their father's death.

"I'm probably the only person who loves them for themselves," Sophie had told me one day not long ago as I checked her vital signs and drew blood. "They are such wealthy young men that people want to get close to them for all the wrong reasons."

"Don't they say it's just as easy to fall in love with a rich man as a poor one?" I asked with a smile.

Sophie laughed. "So they say. But I want the girls Ammon and Peter finally choose to marry to love them like I loved Tom. All the money makes it hard to discern true feelings."

She looked at me speculatively. "You aren't looking for a nice, rich husband, are you?"

We had laughed companionably as I tried to think of a kind way of saying no.

"Don't worry," she said, patting my hand. "I'm teasing."

Now the question of a wife for Ammon was moot, I thought sadly. I glanced at Peter drooping in his chair. And a wife was certainly the last thing on his mind and would be for a very long time.

Suddenly the sirens outside stopped, and the muffled sounds of car doors slamming and people shouting filtered in to where Peter and I sat. It wasn't long until the front doorbell rang.

A uniformed cop entered the front hall and stood with his arms away from his body in that policeman stance accommodating all the gear hanging from his belt.

"Are you two all right?" he asked.

Peter and I nodded.

"What happened?"

"The car exploded," Peter said. "And I was almost in it!"

The cop looked at Peter's neatly pressed chinos and blue oxford shirt under a navy cable sweater. "You were near the car when it blew?" he asked politely.

"No. I was in the house getting my sunglasses, but I was supposed to be in it." He patted his chest pocket where the glasses bulged slightly under his sweater. "I just ran back for them. The glare, you know. I was supposed to be in the car!"

The uniform nodded and looked at me. I could see him assessing my grubby clothes and abraded forehead.

"Are you sure you're all right?"

I nodded, then glanced down at myself. "I had just tucked a lap robe around Mrs. Hostetter and was walking back to the house when the first explosion came. It knocked me into the flower bed. The second one knocked me into the front steps." I indicated my forehead.

The cop nodded. "I want the two of you to remain here and talk to the detective assigned to the case. Why don't you wait here, Ms...." And he waited for my name.

"Rose Martin. I've been Mrs. Hostetter's home health nurse."

He nodded. "That your car outside the hedge?"

I nodded. "I was afraid it might catch fire too."

"Right." He pointed to the chair I'd just vacated. I sat down again gratefully.

"You, sir," he said to Peter, "can wait in the living room."

Peter hesitated. "But my mother and my brother."

The policeman looked questioningly at him.

"The people in the car," I said to the officer. "Sophie and Ammon Hostetter."

The cop looked at Peter. "And you are?"

"Peter Hostetter."

"Well, Mr. Hostetter, if you'd wait in the living room for the detective, I'd appreciate it. And if there is any news from outside, I'll see that you get it. And I'm sorry for your loss."

Peter blinked. "Thank you." He turned and walked to the living room.

It was almost two hours before the police were finished with me. The detective on the case turned out to be a guy named Lem Huber. I went to school with his younger brother Al at Twin Valley High School. I knew Lem as the football star three years older than Al and me, then as the college man who showed up at Al's high school games to cheer for him. Most recently, I had run into him at the hospital a couple of times when my ambulance runs and his investigations overlapped.

"Well, well, Rose Martin," he said when he came in.

I felt my tension level diminish dramatically when I saw him.

"So tell me everything you know," he said as he sat in the companion balloon chair. "Nice and slow and detailed."

He let me talk without interruption. Then he questioned

me politely about what I had said, asking the same questions from several different points of view. I answered as thoroughly as I could, but it all came down to one thing as far as I was concerned: through some terrible accident Sophie and Ammon Hostetter had died.

When Lem finally told me I could leave, I sighed with relief. I grabbed my medical equipment, my purse, and keys and rushed out the front door. Fire equipment and emergency vehicles still filled the drive and lawn, many with lights revolving, all with static pouring from their radios. The fire was long extinguished, but all the attendant chaos of a crisis was present, including men and women in a variety of uniforms talking and laughing, now that the immediate need was met. Police officials were examining what was left of the Town Car under high-voltage lights. Yellow scene-of-the-crime tape was draped all over the lawn.

I was so consumed with relief that I could finally leave, I was unprepared for what I saw. Memories long buried leaped at me, overwhelming me, choking me, a kaleidoscope of emotions tearing reason and control from me. My stomach heaved and I grabbed one of the porch pillars to keep from falling.

"Rose?" Lem spoke behind me, and his hand came out to help support me.

I swallowed once, twice, and tried to contain the incipient panic swelling inside, the great beast who waited in the shadows to devour me whenever my guard was down.

I pushed myself away from the pillar. "I'll be all

right," I said with what I hoped sounded like assurance, though I suspected I was so white he wouldn't believe anything I said even if my voice had been steady, which regrettably it wasn't. "Too many memories."

Lem nodded as he continued to hold my elbow. "This was pretty bad."

I made a little noise he took for assent, and I allowed him to think that it was the horror of today's events that had overcome me. It was safer that way.

Lem raised an arm and waved, and the next thing I knew, one of the firefighters was holding up two fingers and asking, "How many?"

I glared at him. "I do not have a concussion."

"Now how would you know?" he asked with a smile.

"I'm a nurse."

"Ah." He studied the knot on my forehead in the porch light.

"And an EMT."

"Good for you, sweetheart." He poked around the injury. "But even a First Responder like me knows this needs to be cleaned out and disinfected."

"Ouch." I flinched as he got too enthusiastic. "So clean it."

"Inside," he ordered. This time I sat in the kitchen and squirmed as he painted my forehead orange with Mercurochrome.

"Hey," I groused. "Where's the disinfectant cream? Or the saline/hydrogen peroxide? Or even Bactine? Anything less obvious."

"We ran out of solution and cream at the last call and haven't been back to base to get a replacement. And they don't give me Bactine. I personally love Mercurochrome. I always carry some for special cases like you." He stepped back and studied his handiwork. I didn't like his smug grin.

I took my orange forehead and my sagging energy level and went outside again. But this time I was prepared. I had my thoughts firmly in neutral as I walked across the yard and out to my car. I drove into Lancaster and to the Home Health Group office, my mind a careful blank. I pulled into the parking area behind the office and parked the car, concentrating on nothing. I unlocked the back office door and put all my supplies away, signing the supply sheets and requisition orders, thinking only of pleasing Madylyn. I got into my blue Civic and started for home.

I hadn't gone very far when my mind, never very quiet at the best of times, exploded. Images flashed through my mind with the relentless pulse of the light strip on a police cruiser. Fire, crushed impatiens, sirens, static, yellow police tape. Surviving brothers with sunglasses. Firefighters with Mercurochrome. Polite detectives with fine brown hair that floated every time they turned their heads.

And rushing white water, swollen and angry, creaming over rocks.

And the inevitable, "Rose, what happened?"

It didn't take much intelligence to realize just how

close to the edge I was.

"I'm fine. Really. I'm fine." I repeated it to myself like a litany. Maybe if I said it often enough, it would become true.

But coming out of the house and seeing those lights and hearing that static had brought such a rush of agony, I was unlikely to feel fine for quite some time. I hadn't had this strong a flashback in years.

You're being stupid, I told myself. You're a nurse and an EMT. You deal with emergencies much too frequently to be spooked like this.

But that's when I'm the healer, the helper. I fix the problems. I don't cause them.

But you didn't cause the problem today.

No, I didn't, but I didn't prevent it, either.

Like you could have. What are you, prescient?

I shrugged away that bit of logic and went back to the real crux of my distress.

But I was the cause then.

The little voice that had been answering me back was uncomfortably quiet.

Suddenly I knew I wasn't going to make it home. I felt the bile rise in my throat and swallowed desperately against the impulse to vomit. I felt the tears begin, blurring my vision until I could barely see the road. I felt the shaking start deep in my stomach, and I knew it would radiate outward until my whole body shook.

Oh, God!

I blinked madly, desperately.

Oh, God! I have to get off the road before I fail again, before I'm the cause again.

And I saw the answer to my prayer loom out of the darkness, a white farmhouse with green trim, clean, and orderly and known. I pulled into the Zooks' drive, shoved the car in park, and fell to pieces.

Two

I DON'T KNOW HOW LONG I SAT IN THE ZOOKS' DRIVE. MY normal thought processes and emotional responses were very much on the fritz. It was one of those terrifying times when thinking is too horrendous and your mind copes by going blank. I sat gripping the wheel, unable to do anything but sob for a long time. At least it felt like a long time. In reality it may have been only a few minutes.

Then I tossed my glasses on the passenger seat because they suddenly felt too tight for my swollen, overheated face. I hugged myself as I shivered and cried and generally made a fool of myself, though I suppose since no one saw me but me, I didn't, strictly speaking, play the fool. But I felt the pain. Oh, how I felt the pain.

I saw Sophie's smiling face, full of excitement over her foray into the real world.

I saw Ammon's kind face as he helped his mother with the seat belt.

Then the image jumped, and I saw my mother's ravaged face, my father's terrified face, Rhoda's dead face. The ache in my chest expanded until I could barely breathe.

Oh, God, I cried for what was surely the millionth time. *Help me! I don't want Rhoda to be dead! I don't want Sophie to be dead! Or Ammon! Please! Oh, God! Please!*

A sharp rap on the driver's side window made me jump, and a small scream erupted like a little verbal geyser. I spun and saw a dark figure looming in the night, the shape blurry through the condensation formed on the window by my weeping and harsh, heavy breathing.

I was too emotionally drained to feel fear, though I wondered resentfully just who was insensitive enough to bother me while I felt like this.

"Roll down the window," a man requested, his voice made hollow by the glass between us.

I was so depleted with my personal agony that I couldn't respond. All I could do was stare. Tears still streamed down my face, and the relentless pounding in my head continued unabated, but I didn't seem to be shaking anymore, a fact that gave me a strange, foolish pride.

"Open the window!" the voice said, this time an order, courteous but implacable.

He spoke with such quiet authority that I struggled

to obey with hands so uncoordinated that I could barely push the little button on the door panel. After long moments I managed to lower the window a couple of inches.

"What?" I asked in a thready whisper. I began to yearn desperately for a tissue, for several tissues, for a box of tissues as tears dripped off my chin onto my chest. I grabbed the edge of my cardigan and wiped ineffectually across my face.

The man leaned over and peered at me. He wore a broad-brimmed black hat but no beard. "What are you doing here?" he asked, not unkindly.

Now there was a foolish question.

"Crying," I said and sniffed. I lowered my head to my hands where they again rested on the steering wheel. It was too great an effort to hold myself upright. "Crying."

Suddenly a flashlight was shining on me, or rather on the top of my head and what little of my face wasn't blocked by my arms.

"Rose? Is that you?" The man's voice was hesitant, disbelieving.

I nodded without lifting my head. I recognized the voice of Elam Zook. I was parked in his driveway, or rather that of his father, John. Elam and John, staunch and upright Amishmen, worked the family farm together.

I leaned wearily back against the headrest and looked toward the partially opened window, blinking in the glare. "Hi, Elam." I barely made a sound in spite of the great effort the words took.

"Rose!" he said in horror.

Well, now I knew what I looked like.

"Iss die Rose?" another male voice asked, and John Zook peered in the window at me. "Ach, look at her!" He was highly distressed.

"Hi, John," I managed. "I'm—" I swallowed against the constriction in my throat. "I'm just borrowing your driveway for a few minutes. I won't be long." I tried to sound like it was an everyday occurrence that I drove into driveways, parked with my motor running and my lights on, and sat sobbing my heart out.

"Rose." A third voice was both stern and concerned.

I looked as John moved aside and Jake rolled up to the window in his wheelchair, his trusty German shepherd Hawk at his side. I smiled, or at least I tried to. I always smiled at Jake, prickly, handsome, marvelous Jake.

He looked at me, skewered in the stark light his brother held to my face, and muttered something harsh under his breath. "Lower this window," he ordered.

I didn't move.

"Rose," he growled. "Lower the window all the way."

I nodded but still didn't move.

Jake made a disgruntled noise and grabbed the door handle. He pulled. Nothing happened. "Unlock the door. Now."

What a good idea, I thought, but what came out in a weak, quavering voice was, "Stop yelling at me."

"Rose." His voice was full of exasperation and warning.

"Right," I said, looking at the door. It seemed miles away, but I wanted to make Jake happy. I always wanted to make Jake happy. Maybe that was because when we first met, I'd thought he died.

I studied the buttons on the door panel, trying to decide which one was the lock. With great resolve, I reached and pushed. The window slid all the way down.

I sighed and smiled weakly. "Sorry," was all I could manage as two big tears slid down my cheeks.

Jake looked at me and shook his head. I couldn't tell if it was in pity or exasperation. He reached inside the car, pushed the right button to release the lock, and pulled open my door. He maneuvered around it and wheeled his chair right to the edge of my seat. He sat there studying me for a long minute.

"Hi," I whispered, rolling my head toward him and trying to smile. Without warning, my voice broke off in a great sob. I felt myself begin to shake again.

"I'm s-sorry. I'm s-sorry!" And I shook harder. "You're so brave and I'm—"

"Rosie!" The distress in his voice washed over me like a soothing balm, but I couldn't stop the tremors or the tears.

He reached across me to where my hands lay limply in my lap. He grasped them, held them between his palms, and rubbed until they felt warm for the first time in hours. Then he grabbed my wrists and pulled.

"What?" I mumbled as I automatically pulled back.

"Come here," he said as he continued to tug.

I hadn't the strength to continue fighting him. I let him draw me out of the car and onto his lap.

"Jake! I can't sit on you! I'll hurt you!" I tried to pull away.

"A little thing like you? Never." He put a hand on my waist and held me in place. Hawk put his head on my knee.

"But your legs!"

"They can't feel you, Rose. Don't worry."

So I sat stiffly on his knees with my tear-ravaged face, my wild woman hair, and a bad case of the hiccups I'd gotten from all the crying. Elam continued to shine the flashlight on me. I put my hands to my face to block both the light and Jake's view of me. I wasn't surprised to feel tears slide between my fingers. At the rate I was weeping, I'd be suffering from dehydration momentarily.

Jake pulled my hands from my face and held them again in his strong ones.

"Tell me. Tell me what's wrong."

"Oh, Jake, it was awf… I s-saw…" I couldn't articulate a complete sentence. I took a deep breath. "Sophie and Ammon. And the lights! The static!"

He put his hand under my chin and turned me to face him. He looked at me like what I had just said made sense.

"If it's got you this upset, it must have been rough," he said, reaching out to push my hair off my face. For the first time he noticed the abrasion on my forehead.

"Rosie!" He ran a finger softly over my skin, being careful not to touch the injury itself. "What happened? Did you fall? Or have an accident?"

"No," I said, answering the last question. It was too difficult and too confusing to remember everything he asked. I was too tired. "I didn't have an accident."

The flashlight beam moved off of me, and Elam, John, and Hawk began a careful tour of my car, looking for dings and collapsed fenders.

"I didn't," I protested weakly.

"I don't see anything," Elam said when they completed their circuit.

John nodded agreement. "The car's fine."

"I told you." I was irritated that they hadn't taken my word.

"Then what?" Jake asked again. His voice was so gentle. If I weren't already crying, I'd have burst into tears at his concern.

My feelings for this man were so complicated, yet so fierce. I'd known him for two years, ever since the night he was nearly killed outside my mother's home in Honey Brook. I had sat with him in the street in the pouring rain that night while we waited for the medevac helicopter to arrive to transport him to the trauma unit at Brandywine Hospital in Coatesville. I felt his failing vital signs and watched the emergency techs shake their heads. I thought he died. I even planted a little cross by the site of his accident as a memorial.

It was a year before I learned he was alive. I met Kristie Matthews who boarded here at the farm, and she told me he had survived. I took down my little cross, but almost another year passed before I actually met the man. When his mother took a terrible fall on the cellar stairs during the summer, I'd been on the emergency crew that took Mary to the hospital. Then I'd been the home health nurse assigned to her care when she returned to the farm.

Often on my visits to Mary, I'd talked with Jake, lingering after I should have left for my next case. I enjoyed our conversations and apparently so did he. He made it a point to be around when I had a visit scheduled. We talked about everything from his parents' strict faith to why I liked being a nurse to how his life had changed in the past two years.

After my official visits to Mary ended, I stopped by unannounced two more times, ostensibly to check on her but really to talk with Jake. He'd been home one time, and we talked for an hour. He was absent the next time, and I was appalled at the disappointment I felt at missing him. I knew I couldn't stop again unless he specifically invited me. Otherwise, I was setting myself up for heartbreak.

Jake called me after that second visit, saying Mary had told him I'd dropped by. His voice on the phone made my mouth go dry and my palms sweat. Since then he called at infrequent intervals, always surprising me, always getting the same physical reaction. We talked every time for an hour or two. But he never mentioned meeting or my coming to the farm or his coming to my place. Just friends talking.

Only it always felt like more. Or maybe, more accurately, almost more.

One thing I'd never told Jake was that Rose, the home health nurse, was the same Rose who sat in the street with him. He didn't want to meet the latter, a matter of pride as far as I could discern. Rose in the street had seen him at his worst, his most vulnerable. As a man who liked to be in control, he found it bad enough to be confined to a wheelchair. To be reminded of the night his world had collapsed was more than he could handle.

So even though I thought his feelings on this issue foolish, I'd never told him that I was Rose from the street. In all our conversations about life and death and God and salvation, I'd never told him. Someday I would, when the circumstances were right. It certainly wasn't my intent to be less than truthful with him. After all, I was a woman who prided herself in being honest. Soon, I always told myself. Soon.

Now as I sat on his lap, I was thinking only about the comfort he was to me. If I couldn't cope with the memories that plagued me, he would handle them for me. He would take my pain and transfer it to his strong shoulders, barely bending under the load that was driving me into the ground. Against all reason, I knew Jake could fix my troubles. I didn't understand how he could do something that monumental; I just knew he could.

If he wanted to.

The problem was that he'd never shown in the slightest fashion that he wanted to do anything as personal as cope on my behalf. He never showed he wanted to be anything more than my casual friend, just like Elam and the rest of the Zooks. It was only in my dreams that he was interested in being God's man for me. In real life he wasn't interested in being anyone's man, not mine and certainly not God's.

"What happened?" he repeated softly, studying the lump on my forehead in the renewed blaze of the flashlight.

"I fell. When the second explosion came, I hit my head on the step."

"The second explosion?"

I nodded. "The first one just knocked me down. It didn't hurt me, really it didn't, but it didn't do the impatiens any good."

"Uh-huh," he said, just like he understood what I was talking about. "And that's why you're crying? It hurts? Did you see the doctor about it?"

The man has to stop with these multiple questions, I thought as I reached up and felt the knot gingerly. I shook my head ever so slightly. As pain shot through my temples, I winced, stilled, and said, "No."

"No, what? No, it doesn't hurt? No, you didn't see a doctor? No, you're not crying because you hit your head?"

"No, I mean yes, it hurts, and no, I didn't see a doctor. A firefighter treated me. Can't you see the disinfectant he painted me with?"

"I thought maybe you treated yourself."

"I'd never paint myself orange."

"And that's why you're crying?" There was a slight smile in his voice. "You don't want to be orange?"

I tried to frown at him, but my orange forehead wouldn't pucker well. "That's not why I'm crying and you know it."

"So why?" he prompted when I fell silent. His voice was a shade less patient. "Because you fell?"

"No." I shut my eyes against the glare of the flashlight still shining in my face. I knew I was frustrating him with my inability to get the story out. I took a deep breath. I could tell this. I could. But for some reason, I couldn't.

"You're crying because of the second explosion?"

"No."

"Because of the first explosion?"

"No."

"Were you on an emergency call?"

"No."

There was a short silence. I could almost feel Jake looking at Elam and John for help. And I could swear I heard both of them shrug.

"Come on, Rose," Jake said, a faint edge to his voice. "Help me out here."

"The light," I said.

"You're crying because of the light?"

"No," I whispered. "Make them turn it off."

Immediately the light slid away from my face, though it didn't go out.

"I'm sorry, Rose," Elam said. "I should have thought."

I nodded. "It's okay." I looked at Jake beseechingly.

"Father, Elam," Jake said without taking his eyes from me. "Why don't you two go inside?"

That's the way it often was between Jake and me. We understood each other on some wordless level. In the long conversations we had after I treated Mary, we often disagreed, but we also finished each other's sentences. Tonight somehow he knew I wanted to talk to him alone.

The two men hesitated. Then Elam said, "You'll bring her in when she's feeling better? Mom'll be very upset if you don't."

Jake nodded and the flashlight suddenly went out completely. John and Elam walked toward the house where the soft, gentle light of Coleman lanterns and kerosene lamps glowed in the windows. No electric lights for the Zooks. No curtains to block the light, either. They kept the *Ordnung*, the oral collection of laws that governed Amish society.

All except Jake. He'd rebelled, and the rebellion had led to his accident. His mother thought his paralysis was his punishment from God, but she loved him fiercely anyway.

Jake rolled his chair—and me—back until there

was room to shut the car door. The ceiling light went out and the darkness of the autumn night wrapped around us.

"Oh, Jake." I sighed, my voice ragged.

"It'll be okay," he whispered, lifting a hand to wipe at my tears. His other hand continued to rest on my waist. Hawk sat beside us and stared at me.

"No." I whispered, disconsolate. "Never."

"Oh, Rosie." His voice was gentle again. "What happened?"

"Lights," I said, trying to explain. "Static. They died!" And I grabbed him about the chest and buried my face against his denim shirt. I couldn't stop the tears. He wrapped his arms around me and held me, waiting for the storm to pass.

"It's all right," he whispered over and over again as he gently stroked my hair and patted my back. "You're going to be fine. It'll be all right."

"No." I drew a deep, quivering breath. "Even God can't make it right."

I felt his surprise. "Is this Rose the Evangelist making such a statement?"

Immediately I tried to cover my faithless tracks. "Not that God can't get me through it. It's just that what's done is done."

"Ah."

We were silent for a little while. I rested against him, drawing strength from his strength, until I became so self-conscious that I had to sit up. In fact, I needed to get off his lap completely. I needed to remind myself that his lap wasn't mine.

I straightened and stood. He let me.

"Why don't you sit in the car?" he suggested. "Then we can be eye to eye."

I nodded and opened the car door. Out of the side of my vision I saw Jake raise his body from his chair, holding himself suspended by his arms for several seconds. It was part of his routine to prevent pressure sores. Change position every fifteen minutes. Maintaining good health when confined to a wheelchair was no simple matter.

I fiddled with the dashboard until I found the knob that turned off the overhead light. I wanted the cocoon of darkness for a while longer.

When Jake resumed his seat and wheeled to the car, I levered my seat as far back as it would go, then sat sideways, facing him, my feet resting on the ledge of the open door. Our knees met between us.

"Okay," Jake said briskly. "Suppose we start with the first explosion."

I nodded. "Did you ever have any Pockets when you were a kid?"

Jake looked at me strangely. "Yes. Mom always put them in all our pants from Father on down to Elam."

Now it was my turn to look at Jake strangely. "Your father played with Pockets?"

"I doubt he played with them. He carried things in them just like I did."

Realization dawned. "Not pockets. Pockets. Capital

P. The little cars." I made a small rectangle with my hands.

Jake nodded. "Gotcha. And one of them exploded?"

I gave a little laugh. "I wish." I was quiet a minute.

"Hey, there." Jake tapped on my knee with an index finger. "You were saying?"

"Right. Well, one of my clients was Sophie Hostetter. Her late husband Tom was the one who invented Pockets."

"Yeah? I had a Pockets car when I was a kid. I found it at Kauffman's Market when we went to get peaches for jam. Some English kid must have left it behind. I was fascinated with it. There I stood in my straw hat and Amish haircut, my little shirt and black broadfall pants, a horse and buggy waiting outside to take us home, and I had a car! My very own car!"

I was caught by the picture of Jake as a little boy, bangs dangling over his forehead, bare feet hanging out of too short pants, dazzled by the forbidden object. "What did your mother say?"

"I didn't tell her. She was so busy lugging bushels of peaches around that she never noticed. I kept that little blue car hidden for years. I never even showed it to my brothers. One of the first things I did when I was old enough and had some money was buy myself a blue car just like my Pockets."

"Sophie gave me the special collector's set of sixty cars," I said, feeling absurdly proud.

Jake whistled, suitably impressed. "Tell me, do all

the car's doors open or was I just lucky to get a special one?" Jake asked. "I've always wondered."

"I don't know. I've never opened the set."

"What?" Jake clutched his chest. "You have this complete set of Pockets, and you've never played with them? Be still, my heart."

I actually grinned. "Thanks."

He grinned back, the hard planes of his face softening. "You're welcome."

My smile slowly faded as I watched this man I was afraid I loved. "What happened to your Pockets?"

"I still have it."

"What?"

"I do. It's on the end table in the living room. I kept it in my bedside table at the rehab center as a reminder that someday I was going to drive again. It took me a while to get my license, but I owe it all to my trusty blue Pockets."

"Sophie would have loved that story. I wish I could tell it to her."

"She died?" Jake's voice was gentle.

I felt the tears again. "The explosion. She and her son Ammon." I cleared my throat, pushing down the welling emotion. "It was her car that exploded. I was there."

Jake, who had been leaning toward me while we talked, fell back in his chair as if someone had pushed him. "Rose! You saw this?"

"Well, I didn't actually see either explosion. I had

my back turned. That's why I was knocked down on my face instead of my bottom. But I saw the fire." I started to rub my aching forehead only to wince when I dragged my fingers over the lump. "Oh yes, I saw the fire."

"Rose, I don't know what to say!"

I shrugged. "I've seen terrible things before. Scraping up people after accidents or shootings isn't exactly pleasant. But I knew Sophie." Again the welling of tears. "And there were all the lights and the static from the radios." My voice faltered and fell silent. I gripped my hands and pressed them to my chest. I started to tremble again.

Jake reached out and took my hands in his. He pulled them down to his knees and began to rub his thumbs absently over the backs of them.

"You mentioned the lights and the static before." He looked at me closely. "Why did they affect you so much? You've seen lots of revolving lights and heard lots of radio static in the course of your emergency runs."

"Rhoda," I said in a whisper.

"I thought her name was Sophie."

"It was. But it reminded me too much of Rhoda."

He shook his head in a flash of irritation. "Rose, you're rambling again. Who's Rhoda?"

"My sister."

"Was she with you? Was she hurt?"

"Rhoda's dead. She's been dead for fifteen years. This just brought it all back." I started to sob. "I'm sorry. I feel like such a baby." Normally I rarely cried, but tonight I couldn't stop.

"It's okay," Jake said. "Memories can be very painful things."

I glanced at him through my tears. His memories must be excruciating at times. I wondered which hurt him more, the memories of running or of the torture of rehab? And I cried harder.

Somehow I found myself on Jake's lap again, his voice gentling me, his hand soothing me. I don't know when I realized that I wasn't crying for the past anymore. I wasn't even crying for Sophie and Ammon or for Jake. I was crying for myself and the fact that it had been fifteen years since anyone had rubbed my back and told me everything would be all right.

Three

FINALLY I FELT SOME SEMBLANCE OF CONTROL. MY BREATHING had slowed and my weeping seemed over. I still wanted that box of tissues.

"I'd better go." I sounded all cloggy, like I had a major head cold. I stood and sniffed, I hoped discreetly. "I've given you enough trouble for one night."

I reached for the car door, my movements slow and lethargic. I had run on an adrenaline high all through the aftermath of the explosions and the police interviews. This experience of intense energy and superior mental clarity was nothing new to me. It occurred each time I ran with my emergency crew, each time I dealt with the unexpected at some accident scene. The adrenaline was even responsible for my hysterical collapse. Too much juice. As a result I couldn't cope with my usual calm.

Equally familiar was the inevitable languor that

struck with the draining away of the adrenaline. Now I had all the energy of melted ice.

"I need to get home," I repeated.

Jake made a noise deep in his throat, one that said don't be dumb. "Mom wants you to come in before you go."

I thought of the way I must look, the way I felt. "I don't think so."

Jake continued like I hadn't spoken. "And you're in no condition to drive anywhere anyway. You're shaking like a leaf."

Immediately I stuck my hands in my pockets. "I'll be all right."

Jake made that throaty sound again.

"Don't threaten me," I said but with no heat. I hadn't the energy to get angry. What I was was embarrassed. I'd made a blithering idiot of myself in front of Jake and to some degree John and Elam. The last thing I wanted to do was repeat the performance in front of the rest of the family. I wanted to get away so I could blush and squirm—and mourn—in private.

"Besides, what are you going to do if I leave? Beat me up? Send Hawk after me to corner me until you catch up? Tie me to the wheelchair and take me inside forcibly?"

He reached out and poked me in the side. I jumped. He poked me again and grinned. "I'll just tickle you until you do as I say."

I backed out of his reach and scowled. "Don't you dare."

"Get in the house, woman," he said, pointing up the front walk. "Mom'll be angry at both of us if you don't."

"Mary never gets angry," I said. "She's a lady and an Amish one at that."

"Correction," Jake said. "Mom never yells, but she does get angry. It shows in lumpy gravy and under-cooked potatoes and shoofly pie without a wet bottom. Get in the house or we'll all suffer for your pride."

My pride? I glared at him and he stared back, one eyebrow cocked in challenge.

"You're a martinet, Jake Zook," I muttered as I stalked up the walk to the house. "And you're a fine one to talk about pride."

"I bet you think I don't know what *martinet* means, don't you? Well, I'm a college man now, you know, not a junior high dropout. And I recognize an insult when I hear one."

"Good! I'd hate for a fine slur to be misunderstood."

I thought I heard a soft chuckle, but when I swung to look at him in the dim light by the front steps, he merely looked arrogantly back.

"Go on," he ordered in true martinet fashion. "Get up those steps and knock on the door. Mom's waiting. You're keeping her and Father up."

I narrowed my eyes at his gall. I wasn't the one who wanted this visit! He narrowed his eyes back, as clear a dare as I'd received in a long, long time.

Then it hit me and I smiled slowly. "I know what you're doing. And you think you're so clever. You're trying to get me mad so I'll stop being weepy."

He snorted. "You think so, huh?"

"I know so. I bet that's what they did to you in the rehab center, right? Make the guy mad and then he'll fight."

"Well, then, smart lady, start fighting and get up those steps. I'm cold."

Sudden, sharp guilt sank fierce talons into my raw conscience. He was cold, and it was my fault, keeping him out here in this weather all this time. He had been stationary long enough to make any able-bodied person chilled, but he dealt with a body temperature that didn't regulate itself well due to his injury. "I'm sorry."

He rolled his eyes. "Don't you dare take on any more guilt! I've been out here because I wanted to be. Got that? But I don't want to be out here anymore, so get inside. Now!"

I pulled myself up the stairs with all the enthusiasm of a kid going to the doctor's office for a shot. I glanced over my shoulder, hoping against hope that Jake had wheeled himself off and I could escape. No such luck. He sat there, his hooded hawk's eyes staring at me. With poor grace, I knocked on the front door.

When Mary answered, Jake said softly, "I'll see you in the living room in a couple of minutes."

He disappeared around the side of the house, heading for the ramp at his front door. He'd follow that inside, then wheel through his apartment to the connecting door to his parents' house.

Mary was on me like a mama bear on her hurt cub. She tsk-tsked and patted my hand. She sat me in her favorite rocker. She examined my knotty forehead and felt for a temperature.

"Get a damp cloth, Esther," she ordered. "And make Rose a cup of tea."

"I'm okay, Mary," I protested. "Really. I'm fine." But as unwilling as I'd felt about being with people, I had to admit that, like arid soil under a spring rain, my wounded spirit soaked up the love and concern she showered on me.

Jake came through the doorway into the great room that filled the first floor of the Zooks' home just in time to hear me tell Mary I was fine. He snorted. I pointedly ignored him and let his mother pat my hand.

Next thing I knew Mary was wiping my face with the cool cloth, and fragrant tea was waiting for me on the little table beside my chair.

"Thank you," I whispered as I rested my head against the back of the chair. What a luxury, being cared for like this! Usually I was the one who cared, not the one who was cared for.

I felt Jake's eyes on me. When I finally looked at him, he gave me a half smile as if to say, "See? You love being fussed over just like everyone else. And if you need to cry some more, it's okay."

Then he winked, and I swear I blushed.

"Are you sure you're all right, Rose?" Esther hovered over me, her brown eyes wide with concern, her rosy cheeks stained a deeper pink than usual.

Esther wasn't a Zook, but during the summer after Mary fell down the stairs, she had come to serve as a *maud* or maid for the family, something unmarried women often did within the community when the need arose. Expediency dictated that the men of the family, needed in the fields, not care for Mary. So Esther had moved into the room vacated when Mary and John's daughter Ruth had married and moved to Honey Brook with her husband Isaiah.

I smiled at Esther. She was so beautiful with her head of rich chestnut hair caught beneath her organdy *kapp,* but I couldn't tell her she was lovely. Her whole life she had been taught to emphasize community at the cost of self, and compliments called attention to the individual in a most prideful way.

"I'm fine, Esther." I took a drink of tea, jerking as I scorched my tongue. "Really, I'm fine."

I ignored Jake's soft snort of disbelief.

Esther didn't look any more convinced about my condition than Jake, so I forced myself to sit up straight in Mary's rocker. I'd be fine if it was the last thing I did, just to prove to them all that I could do it.

Mary went to the kitchen with the damp cloth in her hand, and I sat up straighter still as I realized she was walking with a limp. "Mary! Your leg!"

She turned and shrugged. "Some days it's better than others, but it's always bad at night when I'm tired."

"Arthritis?"

She sighed. "In the ankle and the hip. I tell John that I am a better forecaster of rain than that forecaster he has in the barn." She walked to me with a freshened cloth that she put across my forehead. "But it's you we're worried about."

"A couple of her friends died today," Jake said. "It's hit her hard."

Mary looked horrified. "I should think so." And she patted my head until I felt like Hawk.

"Mom," Jake said gently, "you're hovering."

Mary immediately withdrew her hand.

"No!" I glared at Jake. "Don't listen to him. Hover. Please."

She placed her hand gently on my head for a minute, then took a chair near me. "You drink your tea," she ordered. "Then Esther can take you up to the empty apartment over Jake's rooms."

"Oh, Mary!" I was touched by her kindness. "I can't stay."

"But Esther's already made up the bed for you."

"I need to get home."

"Why?"

"Yeah," Jake said. "Why?"

I sputtered a bit but could come up with no good reason. No one waited for me there, not even a cat. My landlord wouldn't allow pets. No one would know whether I slept in my own bed or not. Certainly no one would care.

"In fact," Jake said, "I think you should stay the

whole weekend." He looked at his mother who nodded her strong agreement.

"Oh, I couldn't!" But the thought of being around these caring, thoughtful people instead of alone with the nightmares of today was so attractive.

"Certainly you could," Mary said. "Please stay."

Esther nodded.

I wondered what the sleeping John and Elam would think when they rose at dawn and found yet another English girl invading their house. I decided suddenly that I didn't care. I had cried out to God that I couldn't handle my memories, that I needed help. He had given me the Zooks.

"Yes." I felt the tears again, but this time they were good tears. "I'd love to stay."

"Okay," Jake said. "Finish your tea and I'll drive you to your place to get whatever you need."

"That's okay. I can get the things myself."

"No, Rose, you can't." Jake's tone of voice brooked no argument.

I argued anyway. "I'll zip right over and be back in no time." I stood.

"You really have a hard time accepting help, don't you?" Jake said as he wheeled directly in front of me.

"Jake," Mary murmured. "She's had a hard day."

"She's got a hard head, you mean."

I was stung by his comment. "I do not! It's just that I can take care of myself."

"Who said you couldn't?"

"You!" I stared daggers at him.

"All I did was offer to take you so you wouldn't have to drive, upset as you are. I was being nice, for heaven's sake!"

"Yeah. Right. Such a fine gentleman," I said sarcastically and was immediately ashamed. He was being nice.

"Rose, you will let me drive you. You will come along quietly. You will stop being so stubborn." He said it all through clenched teeth.

"Rose," Esther said quietly, "You must allow Jake to help you. You mustn't deny him that blessing."

I stared at her. Helping me would be a blessing to Jake? While I wasn't convinced of that, the better part of wisdom is knowing when you're beaten.

"You're right, Esther." I smiled at her. When I looked at Jake, I couldn't quite sustain the smile. "Thanks, Jake," I said stiffly.

I'll give Jake credit. He didn't gloat, not even once, as we went out to his van.

He drove with confidence and competence, his hands quick on the controls. He parked in front of the house where I had a small apartment on the second floor. I ran in, grabbed a duffel, and packed for the weekend. I stashed two novels and my Bible on top of my clothes. As I pulled the front door closed, I was glad I wasn't going to be here alone for two days.

We made the entire trip back to the farm in silence, but it was a comfortable hush that spoke of friendship and ease. All my anger was long gone as was his frustration with my immature refusal of help. I guess one definition of friendship could be when one friend sees the other at her worst and doesn't hold it against her.

Jake left me at the foot of the stairs to his parents' house. There he whispered, "Sleep well, Rose."

I bent and kissed his cheek. "I'm sorry for being so ungrateful. I don't know what I would have done without you, and I don't know how to thank you."

As I straightened, he ran a finger down my cheek. "Then don't try." And he wheeled away.

When I woke the next morning, I lay in bed staring at walls so white they shimmered in the sunlight's glare. I shivered in the crisp cold and pulled the quilt, a patchwork of crimson and blue calicos, more tightly about my shoulders. I turned my head and saw a cluster of white, yellow, and ruby mums, surely the last of the season, squished rather inelegantly into a Mason jar. I hadn't even noticed them last night, but I imagine Esther had brought them for me from her own room.

I was in the apartment that Kristie Matthews, then Cara Bentley had rented prior to their marriages. I was sleeping in the bedroom directly above Jake's bedroom, occupying one of the rooms on the second floor of the *grossdawdy haus,* or granddaddy house, an ell added to the main house.

Jake's grandparents had originally lived here when they retired from the main responsibility for the farm, turning both the farm and the main house over to John, Mary, and their family. The senior Zooks had been killed several years ago in a buggy-car accident, something that used to be a much more frequent occurrence before the Amish began putting reflective triangles and blinking lights powered by batteries on the back of their buggies. They also added bicycle reflectors around the two sides and top of the buggies, sprinkled there much as the blood of lambs must have been sprinkled on the doorposts and lintels of the homes of the Israelites in ancient Egypt. Now on a dark night, a driver had warning before he was suddenly on top of the slow-moving buggies.

The grossdawdy haus had a small living room, bedroom, kitchen, and bath on Jake's level. On my level were two good-sized rooms, the bedroom I was in and a living room, and a small bath.

I knew that when Jake had come home from the rehab facility after his accident, his parents had realized he'd never be Plain again. The need to accommodate their injured son had caused them to play mental tag with the Ordnung. They had brought in electricity and phone service to this wing of their home, providing exactly what Jake needed: privacy and convenience with help as close as his parents in the main body of the house. Since the electricity and phone didn't go into the main house, Mary and John hadn't actually broken the Ordnung, though a legalist could argue that they had bent it a far amount.

I snuggled down further under the quilt and

thought of Jake somewhere in the rooms below me. For reasons of his own, he'd rejected the Ordnung and the Plain life, refusing the custom to join the church in his late teens. Instead, he'd rebelled and hadn't stopped until his motorcycle landed on his back in the street by our house. And even then, he'd continued to rebel in his heart.

I sighed. Jake and his complexities were more than I could deal with this morning, at least before a shower and a cup of coffee. I glanced at the window again and could see rime about the edges of the glass, crystal shards growing across the pane in an intricate and beautiful pattern. If I hadn't already done in Sophie's impatiens, the morning frost would have.

I shivered. The room was frigid with a late November chill, since in the chaos of last night, no one had thought to turn on the electric strip heater.

The chaos of last night! I began to shiver in earnest.

Sophie! And Ammon! And poor Peter, left all alone!

And flashing lights and crackling radios and memories long feared.

I sat up abruptly and felt the fear lessen as the cold wrapped its tentacles about me.

Don't think of explosions and fires and screaming. Don't think of static and flashing lights! *Oh, God, please don't let me think about it! Help me remember how wonderful Sophie was, how funny she was, always with spirit and pluck even at the worst of times.*

I thought of her love for Ammon and Peter and the way her face softened when she talked about them.

"People say Pockets is our greatest achievement," she told me once. "But Tom and I knew it was the boys. Our boys."

Ammon was tall, fair, and blue eyed like his father had been. In fact, he looked amazingly like the pictures of Tom Hostetter that sat in marvelous ornate frames all over the house.

Sadly, I often suspected that this physical resemblance was the extent of Ammon's similarity to his brilliant and principled father. Not that Ammon was weak or unintelligent. He was just...ordinary. A regular person. Someone most families would be proud of, even boast about, but who didn't hold a candle to his clever, inventive father.

But Sophie saw him as his father's equal, and even as I disagreed, I appreciated her mother's heart.

Peter, in contrast to his brother, was Sophie's image: short, dark, and with her intensity, if not her God-heart. He was handsome, but her fine, aristocratic features were blurred a bit in him, like he was a poor copy in which the colors all ran a bit about the edges. Her great, almost black eyes gleamed with life; Peter's merely saw things. Her quick mind made her conversation lively and thoughtful; Peter merely talked.

But again Sophie never saw her son as less that wonderful. Her mother's love wouldn't let her.

"Ammon is the older son and his path has always been to become CEO at Hostetter, Inc.," Sophie told me one day.

"Sort of like primogeniture in Olde England?" I asked.

"It's what Tom always wanted. Besides, no company can have two men in charge. Someone has to be the one who calls the shots. First it was Tom. Now it's Ammon."

"So what's Peter supposed to do?" I asked with more acid than wisdom. "Go into the military or the clergy like younger sons used to?"

"Whatever he wants," Sophie said, ignoring my sarcasm. "Whatever he wants."

But what if he wants Hostetter, Inc.?

"He's so smart," she said. "He's going to do very well making his own way." She smiled sweetly, her pride in her son blazing in her eyes.

I must have looked skeptical because she hastened to explain. "Tom owned three-quarters of Hostetter, Inc. His younger brother Ernie, the company's chief financial officer, owns the other quarter. When Tom died, he left me half of his shares and the boys split his other half evenly."

It didn't take much figuring to realize that Sophie held the majority of the shares and therefore the power at Hostetter, Inc. I wondered how Ernie felt about being dependent on a woman. Some men still resented that situation with all that was in them.

"Ernie doesn't mind the younger Ammon being CEO?" I asked, deciding that question was safer than the woman one.

She smiled briefly. "Ernie doesn't have a choice. He

tried a takeover after Tom died. I guess he thought I would be too grief stricken or too dumb to understand what he was trying to do. He offered me a pittance for my shares 'to spare me the pain of having to think.'"

I almost choked. "He actually said that?"

She looked grim. "That's when Ammon took to calling him Evil Ernie."

I couldn't help it. I laughed.

"It is funny," she agreed. "But unfortunately there's truth there, too. I told Tom twenty-five years ago not to take him into the company, but Tom was a softy." She sighed. "We've all had to put up with the man ever since."

"You almost make me glad I don't have a brother."

"We'll give you Ernie," she said. "For free."

I stowed my supplies and prepared to leave. "Thanks but no thanks."

"So you needn't worry about Peter," Sophie said, returning to the topic dear to her heart. "He may not get to run the company, but there's more than enough income from his stock for him to try his hand at making his own fortune without having to sell his shares." She spoke with total confidence in her son's abilities and the company's health.

He can make his fortune if he's clever enough, I thought. And if his income from the stock continues. And it continues only if Ammon's savvy enough to keep the business going, which I wondered about since Ammon made the decision to replace the sturdy metal cars with plastic ones that looked remarkably like every other plastic car on the market. And what if someone comes along with a new company that knocks Hostetter, Inc. from its pedestal? And what if the economy doesn't stay healthy? And what if. And what if. And what if.

What a lot of ifs.

Now it didn't matter whether Ammon had the ability to run the company or not. But at least Sophie wouldn't be disappointed in her son. I wondered what happened to both Sophie's and Ammon's shares now. Peter or Ernie? Or someone else entirely? Someone I knew nothing about?

I sighed. "I'm going to miss you, Sophie," I whispered and actually saw my breath in my frosty room.

I pushed back the quilt and hurried to turn up the electric strip heater. I ran to the bathroom and turned on the shower as hot as I could get it. By the time I finally climbed out, slightly pruney, the room was warm. I pulled on jeans and a thick red sweater over a plaid turtleneck. I tied my sneakers on and clipped my pager at my waist. I was part of the backup on-call first response team for the weekend. If more than one thing at a time went wrong or if there were a major catastrophe, I'd get buzzed.

Oh, Lord, I could use a quiet weekend if it's okay with You.

I went into my living room with its overstuffed chairs, big old-fashioned desk, and wonderful view of the patchwork countryside from each of the windows. I'd always loved the way the small, family-sized Amish farms quilted the countryside with squares of plowed field and fallow field, great barns and white houses. Just miles to the south, great expanses of rolling green fields heralded the great horse farms and Olympic training centers of southern Chester County, but here in Lancaster County, the vistas were close and cozy and somehow comforting.

I went downstairs where Mary and Esther insisted on making me a breakfast of eggs, fried potatoes, and toast. They tried to foist scrapple on me, that mixture of cornmeal and unthinkable ground animal parts, but I managed to convince them not to bother. Esther made me another cup of tea that she served in a mug that advertised International Harvester.

While I ate, Jake came into the room.

"Any extra coffee?" he asked, and Esther quickly brought him a cup.

"What are your plans for the day?" Mary asked her son as she slid a pie in the oven.

"Mom." There was a hint of warning in his voice.

Esther smiled gently, but Mary looked decidedly unhappy. The two women glanced at each other, nodded, and disappeared upstairs.

"What was that all about?" I asked.

"Mom was hovering. We're trying to break her of the habit."

"She does it a lot?" I thought of how much I had liked her hovering last night.

"All the time."

"So?"

"It drives me crazy. It's like I'm five years old. She always wants to know what I'm doing, where I'm going, who I'm going with."

"She cares."

He nodded, acknowledging that truth. Still her abundance of concern obviously rankled. "She smothers if I'm not careful."

I looked at him and couldn't resist. "So," I said brightly, "what are you doing today?"

He turned and looked at me in disgust. I smiled sweetly back.

Slowly his expression turned narrow-eyed and speculative. "Why? Do you want to come along?"

I narrowed my eyes back and answered just as softly. "Do you want me to?"

We stared at each other for a minute before it suddenly struck me: I was flirting! With Jake! Me!

The thought was so surprising that I blinked and sat up straight, flustered. Jake smirked and buried his face in his coffee mug. After a minute of silence during which I tried frantically to think of something to say that didn't sound inane, he set the mug on the table, turned, and rolled to his room.

"See you, Rose."

I never did find out what he was going to do.

I passed the day reading, napping, and taking a walk down the road to the Stoltzfus farm. I had been to that farm in early fall as a home health nurse, caring for a newborn infant with the improbable name of Trevor Stoltzfus. Not that either Trevor or Stoltzfus was unusual. It was just that the combination in an Amish household was far from common.

"What a lovely name," I told his young mother Becky as I weighed the baby.

She grinned. "Not very Amish, is it?"

"How did you decide on it?" I asked.

"I read it once in a novel and liked it. The hero was Trevor."

I cuddled little Trevor, praising him to Becky as a fine boy, but he was so ill that I secretly doubted he'd ever grow up to be anyone's hero.

As I passed the house, I wondered how the little guy was doing. Indeed, as I thought of the tiny chest with the great red wound from palliative heart surgery, I wondered if he were even alive. I hoped so for Becky's sake. Being a single mother at her age was hard enough even when there were no health complications.

I heard the clop of hooves and moved to the side of the road as a buggy pulled from the Stoltzfus's drive. I smiled at Old Nate Stoltzfus and his wondrous white beard, but he kept his eyes fixed straight ahead. He'd never acknowledged me when I came to the house to visit Trevor, either. His impoliteness was doubly obvious since the Amish were most gracious to visitors, even English ones like me.

As I turned and walked back to the Zooks', I decided

that every group had its prickly pears.

It was midafternoon when Mary, Esther, and I sat down at the kitchen table for a cup of tea. We had just begun a conversation about the best way to put up pumpkin, something about which I knew very little and desired to know even less, when there was a knock at the door.

Esther answered and welcomed Becky Stoltzfus in. She was bundled against the chill, little Trevor wrapped in so many blankets that he resembled a roll of cotton batting.

Esther immediately took the baby and began unwinding. Mary rose and took Becky's coat. I got another mug from the cupboard, this one reading John Deere, and poured Becky some tea. When we sat back down at the table, Esther kept little Trevor, cooing and smiling at him. The baby looked back, smiling, and grabbed one of her fingers. Esther melted.

"He's so wonderful, Becky." She bent and kissed his cheek. *"Du bischt an scheeni bubbli."*

He might be a nice baby, I thought, but he was still a very sick one. He should weigh more than he did, and he had the coloring of someone whose system wasn't getting enough oxygen.

"How is he, Becky?" I asked, keeping my voice casual.

"He's doing fine," she said, eyes shining. "We were at the doctor's last week." I didn't know what the doctor had told Becky, but my instinct and training didn't say fine.

Oh, Lord, it doesn't look good. Please intervene on Trevor's behalf.

Esther's tea grew cold as she played with the baby. She rocked him, cuddled him, offered him her finger to grasp. She lifted her hand with his fist clamped about her index finger to her mouth and kissed his thin little hand. He giggled.

"*Scheeni botchi,*" she said, stroking his little hand. "*Scheeni botchi.*"

While Esther entertained Trevor, Mary and I talked with Becky.

"Some days with a baby is hard, ain't?" asked Mary.

Becky nodded. "But he's not really any trouble."

"Does he sleep goot?"

"He sleeps goot but not long." She smiled wearily. "I'm always tired."

"Does your grandmother watch him sometimes so you can get some sleep?" I asked, setting down my almost empty mug. The tea spiced with spearmint Mary had grown was both delicious and refreshing.

Becky hesitated a minute. "No. My grandfather has told her not to touch the baby."

I was stunned. Such action was not at all the typical attitude of the Amish toward babies and little children. They were loving and indulgent toward their offspring for the first two or three years of their lives, giving them unlimited love and lots of attention. Whenever I went into an Amish home for home health reasons, I enjoyed watching how the whole family doted on the babies and toddlers.

"Whyever not?" I asked. "Certainly they don't think that Trevor's illness is contagious."

"It isn't Trevor they have a problem with," she said. "It's me."

"They are very strict," Esther said neutrally. "They have always taken the Ordnung and applied it strictly."

"Not because they are mean," Mary hastened to tell me. "They do not want to hurt Becky. They want to obey *Herr Gott.*"

The thing that always fascinated me about the Ordnung was that it was both elastic and brittle. It changed constantly as the bishops regularly evaluated modern life to see if new inventions and products would aid or disrupt family and church. Seen as acceptable were John's weather forecaster in the barn and the iron-wheeled tractor for stationary use in the barnyard, its power used to run other tools. But if he drove that tractor into the fields or if he traded that forecaster for a regular radio, he would be in big trouble with the church authorities.

Accommodation, I thought. Yet these hair-splitting laws weren't arbitrary, even though they frequently seemed so to us fancy folk. They were designed to preserve family and church, to insure the well-being of the community as opposed to the tastes of the individual.

Tractors in the fields would make the small Amish farms too small to be family undertakings. Children wouldn't be needed to work alongside and be trained by their fathers. Grown sons and daughters would have to go elsewhere to seek employment. Family would disintegrate.

Radios brought godless music, vain teachings, and the outside world to a people who knew their closed community was God's chosen way. The unvetted ideas, greed, and individuality promoted on the airwaves were certain to overwhelm the people unless the very presence of these dangers was forbidden.

If the Ordnung was broken and the community was threatened, it was serious indeed. It was sin and a shunnable offense.

But how did all this legalism apply to Becky and Trevor? It made no sense. Unless it had to do with her unwed pregnancy.

"I'm here because my mother begged them to take me in," Becky said. "They feed me and keep a warm roof over our heads. I am not complaining. I know I'm an embarrassment to them even though they know I confessed my sin before the church."

"Here," Mary said. "Let me get us all some warm tea. If your cup is like mine, it is lukewarm. We don't want lukewarm. The Lord will spew us out of his mouth."

And that quickly the topic was changed. Shortly afterward, Becky wrapped Trevor again and they walked down the road to her grandfather's farm. Mary and Esther began preparing supper and refused to let me help. I went to my rooms and pondered the anomaly of Amish great-grandparents not touching their great-grandson.

At the evening meal Jake made it a point to sit next to me. We both made believe we didn't see Esther and Mary exchange a meaningful glance as they took their places, Mary next to John who sat at the head, Esther between Mary and Elam who sat at the foot. Everyone bowed his head.

I waited for John or maybe Elam to say grace, but no one said anything. Head still bowed, I glanced around. I watched as one by one, heads came up and the food was passed. I found out that sometimes the meal was almost as silent as the grace. John and Elam talked briefly about the harness repair work they were doing in their little smithy in the shed by the barn. Mary said that all the food was prepared for the big meal tomorrow after church at Old Nate Stoltzfus's.

"That's Becky's grandfather?" I asked.

Everyone nodded.

"He pulled out of his lane just as I walked past earlier this afternoon," I said.

"Did he speak to you?" Elam's gray eyes sparkled.

"No." I pictured the frosty old man with the white beard down his chest. "He ignored me."

"He didn't glare or snarl?" Elam grinned at his brother.

"Or shake his fist?" Jake said, grinning back.

"Elam. Chake." John spoke quietly, but both young men immediately wiped their faces clear of emotion. Their eyes, however, continued to dance. I was taken with John's *ch* sound when he said Jake. So Dutch! I had to stifle a grin of my own.

"Becky and the baby walked up this afternoon," Esther said.

"Poor thing," Mary said, and I didn't know if she meant Becky or Trevor.

"Ah yes, the baby." Jake's voice was suddenly sarcastic, though I couldn't understand why. "Conceived in sin and born out of wedlock."

"She repented before the congregation, Jake," Mary said quickly.

Jake nodded, his face closed and dark. "But she's still being punished, isn't she?"

No one said anything for several minutes. Then Esther spoke rather hesitantly and to me. "Will Trevor be all right? He's so small."

I shook my head. "I don't know. I'm worried about him, too."

"What's wrong with him?" Again it was Esther, her face full of sorrow.

I went for the simplest explanation. "He was born with a bad heart."

"Undoubtedly because of her sin," Jake said.

I glared at him. He was baiting his family, and I thought it rude and unkind. He refused to look at me.

"She's not from our district," Mary said. "Her parents moved to Ohio shortly after they married."

"So?" Jake said, a challenge in his voice. "That means what? Our district is unsullied?"

"Chake," John said again.

"I chust meant that she has no one here who is close to her," Mary said quietly. She looked at me. "Her mother and father didn't want her at home after this happened. She's the oldest, and they were afraid she'd lead the rest astray. So they sent her to her grandparents."

"In the late summer before the baby was born, she often walked up here," Esther said. "She would sit with me on the porch for a few minutes drinking root beer. Then she'd walk back to Old Nate's." As she talked, Esther tore a piece of Mary's homemade wheat bread to shreds. "The baby is so tiny and frail."

No one spoke for the rest of the meal. When Esther cleared the fried chicken, mashed potatoes, and Mary's canned green beans from the table and served her own apple pie, silence reigned. The only noises were the scraping of silver on plates and the thump of glasses and cups set on the table. When we were finished eating, everyone bowed his head again for another silent prayer. I wondered what Jake thought about during this time.

I helped Esther clear the table and wash the dishes. As I wiped down the oilcloth that covered the table in the center of the kitchen portion of the great room, Jake wheeled his chair to me.

"You doing all right?" he asked, his dark eyes intent.

I nodded. "Better than I thought I'd do." I smiled. "You were right. Staying here has been good."

He nodded, pleased. "How about going to a movie tonight? That'll really take your mind off things."

"A movie?" Talk about being astonished at an invitation. I could have been knocked over with the proverbial feather. "You and me? Tonight?"

He gave me a half smile. "You may be sure that no one else in the room would stoop to an activity like a movie."

I glanced at Mary and Esther in their long caped dresses, their heavy black hose, and their kapps. I looked at Elam and John in their white shirts and black broadfall pants, relaxing in their living room chairs, their stockinged feet propped on a hassock. No, these folks certainly weren't moviegoers.

"And can't two friends go someplace together without it being a big deal?" he asked, suddenly embarrassed.

I swallowed a laugh at his discomfort. "I'd like to go," I said, my voice as prim as a Victorian maiden accepting an invitation to stroll with her beau by the river on a Sunday afternoon. "Especially with someone as charmingly and unfailingly pleasant as you."

He made his deep-in-the-throat noise. "There's a show at 8:15. We've got an hour before we have to leave."

"Then you can play a game with me," Esther said, her eyes bright.

Jake groaned. "Come on, Esther. Give me a break."

"You're just upset because I won last time," she said, going to a chest in the living room and taking out a board game. As she set it on the kitchen table, I saw it was Parcheesi.

"I haven't played this in years." I took a seat on one side of the table.

"Are you sure you want to play?" Jake asked.

"Why not?" I looked at him, puzzled.

He grinned broadly. "You'll find out."

Esther and I began arranging the board for play.

"Elam!" Jake looked at his brother, oblivious as he read his newspaper. "If I have to suffer this travesty called playing a game with Esther, you have to suffer too."

Elam showed no response.

"Come on, Elam," I called. "It's the least you can do after that delicious apple pie."

"Yeah, Elam," Jake's dark eyes sparkled maliciously. "Be nice."

Esther walked to Elam's chair. "Come, Elam," she said sweetly. "It would be fun with four."

Elam knew when he was beaten. He folded his paper, padded across the floor, and took the chair across from me. Esther was radiant over the fact that he had joined us.

"You have no idea what you're in for," he told me as he put his hands together and stretched them in front of him.

I couldn't imagine why both Jake and Elam were making such a fuss over a game of Parcheesi. It was only a child's game, for heaven's sake.

"I'm red," Esther announced as she gave a little bounce in her seat.

"She's always red, no matter what the game," Jake said. "It's her lucky color."

"I don't believe in luck," Esther said in gentle reproof.

"Then I'll be red tonight," Elam said, reaching for the red men.

"No!" Esther grabbed the four red men from the box before Elam could get them. She cleared her throat delicately. "I like red."

We set our men in our squares and began throwing the dice to see who went first. When Esther won the right to go first, she jumped in her chair and shouted, "Goot!" Elam and Jake looked at each other and rolled their eyes.

On our first turns none of us rolled the requisite five to move onto the board. As she threw for the second time, Esther got a three and a two. She clapped and moved a man onto the board. "Just watch. Just watch," she said, a taunting quality in her voice. "I'm going to beat you all!"

As the game moved on, I watched Esther in amazement. She got more and more competitive, more and more intense. She counted every move with every player. She mocked, she teased, she hooted, she trash-talked Amish-style.

"I'm sending you back to the beginning, Rose. And I don't want that blue man of yours to get back on the board until Christmas. He's an ugly color. Keep him out of my way!"

"Is she always like this?" I asked Jake.

"She's usually worse. I think she's got her good manners on for company."

"Ha, Elam! I've got you blockaded!" Esther couldn't sit still. She walked around the table to Elam and pointed to her pair of men blocking Elam's green man. "You aren't going anywhere and I'm going Home. Look! I'm taking this little red man all the way Home." And she marched her man up the last stretch and Home.

"I don't know, Esther," Elam said calmly, his eyes studying the board. "I don't think he goes Home. I think you miscounted."

"What?" Esther, filled with tension, put her finger on the board and began to count again. "No, I did it right."

"Only if you started at this place." He pointed where her man had stood at the end of her last turn. "But you were here." And he pointed back a space.

"I was not," she said hotly. "I was here!" She pointed to the spot where her man had been. "Wasn't I?" She looked at me.

I looked from her to Elam and saw the gleam in his eyes. "I think he's teasing you, Esther."

"What?" She spun to Elam, appalled. "You can't tease about something like this."

"No," he said kindly. "You can't tease about something like this. I can."

She sat back in her chair, her expression distressed, her cheeks scarlet. She looked beautiful. "Oh no! I've done it again, haven't I? I've been praying so hard that God would take my winning spirit away."

She looked so genuinely penitent that Elam smiled.

"You were right in your counting. Your man is Home."

Her eyes lit up and she opened her mouth to let out some huzzah of some kind when she caught herself. "That's nice," she said softly. "I'm pleased."

She stayed gentle and sweet for two more turns. Then she landed on one of Jake's men's spots. "Hah! He goes back to the beginning, Jake. This is my space now! Back, back, back! Come on, get him out of here."

"What does she do when she loses?" I asked Jake later as we drove to the movies. Esther had won and done a discreet victory dance around the table. Then she had gathered up the games pieces, put the box away, and become Esther again, sweet, docile, gentle, the cover girl for Amish life.

"She swallows real hard, puts the game away, and goes to her room for a while. When she comes out, she's Esther again."

Grinning, I said, "I love people. They are so full of contradictions and surprises. Never in my wildest imagination would I have expected Esther to be as driven as any professional athlete. She'd make a great lineman if we could find shoulder pads small enough to fit."

"How about me?" Jake asked. "Am I a man of contradictions?"

"Are you kidding?" I laughed, a short burst of air. "You're kind and comforting one minute, grouchy the next, sunk in a black fog the next."

Jake made a face, not exactly pleased with my analysis. "And you are sensitive and weepy, then sassy and

GAYLE ROPER

independent. You're Rose the Evangelist and Rose the Caregiver, Rose the Comedienne and Rose the Heartbreaker."

I looked at him, amazed, especially at the last description. To my knowledge I'd never broken anyone's heart. So where had that thought come from? I longed to say, "Me? A heartbreaker? Tell me more!" But I didn't have the nerve. Instead I said, "I'm all that?"

"And more." He pulled into a parking spot.

And more. I shivered as I climbed out of the van. Something else to ponder.

We bought our tickets for an adventure movie that was all the rage and entered the lobby.

"Popcorn?" Jake asked as he paused.

Knowing full well that the last thing I needed was more food but a sucker for popcorn, I said, "Sure."

"Soda?"

"Why not?"

We joined the line by a counter where I told myself that I didn't want that phony butter dripped all over my popcorn. It was bad for me, it would make me fat, and it would get my hands all messy. But it tasted so good!

I was dimly aware of others taking their places behind us, but it wasn't until a young woman said, "Rose?" in a too-pleased-with-herself voice that I paid attention.

I turned and found myself facing Allie Priestly, a "friend" from high school whom I hadn't seen in years

72

and hadn't missed. Standing beside her was Ben Abrams, my ex-fiancé.

"Look, Ben. It's Rose. Isn't this wonderful!"

Not a Kodak moment.

Four

AS I STARED WITH A DREADFUL FASCINATION AT MY OLD nemesis and my ex-fiancé, two mental pictures formed.

One was of Allie in tenth grade. She and I had both wanted to be cheerleaders. She was leggy, blond, just out of braces, and unencumbered by conscience. I was slim, my euphemism for straight as a board, could never make my hair obey, and I wore glasses, my astigmatism making contacts impossible.

We both went to tryouts that day long ago, she arriving on time, I arriving fifteen minutes late because of a makeup quiz I had to take. I slid into the bleachers beside her and asked, "Did the coach give any special directions?"

Allie shook her head. "She said we should just get out there and give it our best. Be bouncy."

I nodded as I watched a couple of candidates. I felt

certain I could do better than they. When my name was called, I ran onto the gym floor and gave it my all, trying to look so bouncy that I gave Tigger a run for his money.

Allie was called after I was, and she ran out onto the floor. Just before she began to cheer, she looked over at me and smirked. Then she looked down at the floor. For the first time I saw a circle of tape. Allie carefully stood in the center and began.

With a sinking feeling, I leaned forward to the girl sitting in front of me. "What's with the circle?"

"You have to stand in the center the whole time," she whispered. "The coach said how important it is to her that you listen to instructions, and if you can't remember that little bit, you'll never remember other things."

I looked at Allie with her blond hair and straight-toothed smile and knew she had deliberately not told me about the circle. It took me a long time to accept that God also knew about the circle, yet He not only allowed me to be late, He allowed me to sit next to Allie and ask her my question. Obviously He had other things besides cheerleading for me, and I gradually came to terms with that fact. Still, every game as I sat in the stands and watched Allie jump and tumble, I fought my resentment. Now here she was right behind me, all smiles. I'd soon know how mature I had become.

The other image that flashed through my mind was of Ben the night I broke our engagement. I had come to realize that even though he was a Christian, he wasn't the Christian for me. Something I couldn't even define wasn't right.

"I'm sorry, Ben," I said one night when he came to my mother's house to visit me. It was my senior year in nursing school, and I was home for the weekend. "You're a great guy. It's not your fault. It's mine. I don't love you as I should if I'm to be your wife. I just have to be fair to you and release you. You'll find someone who will love you as you deserve to be loved." And I handed him my engagement ring.

I'd worked long and hard to come up with lines that sounded as kind as I could possibly make them. Always Miss Nice Person, that's me, even though I had begun to suspect he was not being faithful to me. But since I couldn't prove it, I didn't want to decimate the guy. I just wanted to break our engagement and be free of what had become his cloying and increasingly annoying presence.

He chose to be decimated. He shouted. He ranted. He turned scarlet. Finally, in a great rush of anger, he ran across my mother's lawn and threw what had been my beautiful diamond ring across the street into a field.

"If you won't wear that ring, Rose, then no one should wear it!"

He stormed to his car and roared off. I wasn't even in the house before I heard the screech of metal that turned out to be Jake's accident.

As these thoughts raced through my mind in a second or two, I stared at Allie and Ben. I became aware of

GAYLE ROPER

Jake, sensing my consternation, looking on with great interest. Gritting my teeth, I smiled sweetly and made the introductions. Jake shook hands with Ben with great aplomb and smiled charmingly at Allie. But then he had no history with them.

"Guess what?" Allie asked me while Jake turned to order our popcorn.

I spread my hands, at a loss as to what to guess.

Allie grabbed Ben's hand and looked at me with a great, smug smile. "Ben and I are engaged!"

I blinked. "How wonderful." I think I managed to sound somewhat pleased. In fact I was pleased. They deserved each other.

"Just look!" She stuck her left hand under my nose. I couldn't imagine how I had previously missed the sparkling stone on her third finger. The solitaire sat on an S-shaped shank with a tiny baguette on each side of the central stone.

"Very beautiful," I said as I stared first at it, then at Ben who was suddenly busy studying the candy in the display case.

A giant tub of popcorn was shoved into my hands.

"Come on, Tiger," Jake said. "We need to get our seats." He wheeled off and I had no choice but to follow.

As I walked away, gnashing my teeth and screaming inside, I heard Allie say, "Tiger? Oh, please!" I'd never known anyone who could drip condescension like she could. The fact that I'd been thinking the very same thing only made me angrier.

I stalked after Jake. I grabbed a handful of popcorn and shoved it into my mouth. Yes! Phony butter. Maybe the evening could be salvaged.

Just outside the auditorium where our film was showing, Jake stopped. He looked at my clenched jaw and stormy expression.

"I seem to be asking this of you a lot, but are you okay?"

"I'm fine," I ground out.

He raised his eyebrow. "I can tell."

"Did you see that ring?" I demanded.

"Not really. I'm not into engagement rings." Jake studied me. "Why does the ring bother you? Do you still love him or something?"

"Ben?" I stared, aghast. "Are you kidding? It was one of the greatest escapes of recorded history that I got away from him before it was too late."

"Then are you upset because you resent Allie so much? She got your man and all that, even though you no longer wanted him?"

I sputtered at the idea. "Hardly. They deserve each other."

"Then what's the problem?"

"The ring!" I held out my left hand and pointed to the third finger with my popcorn tub. "It was my ring! I picked it out! He bought it for me and now he gave it to her!"

"It was your ring?"

"My ring!"

"And you want it back?"

"Never!"

He shook his head and shrugged his massive shoulders. "Then what?"

"He threw it away!"

Jake looked at me, confused. "He threw it away?"

I nodded. "He was so mad when I broke up with him that he raced to the bottom of my mother's yard and tossed the ring as far as he could, right into the field across the street!"

Jake picked up a handful of popcorn. "He actually threw away a ring worth all that money?" He stuffed the popcorn in his mouth. "No wonder you broke up with him. He's too dumb to be on the loose."

I stilled for a moment. Dumb? I'd always thought egotistical, but dumb might be better. If he'd thrown it away. There was the rub.

"But he never threw it away, did he? What a grandstander!" Jake was right with me, as usual. He grabbed another handful of popcorn. A huge grin spread over his face as the absurdity of it all hit him.

"Don't you dare laugh!" I ordered. I was livid at Ben, my jaw so tightly clenched I might have had tetanus. "This is no laughing matter! Why, he probably didn't even care that I broke up with him! He probably never really loved me after all!"

"You're just mad because he put one over on you," Jake said peaceably.

"And that's not the worst of it!" I spun around in a

circle in my frustration, several kernels spilling from my tub onto the rug. Jake pointed to them, and I picked them up without being totally aware of what I was doing. My mind was going in agitated spirals, and I stood staring at the popcorn in my palm.

"Trash receptacle," Jake said.

"Right." I walked across the hall and dumped the popcorn. I was still frowning when I came back. "Mom and I spent hours over in that field looking for that ring! Hours!"

Jake stared at me for a moment. Then he began to laugh. "Oh, Rosie, I can just see you out there, down on your hands and knees, sifting through the dirt and grass, hoping against hope that you could find the thing, thinking of all the stuff you could buy when you traded it in." And he began to laugh harder.

I stared at him through slitted eyes. He was much too close to the truth for comfort. All those hours searching for the ring, and it was never even there!

Suddenly the absurdity of the whole thing washed over me. I started to laugh too, and soon we were wheezing, gasping for breath. I had to use the wall to hold myself up.

Into this scene of great merriment walked Allie and Ben. Ben took one look at the two of us and spun Allie around on her heels, rushing her into the first auditorium they came to, the one showing a bland kiddie flick that had been creamed by the critics as less than stellar.

"But Ben this wasn't what I wanted to see," Allie

cried as the door swung shut behind them.

We found our movie to be vastly entertaining. In fact, we laughed so readily that the people around us began looking at us askance. I didn't care. I kept imagining Allie looking at the wrong movie, getting more agitated with Ben by the moment, and Ben sitting there worried about seeing Jake and me again. After all, what if I told Allie what I knew about her ring? I was willing to bet anything that she had no idea of its previous history.

I started to giggle again, only to feel Jake's elbow in my side. I looked at the screen and saw I was giggling at a death scene. That made me laugh harder. Soon he joined me, and the people behind us actually moved.

The upshot was that I went to bed feeling much better than I had the night before. That's why the nightmare took me so by surprise.

I sat bolt upright in bed, my heart pounding. My dream wrapped dark tentacles of terror about me, gripping me as tightly as imprisoning chains. I was sweating, trembling, almost hyperventilating. It seemed impossible that I was staring into ordinary darkness in an ordinary bedroom, so vivid had been the flashing red lights and the crackling static. And the bodies! They lay in the road, floated in the water, and sat in burning cars.

They all looked at me and chorused, "You! You! You!"

I slashed at the tears on my cheeks and reached for my bedside lamp. Immediately, in the glare of the light, the phantoms disappeared. I stared with relief at my coat hanging on a peg on the wall and reveled in the sheer normality of the sight.

But the feelings of horror clung, sticky cobwebs of emotion that refused to release me.

I pushed back the covers and climbed shivering from bed, then padded into the bathroom. I'd discovered long ago that movement or a different location banished the emotions that clung long after the visions had ceased.

I drank two glasses of water, wet the cloth and wiped it across my face, and brushed my teeth.

Still the clammy terror remained.

A cup of tea. That's what I needed. Chamomile to help me relax and sleep again.

I started out of the bathroom only to realize I wasn't in my place. I was at the Zooks'.

If I lived here, one of the first things I'd buy would be a microwave to keep up here for just such emergencies.

I padded into my darkened living room and stared out the window at the quiet countryside silvered by a three-quarters moon. Everything looked so peaceful, so tranquil, so at odds with what I felt.

Oh, dear Lord, help me. Calm me down. I feel like I'm coming apart here.

I took my shivering body back to the bedroom and tugged on a set of sweats over my nightshirt. I grabbed my sweater and pulled it on over the sweatshirt, then added my bathrobe. I felt like the little brother in "The Christmas Story," the one who couldn't move because of so many layers of winter clothes. I could barely bend enough to tie my sneakers. It was sheer habit that caused me to attach my beeper to my bathrobe belt.

When I no longer shook with cold but merely shivered, I grabbed my emergency flashlight and made my way downstairs. Maybe there was enough heat left in the woodstove for me to heat a cup of water. I didn't think Mary would mind if I rummaged until I found her wonderful spearmint tea. To be honest, though, I didn't care whether she minded or not. My nerves were jangled enough to make me less than the ideal houseguest.

Moving quietly I put some water in the teakettle and set it on the still-warm stove. It might not boil anymore, but it would at least get warm. I began opening and closing cupboards as quietly as I could, shining my flashlight into all the nooks and crannies. I found the tea in the third place I looked. Not too bad, I thought with misplaced pride.

I was getting a mug from the cabinet when I heard the whoosh of Jake's wheels.

"Who's there? What's going on?" He didn't sound too happy.

"It's me," I whispered, shining my light at my face. I probably looked like a Halloween ghoul.

"Rose." His voice was decidedly testy.

"Don't be so grumpy. I'm not stealing the family jewels. I'm making a cup of tea. You want one?"

"Why not?" He wheeled over to the table and lit the Coleman lantern that sat on it. The sudden bright light made me blink.

"That's too bright." I shielded my eyes. "Midnight escapades call for soft light." Also soft light might disguise how strange I must look with my combination of clothes, my uncombed hair, and my nighttime face cream.

Jake grunted and turned to an end table. He lifted the globe and lit a kerosene lamp. As soon as it took hold, I turned the Coleman off.

"Much better," I said.

Jake had on a T-shirt and sweatpants. He had a blanket across his knees and another wrapped around his shoulders.

"How did you know I was here? I tried to be so quiet."

"It wasn't your noise. It was the flashlight flickering. I wasn't asleep yet, and I kept seeing streaks of light. I don't close the door to the house at night."

I handed him a mug of tea. We sat at the table with hands wrapped around the warm mugs. The tea hadn't steeped too well because the water wouldn't boil, but warm and flavored were really my only requirements at the moment.

"Do you always have tea in the middle of the night?" Jake asked.

I shook my head. "Bad dream."

"I'm not surprised."

"I am." I stirred my sugar slowly. "I felt very light-hearted when I went to bed. Laughing about Ben was such a wonderful feeling. I expected to sleep like a baby. The nightmare was unexpected."

"The explosion?" Jake looked at me, his face shadowed by his angle to the lamp. He looked stern, but his voice was gentle.

"Partly." I stared into my tea, my mind re-creating what little I could actually recall of the dream. "It was a mishmash of the explosion and Dad and Rhoda and you. There were flashing lights and static and shouts. I'd forgotten about the shouts."

"Shouts?"

"Over the roar of the water for Dad and Rhoda. Over the noise of the fire for Sophie and Ammon, and over the roar of the rotor blades for you."

"For me?"

"It's funny. I hadn't realized how the voices giving orders and issuing instructions meshed so firmly with the other memories until right now." I looked at him. "Isn't the mind a funny thing? I heard those voices at the time, but I didn't consciously remember them until now. Not that I remember specific things said. It's just the people calling."

"How do you know about me?"

"I suppose at some emergency scenes, I've been the one shouting to be heard. Usually things are relatively quiet, and we talk in normal tones. The last thing we want to do is upset the victims or their family and friends. But some scenes are so chaotic that you have to yell."

"How did I get into your dream?" Jake demanded as he laid a hand on my wrist.

"What?" I blinked at him.

"How did I get into your dream?"

"I think I dreamed of the three accidents where I wasn't part of the responding team but rather personally involved somehow. Of course, I wasn't as involved in any of them as I was in my father and Rhoda's, but I was there with you, and there with Sophie and Ammon."

"You were there with me?" His voice was fierce.

I nodded. "Sure. Sitting there in the rain in the street. I thought help would never come!" Then I froze. My mind caught up with my mouth, and I realized I'd said things I hadn't intended to. I stared at his shadowed eyes.

He stared right back.

"You said you never wanted to meet me," I said defensively. "That's what you told Kristie when she found me. You didn't ever want to meet me. Then we met anyway this summer when your mother fell. I knew how you felt so I never said who I was."

"So," he said quietly, "Rose at the table with me is Rose from in the street."

I nodded. "Same one." I looked at his shuttered face. "Say you're not angry. Please." It mattered a lot that he wasn't angry.

"And you never bothered telling me."

I shook my head. "It's like I said. I knew how you felt. Some pride thing about being at your very worst or something."

"Well, I was that."

Did I hear humor in his voice? Was that possible? I wished the light shone on him instead of me. I wished I could see his face. But deep inside somewhere, I was glad to have this little fact out in the open. If he was going to be furious or see it as deception, at least we could confront it and get it done with.

"It was the night that Ben threw the ring away—or rather pretended to," I said.

"The night of the great performance?" Jake seemed more intrigued than angry.

I nodded. "We'd just had that terrible row. He went raging out, threw the ring, got into his car, and stormed off. Next thing I knew, I heard screeching metal, saw sparks as your bike slid along the road, and I heard you scream." I shuddered. "I ran to the intersection, and there you were with the bike on your back. I ran back home and called 911."

"Then you sat in the road with me."

"For about twenty minutes until the medic unit from Brandywine Trauma Center arrived."

"I have this vague recollection of someone who never shut up, sort of like a fly buzzing and buzzing and never leaving me alone."

"That was me, I guess." I looked back into the past. "I think I talked because I didn't know what else to do."

I shivered again. "I thought you died, you know. I even put up one of those white crosses in your memory, though I didn't know who you were."

"Yeah, I knew that."

"You did?"

He nodded. "Kristie told me when she found you last summer."

I suddenly felt very angry. "You mean you knew I had done that for you and you were still too stubborn to meet me? You had the gall to deny me the comfort of seeing you were okay after all I'd done for you?" I stood and glared at him.

"Well, you had the nerve to work your way into a friendship with me in spite of my wishes," he countered defensively.

"I had nothing to do with meeting you!" I was seething at his colossal ego. "Your mother fell down the steps, and I happened to be on call that night. It was a God thing!"

"But you were her home health nurse too!"

"Well, I didn't assign myself the case!"

We glared at each other in the soft light of the lamp.

"Did you know," I finally said, my voice crisp and edgy, "that I began classes to become an EMT because I felt so helpless that night? I felt another person had died because of me, and I vowed it would never happen again."

"Another person?" Jake asked.

Suddenly my anger evaporated and I collapsed into my chair.

"What do you mean, another person?" He wheeled around the table to me.

"Forget it." I stared into my tea mug. "I didn't mean to say it."

"Forget it, my eye." He took me by the chin and forced me to look at him. There was no anger in his face now, just concern. "Tell me what you meant."

I shook my head. "You resent me already for not telling you who I am. I couldn't bear it if you hated me, too."

"I do not resent you."

I snorted.

He skewered me with his black eyes. "You saved my life. I could never hate you."

"That's easy to say now."

"Talk, Tiger." He flattened his hand gently against my cheek. "I won't let you alone until you tell me."

"Please…no."

"Yes."

My shoulders slumped and I shut my eyes. "I killed my father and sister." I died a little as I breathed that terrible truth. "I killed them."

There was a charged silence. I felt the hot flush of guilt and shame and knew that he hated me now, just like my mother did. I turned my face to hide from his gaze, and his fingers, still resting lightly on my cheek, slid into my hair.

"No." His fingers tightened in my hair and forced me to face him. "Whatever happened, you did not kill anyone. I know you. You're the woman who sat with me in the road in the rain, the woman who saved my life by her kindness. You did not kill anyone."

"I didn't mean to," I said in agony. "I really didn't."

We sat knee to knee and I told him of that long-ago sweet summer day. We had gone on a picnic, Mom, Dad, three-year-old Rhoda, and I. It had rained for a week, and the sunshine was so golden and warm. All we wanted was to revel in its return. We went to the Conestoga River, swollen and rampaging from the rains.

"Rhoda and I were fascinated by the wild water."

"Don't you go near that water," Mom said.

"I won't," I assured her.

"Keep an eye on Rhoda while Dad and I get the food from the car."

"Here, Rhoda. Come with me," I called and held out my hand for her. She came running to me, and we played with our dolls for a bit, me with my Barbie in her pink evening gown and Rhoda with her baby doll in its blue nightie.

"But the water drew Rhoda. I became distracted with Barbie, taking off her gown as inappropriate for a picnic and putting on a pair of shorts and a top. I wasn't even aware Rhoda wasn't beside me until I heard a scream from my mother."

I stopped and swallowed. I could still feel the terror of that moment and the indelible stain of the guilt that had splashed across my soul.

"Rhoda had fallen in, and all that we could see was

her bright yellow sunsuit as she was carried away. My father raced to the water and dived in to try and save her." I took a deep breath. "He never surfaced."

We were silent as I relived that sorrow-filled day and Jake tried to assimilate the terrible repercussions of my neglect. I clasped and unclasped my hands in my distress.

"You were how old?" he finally asked.

"Ten."

"Oh, Rosie." His voice was full of sorrow, and I realized with a start that the sorrow was for me, not for Rhoda and Dad or even Mom who lost two-thirds of her family. It was for me. It was the second time he had carried my sorrow with me.

"I killed them," I said again, just to make certain he understood.

"Not at all," he said. "Not at all. It was an accident." He took my hands in his, calming their movements by running his thumbs across the backs of them.

"I was supposed to be watching her."

"Rose, you're an intelligent woman. You can't tell me that you accept the blame for what resulted from your parents' ill-advised decision to have a picnic on the banks of a raging river."

I struggled to explain. "In one sense, I know it wasn't my fault. Things happen. But when they happen to you, how do you not accept the blame?" By the end of the sentence my voice was a mere thread of sound.

He ran a hand over my bowed head. "I know what you mean," he said quietly.

It took a minute for his words to register. "You do?"

"Guilt," he said. "There's more than enough for all."

I looked at him in question.

"You feel guilty about a situation that was not in any way your fault."

I decided not to argue the point. I wanted to hear what he had to say.

"I feel guilty because of what I've done not only to myself but to the people I love."

This statement I would argue. "What do you mean by that?"

"If I hadn't been such an ornery reprobate, such a rebel, I wouldn't have made such a mess of my life and become such a burden to my family."

"And what makes you think you're a burden?" It was my turn to pat his hand. "Do you honestly think your family would prefer you dead?"

"No. I know better than that. But I also have eyes and ears, and I know I require too much of their time and energy. That's just the reality of our lives. What's hardest, though, is knowing I've brought them perilously close to breaking the Ordnung—which would break their hearts."

We sat back in our seats, no longer touching physically but connecting on some inner plane of understood pain.

"So we live with guilt, you and I," he said. "You can't forgive yourself—"

I nodded. "Um. That's certainly the truth."

"And I can't believe God would ever forgive me."

It took a minute to process the end of his sentence because I was so caught up in the miracle of someone understanding me. When I finally grasped what he'd said, I protested. "What do you mean, God wouldn't forgive you?" I was indignant on his behalf. "You haven't done anything worse that millions of other people."

"How do you know that?"

"Well, you haven't, have you?"

He grinned slightly. "Probably not. But all that proves is that they aren't worthy of His forgiveness, either."

"Of course they're not. No one's worthy. He just gives it."

"*If* you earn it."

"No." I shook my head. "Haven't you ever heard of God's grace? That means His forgiveness is free in Christ whether you deserve it or not."

"That's not what I heard as an Amishman. It's more the law. Follow the Ordnung, and maybe when you die, you'll be good enough for heaven. I blew my chances when I became a rebel. Just ask Father. He's a good Amishman. He'll tell you." There was a bitterness in his voice that I didn't like.

"But he's wrong!"

"That's what my brother Andy says, but why should I believe Andy instead of Father?"

"Your brother Andy? I don't know him."

"He left the community several years ago over the issue of law and grace."

"Really?" I felt a surge of hope for Jake. If Andy could understand grace, why couldn't his brother?

Jake nodded. "He says he believes in salvation by grace rather than works."

"God saved you by his special favor when you believed. And you can't take credit for this; it is a gift from God. Salvation is not a reward for the good things we have done, so none of us can boast about it."

Jake looked at me and shrugged.

"Jake, if I didn't believe that truth, I'd have gone crazy long ago. But God forgave me for not keeping a better eye on Rhoda. He promised He would and He did, even though I didn't deserve it. That's grace."

"So you believe God forgave you, but you can't forgive yourself?"

I nodded.

"And I forgave myself because I know I didn't do anything to hurt anyone on purpose, but I can't believe God can forgive me, not just for the accident but for all the living before it and the bitterness after."

We sat in silence in the gentle glow of the kerosene lamp, contemplating the irony of our opinions until I jumped.

"You're chilly," Jake said.

"No." I got out of my chair. "My beeper just went off. I've got to go!"

"What? After the night you've had? Let them send someone else."

"Can't. I have to go regardless of the kind of night

I've had." I dashed for the stairs to run up, change my clothes, and grab my coat and car keys.

I stopped with one foot on the first step. I looked over my shoulder at him and my heart tripped over itself at the sight of him, all dark and compelling. I smiled at him.

"Besides, contrary to all expectations, the night has turned out to be pretty fine.... Thanks to you."

Five

THE CALL WAS FOR THE STOLTZFUS FARM RIGHT DOWN THE road. I was certain something had happened to Trevor, and my heart was breaking before I even got to the house.

I couldn't imagine the terror and heartbreak of having a baby die. If I wept all these years over Dad and Rhoda, how did a mother deal with the death of a child she had carried within her own body for nine months, had fed at her breast, and cradled against her heart?

But it wasn't Becky and her baby that the call was for. It was Old Nate himself. And he didn't need us by the time we arrived.

His body lay crumpled at the bottom of the stairs that led from the living room to the upstairs. Whether a fall down those stairs had caused his death or some sort of attack had caused both his fall and his death or whether there was some other not-readily-apparent cause, my partner Harry and I didn't try to determine. That was for the coroner.

Becky told us she found Old Nate when she went downstairs to get a glass of root beer.

"I only had a small flashlight, and I almost stepped on him in the dark," she said and shivered. I shivered too. What a terrible mental image that was.

"Root beer at this hour of the night?" Harry Mast said.

Becky shrugged. "I had been up with the baby and was thirsty."

She watched her grandmother with worried eyes. "After I wakened Grandmother Annie, I ran down the road to the phone shanty and dialed 911."

Harry and I nodded and settled down to wait for as long as it took the coroner to arrive. While I as a nurse and both Harry and I as EMTs could declare a person dead, we needed the coroner because of the unknown cause of Old Nate's death. He would also oversee the removal of the body. Though there was no evidence of a crime, we treated the situation as a crime scene. It was the old better-safe-than-sorry philosophy.

I stared with interest at the benches lined up in the living room and the kitchen.

"They were supposed to have church here tomorrow," I said softly.

Harry nodded. "They'll all come anyway. It's proper to come sit with the bereaved. She won't be alone from now until the funeral."

Harry was a lay scholar, full of information about all kinds of arcane cultural things. He was a Mennonite farmer, raised in Lampeter just down the road. The only time he'd been out of Lancaster County was when he'd done alternate service as an army medic in Korea. There he found he loved helping people in so practical a manner.

"Just like a Mennonite," I often teased him. "Always taking care of the world."

He'd grin and say, "Well, someone's got to do it, you know. The rest of you Christians are so busy arguing among yourselves that we peaceable Mennonites have the helping fields to ourselves."

While we both knew that these were gross overstatements, we also knew there was a painful amount of truth there.

"How come you're not burned out yet?" I asked him once as I studied the circles under his seventy-one-year-old eyes. "How many gruesome late-night accidents like tonight's can one person take?"

"I ought to be burnt to a cinder by now," he agreed. "But, boy howdy, I love this rescue work. Don't tell my pastor, but I thank the Lord for the army every day. If I hadn't become a medic, I'd have missed all this great stuff!"

Quite simply, Harry was wonderful and I loved being his partner.

"Are there other children besides Becky's father?" I asked Harry.

"It's Becky's mother who's the Stoltzfus's daughter. She just happened to marry another Stoltzfus, no relation."

"Ah." In a community where many were closely related and surnames were often the same even without relationship, things could get confusing, especially to an outsider like me.

"There is a son," Harry said slowly. "His name is Davy. But I don't know if there's been any contact with him since the day he was shunned."

I blinked. "A son who was shunned?" Was that why Old Nate was so unforgiving toward Becky? "What did he do?"

Harry grinned. "He's a driver on the NASCAR circuit."

"He races automobiles?" I was flabbergasted.

"Our own Richard Petty, though not as successful. At least not yet."

Just then I heard the clop of hooves, the rattle of a buggy, and the jingling of a harness.

"How do they know so fast?" I wondered as I peered toward the window.

"Becky," Harry called, "did you phone the bishop when you called us?"

She turned toward us and nodded. "Grandmother Annie gave me the number of his next door neighbors. I called them, and they said they would get him for us."

"Good girl," I said, thinking what a jolt that call must have been to the sleeping neighbors. But such was life in Lancaster County. "Is there anyone else you want to call? I have a cell phone here." And I pulled my phone out of my backpack.

"Nay," she said. *"Denki."*

Annie touched the girl's hand and whispered something.

Becky turned to me. "Maybe later?"

I nodded.

Becky rose and got a scrap of paper and a pen. She returned to her grandmother and was soon writing down something Annie told her.

Becky had just put down the pen and tucked away the scrap of paper when two older couples came into the house without knocking. The women went straight to Annie, but the men checked their stride when they saw Old Nate still lying on the floor where he'd fallen.

They spoke quickly to Annie in Pennsylvania Dutch, a language I didn't understand well. I could follow Esther when she said Trevor was a scheeni bubbli or a nice baby, but when things got much more complex, I was lost. But Harry understood.

"They want to put him to bed to prepare his body," he muttered to me as he pushed off from the wall. "They think it's undignified that he's lying there."

"It is," I said as Harry walked across the room and stood by Old Nate.

"We can't move him," he told everyone. "We don't know what killed him. It's not like he died in his bed from an illness he'd already had. The law requires the coroner take him and determine what happened."

"He fell," said one of the men. "Iss what happened."

"Probably," Harry said. "But we don't know that. Maybe he had a heart attack. Maybe a stroke. Maybe he heard something down here and was coming to see what was wrong and missed his footing."

The Amishmen didn't look happy. I was sure they wished we hadn't been called, but since we had been, they knew they had to accept our presence and its consequences. But how much simpler it would have been to carry Old Nate to his bed and go on from there.

One of them turned to Annie and must have asked who called for us. Annie spoke and everyone looked at Becky. She blushed and looked uncomfortable as she stood quietly beside her grandmother. Her long hair hung down her back in a braid, and she was wearing a flannel gown and robe. Her grandmother had on much the same thing, and it was a sign of her grief and disorientation that she didn't even realize her head was uncovered.

Suddenly pitiful little cries sounded.

Becky turned immediately and raced for the stairs. She stopped a minute with her foot on the lower tread.

"Will you come with me, Rose?" she asked. "Every time I go into his room, my heart beats with fear for what I'll find."

Becky turned to her grandmother's visitors. "Rose was Trevor's nurse. She knows how to help me with him."

The women nodded as though they knew Becky needed help.

"Go on, Rose," Harry said. "I'll call you when the coroner comes."

We both knew that might be a while yet. A big pile-up on the Route 30 bypass had all the emergency services stretched. The fact that the coroner had been called to the scene of that accident did not augur well for the victims—or for a quick resolution here.

I picked up my backpack and followed Becky upstairs and along the hall to the little room she shared with Trevor. It was a far cry from the room I'd had as a fifteen-year-old, a pink and white Victorian excess, much to the dismay of my friends who were into hard rock and the color black. Then there were my TV, stereo, computer, and private phone line, to say nothing of a closet stuffed full of clothes.

It was more than typical Amish spartan furnishings that set Becky's room apart. It was the tattered quilt on her bed when I'd seen beautiful new quilts on the beds in the two large, airy, empty bedrooms we passed to get to her tiny closet of a room. It was the wicker laundry basket that was the baby's cradle and the faded blankets that covered his wasted little body. It was the pathetic stack of worn, gray, holey diapers that Becky hand washed and hung on the line daily because she had no funds for disposables.

The truth was obvious to any observant person, even if I hadn't already known the facts. Becky was not welcome in her grandparents' house. They were highly embarrassed to have her here, first as a pregnant girl and now as an unwed mother. For someone as filled with moral rectitude as Old Nate apparently had been, Becky was a blot on the family name, a name already blackened by Davy, the race car driver. But even Old Nate realized she had to live somewhere. She was simply too young to be on her own.

Becky and I walked into the little bedroom, and she picked up the baby. Her face was filled with love as she held the wailing little boy, a child who was not attractive by even the kindest criteria. His frail little fists with their cyanotic nails waved in the air and his cry was more like that of a lamb's bleating than a two-month-old's usual wail.

"Hello, my Trevor," Becky crooned to the baby. *"Ich leibe dich, mein liebchen, mein bubbli."*

She lay him gently on her bed, placing him in the indentation her head had left on her pillow. He rested there a minute before he resumed his thin cry. She sat on the bed, leaned against the headboard and picked him up. He began to nurse with more energy than I'd have expected.

We sat in silence for a few minutes, the only sound that of Trevor suckling.

"Rose, can you do something for me?" Becky asked suddenly.

"If I can."

"I need to contact my uncle Davy and tell him his

father died. All I have is this address that Grandmother Annie gave me."

I looked at the scrap of paper she handed me and saw that Davy and Lauren Stoltzfus lived in Denton, Texas.

I nodded and took my phone out of my backpack. I got the area code from Information, then dialed Denton, certain that the number would be unlisted. After all, Davy was a race car driver. Wouldn't he have fans he was trying to hide from?

With surprise I wrote down the number the operator gave me. As Harry said, Davy wasn't famous yet. I dialed the number and was again surprised when a woman's voice answered.

"May I speak to Davy Stoltzfus?"

"I'm afraid he's out of town. May I take a message?"

"Am I speaking with Lauren?"

"Yes."

"Lauren, I'm going to hand you over to Davy's niece Becky who has some news for Davy."

I listened as Becky told Lauren about Old Nate's death.

"I don't know when services will be," Becky said. "Probably Tuesday."

"Tell her I'll call her when we know," I said. "And give her my number."

Becky did so, hung up, and looked at me in surprise. "She said to tell Annie she loves her."

"That's nice."

"But how does Lauren even know Grandmother Annie?" Becky asked. "Davy met her after he left home. At least that's the gossip I heard. She's from Texas. Is that far?"

I blinked. "Yes, it's pretty far."

"Do you think…" Becky's eyes narrowed in thought. "Do you think maybe Grandmother Annie has been in contact with Davy and Lauren all these years?"

"Would your grandfather have allowed it?"

Becky shook her head emphatically. "Absolutely not." She put her hand over her mouth. "Grandmother Annie's gone behind his back!"

"Now you don't know that," I cautioned.

"But she had the address right to hand."

We looked at each other and grinned. Wicked, wicked.

Trevor gurgled and Becky looked down at him. She smiled and ran her finger softly over the baby's bald head.

"All I ever wanted was to have a baby," she said. "Lots of babies. To be a mutter."

"But you've done it the hard way, honey." I sat on the edge of the bed, filled with regret on her behalf.

"True," she said. "And I'm sorry about that. But I'm not sorry about you, Trevor, my sweet. You are just wonderful."

I smiled at them. "You're wonderful, Becky. You do far more than any fifteen-year-old could be expected to do, and you do it so capably."

Becky cleared her throat. "You need to know something, Rose." She looked at me, her brown eyes filled with resolve and something I read as trust. "I'm not fifteen. I turned eighteen last week. They said I was fifteen when I came because it made everything look less like a willful sin and more like the foolish mistake of an ignorant girl. But I knew what I was doing, and I know what I'm doing now.... And I know my baby is going to die."

My heart skipped a beat at her quiet statement. I wished with all my heart that I could tell her she was wrong, but in truth, I thought Trevor had survived this long due only to the extraordinary love of his mother.

Becky looked at me with a sad smile. "Denki for not lying to me."

I squeezed her hand gently. "I wish I could tell you differently, honey."

"And thanks for not telling me his illness is punishment for my sin."

My heart contracted again, and I thought of the story in the Bible about the man born blind.

"Teacher," Jesus' disciples asked him, "why was this man born blind? Was it a result of his own sins or those of his parents?"

"It was not because of his sins or his parents' sins," Jesus answered. "He was born blind so the power of God could be seen in him."

As I watched the mother and child, I thought that in a strange way, God's power was seen right in this crude room, in a mother's care for her dying child, her total commitment to his well-being. It was just that same totality of love that had sent Jesus to the manger in Bethlehem and the cross at Golgotha.

Becky lifted Trevor to her shoulder and soon we heard a little burp. She lowered him to her other breast.

"Is your boyfriend waiting for you back home?" I asked.

"I think so. He said he would wait, and I believe him. But when my parents found out about the baby, they sent me away so fast that I never had a chance to speak with him."

"And he hasn't tried to contact you?"

She shook her head.

"Oh, Becky!"

"No," she said quickly. "It's not like you think. He's *meidung.*"

I shook my head. "I don't know the word."

"He's shunned. No one will talk to him or tell him where I am."

"Oh." The enormous life-altering power of shunning struck me again. "Is he shunned because of Trevor?"

"No. He was under the ban before Trevor." She smiled sadly. "I wasn't supposed to see him or have anything to do with him, but—" She shrugged. "Obviously I did."

"Are you being shunned, too?" I was appalled at the idea, but maybe it explained the way her grandparents were treating her.

"No. I hadn't joined the congregation yet."

"But he had?"

"Samuel had. He's twenty-two."

"Why was he shunned?" I feared all sorts of terrible things.

"He bought a pickup truck for his construction work."

"Oh, Becky." I was overwhelmed that something so commonplace in my world should be so costly in hers.

She nodded with understanding at my reaction. Then her expression darkened. "When I go home," she said fiercely, "I will be like you. I will be fancy. I will buy a sweatsuit and wear it all day, even the pants. I will learn to drive Samuel's truck, and we will marry and have many more babies, healthy babies, and we will live in a house with a washing machine and electric lights and an electric can opener. And I will wear lipstick."

I couldn't help but grin at her and her plans for a wanton life. "You are a rebel, Rebecca Stoltzfus."

"I am. And I talk to Herr Gott about it all the time. I could not leave my people if He would not come with me, not even for Samuel, I don't think."

"He'll go anywhere with anyone who believes," I said.

Becky nodded. "I think so, too."

"I'm a Christian, and I know He's with me. I know lots of English people who are believers and will tell you the Lord is with them, too." I used the traditional term *English* to denote anyone who wasn't Amish.

"I had a job cleaning for an English lady back home." Becky said. "She was a Christian, too. She talked to me about Jesus, and she gave me an English Bible that was easy to read." She reached under her pillow and pulled out a much used paper-cover Bible.

"When I learned I was going to have a baby, I went to her. I told her about Samuel and how much I loved him. I thought that because she was fancy, she would say what we did was okay. She didn't. She agreed with Mama that I was wrong, that we were wrong. But not because of Mama or the Ordnung, she said. Because of the Bible." Becky ran her hand across the cover of her obviously cherished book.

"Then she told me about grace. About Jesus. I heard about Him all my life, but finally I understood. Now He's my Savior."

I thanked God for the English woman who had such a great heart.

Becky slipped off the bed and laid Trevor in his nest in his basket on the floor. She began covering him with blankets. "I brought Samuel to my lady, too. I wanted him to know Jesus like me." She stopped and blushed as she glanced at me. "He needed to understand why I wouldn't get into bed with him anymore."

She stood, suddenly concerned lest I misunderstand. "Samuel is not bad," she said. "He isn't, even though he's meidung. He's practical. That's what he always tells me. That's why he got the truck. 'Because it's practical, Becky.' That's what he says."

"Becky, if you love him, I'm sure he's a fine man. You wouldn't love him otherwise."

Her smile was so bright that my breath caught. I realized that she rarely had the luxury of talking about Samuel. That was part of shunning.

"So has Samuel trusted Jesus, too?"

"I don't know," she said, tears gathering in her eyes. "I haven't seen him in so many months. No one will talk to him and tell him where I am. He doesn't know about Trevor, that he was born, that he's sick. My heart breaks that he doesn't know."

My heart broke a bit too. "Have you ever tried to call him at the phone shanty?"

"I tried when I first came, but they saw me. My grandfather said I would have to leave if I tried again. I was seven months pregnant. Where would I go?"

My heart ached. What would I have done under an ultimatum like that? Honored my dictatorial grandfather or followed my heart? It was a hard question to answer because I viewed the whole question from what I considered a normal perspective, while Becky had been immersed in another way of thinking her whole life. Certainly she was rebelling and planning to break free, though that was with Samuel by her side. But here, alone, knowing no one?

"I did try again." She glanced at the door as if afraid of being overheard. "But no one answered the first two times I tried. Then I got a message saying the phone was disconnected. Samuel had moved, I guess. I don't know.

GAYLE ROPER

I didn't worry too much at first. I would only be here until the baby was born, and then I would go home. Somehow I would go home."

We looked at Trevor.

"And now you can't leave," I said.

"I can't risk the travel, the cold. And I can't leave his doctors."

I reached out and hugged this young woman who was enduring such pain on so many levels. She clung to me like a limpet to a rock. I wondered when the last time was that she had been hugged.

Dear Lord, if I can offer her comfort, let me be used in this way.

"It'll be all right, Becky," I said. "It'll be all right."

Why, I wondered even as I spoke, do we say such inane things, such impossible-to-be-true things?

"It is all right," she said softly as she loosened her death grip though she did not let go completely. "I have my baby. I have you. I will have Samuel. And I have Herr Gott."

What a combination of deep wisdom and pure naïveté.

Footsteps sounded on the stairs, and Becky jumped away from me. She turned her back to the door, but not before I saw the tears wetting her cheeks.

One of Annie's female visitors stopped in the doorway, looking around the small room with a frown.

"Yes?" I said.

"The coroner is here. The other man asked could I get you."

"Thank you," I said in my best professional voice and moved to the door. "You keep that baby covered and warm, Becky. I'm depending on you to take good care of him, just like you've been doing. Drafts would be very bad for him. And you need to make another doctor's appointment as soon as possible. I don't like his coloring."

Without turning, she nodded and bent over the baby's basket. "I will," she promised, playing my nurse/patient game with me for the benefit of the woman. "I will."

I got back to the Zooks' at four in the morning and, flashlight in hand, was halfway up the stairs to my rooms when a deep voice stopped me.

"Are you okay?"

I turned and looked at Jake as he stared up the steps at me. The darkness at the foot of the stairwell hid his face, but his voice held a palpable concern.

"I'm fine," I whispered, surprised and pleased that he had waited up to be certain I was all right. I also wondered just what this solicitude meant in the scheme of life.

"Really?" he said. "It didn't upset you again?"

"Really. Remember, I do this stuff all the time."

He made that deep-in-his-throat sound, the one that meant he sort of disagreed about something but wasn't going to say anything at the moment. I took the noise to mean that he didn't like me running around the county in the dead of night.

"You won't have to go out again tonight, will you?"

I shrugged. "You never know."

He looked away, and the light filtering from his apartment showed his disapproving expression.

"Someone had to go out in the night to save you, Jake," I said softly.

"Someone is more than welcome to go," he said. "I don't worry about someone."

I smiled to myself. For a man so opposed to hovering, Jake Zook definitely practiced the art well.

"I didn't have to go far tonight," I said as I came back down the stairs and sat on the step second from the bottom. I set the flashlight beside me, the beam pointing at the ceiling. "It was Old Nate. He's dead."

A burst of air indicated Jake's surprise, and when he spoke, his voice was sardonic. "I'm amazed God was willing to take him—if it was God."

"Jake!" I reprimanded. "What a terrible thing to say."

He shrugged, unrepentant. "He was not a man I had any respect for when he was alive, and I'm certainly not going to start honoring him now that he's dead. In fact," he looked at me thoughtfully, "he is probably the only person I feel actual hostility, maybe even hatred, toward." There was steel in his voice and more than a little bitterness.

I laid my hand on his. "Why do you dislike him so?"

"For what he did to his son Davy. He was my best friend."

Somehow that didn't surprise me. "I spoke with Davy's wife a while ago."

"What?"

"I called Lauren for Annie to tell them about Old Nate."

He whistled, clearly startled. "Annie knew how to contact her?"

I nodded. "She had her address."

"Amazing." He smiled. "I always did like the old girl, and not just for her apple dumplings." Then his lip curled in a travesty of a smile. "I bet anything Old Nate didn't know she even knew about Davy's marriage, let alone how to contact them."

"Come on, Jake." I was uncomfortable with the depth of his aversion to Old Nate. It was one thing not to like someone all that much, to have a passive lack of appreciation for someone. It was entirely another to harbor feelings the depth of Jake's.

"Come on, yourself," he said, his eyes hard and cold. "I lost my best friend when Old Nate made them shun Davy."

"It wasn't Old Nate," I said, trying to get him to be reasonable, knowing it was probably a foolish hope. "It was the Ordnung. You know that."

"Then how about how he's treated Becky? Is that the Ordnung?" He stared at me, fists clenched on the arms of his chair, waiting for my answer.

"You sound so bitter and judgmental." I grabbed my flashlight and shined it in his angry face. "You'd better

115

watch it or you're going to become as bad as Old Nate was."

He grabbed my arm, twisting it so the light danced on the stairwell walls instead of in his eyes. He leaned in and spoke through his gritted teeth, very slowly and very distinctly. "You're right, Rose. I'm bitter. I'm judgmental. And I'm absolutely repulsed by that man. But don't ever try to tell me I'm going to be like him, not ever, not if you value our…" He paused, searching for a word. "Our whatever it is we have!"

He released my arm, turned, and rolled to his apartment, all in one angry movement. He paused at the door. "And I'm glad you're home safely!" He all but shouted it at me. And he was gone.

I sat frozen for a moment, stunned by his vehemence. Finally I sighed and rose, pondering his clenched fists and our whatever it is that we have. My shoulders sagged under the weight of it all, and I knew I didn't have the emotional stamina to think on such volatile topics anymore tonight.

I barely had the strength to tear off my clothes and drop them in a heap on the floor. I tossed my glasses in the general direction of the night table and fell into bed, totally exhausted. I was asleep almost before my head hit the pillow and I slept deeply, untroubled by nightmares or dreams or angry young men.

Six

WHEN I AWOKE, A GLANCE AT MY CLOCK SHOWED THAT I could just make church if I really moved. I washed, dressed, and generally made myself presentable as quickly as I could. When I came downstairs, the family was gone, off to worship or sit the Amish version of shivah with Annie. Of Jake there was no sign.

I slid into the back pew as the singing began, a definite change of pace for me. I liked to sit in the front because the congregation's voices washed over me and made the music so alive. When I got to heaven, one of the things I looked forward to most was being able to sing like I wanted. In fact, I'd probably sing better than I hoped because right now I was too human to imagine what heavenly singing sounded like.

This morning I found that the music made me teary and the message moved me more than usual. While I enjoyed a wonderful time of respite and release in worship, I slipped out during the closing prayer. I was too emotional from the past two days to make small talk.

I drove back to the farm in silence. In a few hours I'd be back in my apartment, sitting on my lumpy couch, watching TV as I did some needlepoint. I'd flick the dust cloth over surfaces that didn't get dusty because nothing happened in the rooms to cause dust. I'd climb into bed and fall asleep until my clock radio blasted me awake. I'd eat a quick breakfast of granola and yogurt while I read a magazine or a novel.

And I'd do it all alone.

Not that I minded solitude. I didn't. I liked being by myself. The rub was being alone all the time.

Sighing, I pulled into the Zooks' drive and went into the house. I didn't even have the door shut when Jake wheeled in from his rooms.

"Where've you been?" he asked, frowning.

"Church," I said, wondering where he thought I'd go on a Sunday morning.

"You should have slept in. You were out late last night."

I smiled at his show of concern and shook my head. "If I slept in following every night I had an emergency run, I'd have been fired by Home Health long ago."

He harrumphed, apparently deciding he wasn't going to get anywhere with this discussion because he said, "Mom left some food for us in the refrigerator."

Suddenly I missed the breakfast I hadn't had time to

eat. "Great! I'm famished. Let me change, and I'll be right back down."

We sat at the kitchen table with a round of ring bologna, a half dozen pickled eggs, a wedge of Muenster cheese, and a loaf of Mary's honey-oat bread. There were a couple of pieces of Esther's apple pie for dessert. We had just cut ourselves slices of meat and cheese when the front door banged open and Elam exploded into the room.

"Well, hello," Jake said. "I didn't expect to see you for several hours. Have some lunch." And he indicated the food on the table.

Elam gave us a lowering glance, his gray eyes hostile and unhappy. He hung his hat by the door. I thought it a wonder he didn't tear the brim off, given the violence with which he impaled it on the peg. He unbuttoned his plain black jacket and pulled it off roughly as he started up the stairs. In a moment we heard him clomping down the hall, his boots striking the floor like a boxer's fists thudding into a practice bag.

Jake and I looked at each other as a door slammed overhead.

"Mary Clare Epp," Jake said with a sardonic nod.

"Who's she?"

"The girl Elam fancies himself in love with. I bet they read the banns for her and Young Joe Lapp this morning."

"You mean they announced their intent to marry?" I looked at the ceiling. "Poor Elam."

"I tried to warn him once, but he wouldn't listen. And if I knew Mary Clare was interested in Young Joe, so did everyone else, believe me."

"Everyone but Elam." Thoughtfully I chewed a piece of cheese. "When I was here this summer, I got the idea that Esther and he were an item."

Jake grunted. "They would be if Esther had her way. She's certainly in love with him. I think the only reason she's still here is that she and Mom hope he'll come to his senses. Personally I think he's crazy to prefer Mary Clare to a wonderful girl like Esther." He savored a piece of her pie, a look of bliss on his face. "Any woman who can cook like this is worth marrying."

When we finished eating, I rose. "Why don't you bring the dishes over and I'll wash?"

Jake eyed me without moving, a strange look on his face.

"Oh, come on," I said. "You aren't an Amishman anymore. You're allowed to help in the kitchen. It's good for you. Remember I was the one out for half the night last night. Of course, you were up half the night too, weren't you?"

He began collecting our dishes. "It's not that I mind helping you. No, that's not it," he said. "It just struck me that you're the first person who's asked me to help around the house since I came home."

I looked at him. "You can't mean that you sit like a lump all day while people wait on you."

He took the jar of pickled eggs, the bologna, and

cheese and rolled to the propane refrigerator. "I don't mean that at all. I do all kinds of things. I've got weights and an exercise machine for my legs. I take 'walks' up and down the road. I pick up my place and work on my van. Now I've got college. But no one *asks* me to do anything."

I rinsed off the plates I'd washed in hot water heated on the cookstove. "They should have you doing all sorts of jobs if you ask me. It should be part of your rehabilitation, just seeing how much you can do. Surely your therapist suggested it."

"Father and Elam have had me working some, and I helped paint the fences and porch before my sister's wedding. But no one asks me to do anything inside."

"And you never noticed until today?"

"I didn't." He was as surprised as I. "I think it's cultural. Men don't help around the house because they do so much outside. Women care for the house. It never occurred to Mom to ask me to do stuff. Not that she waited on me. She didn't. She and Esther just cared for me."

"Coddled you, you mean," I said as I handed him a wet cloth. "Here. Wipe off the table."

"Interersting, interesting," he said.

"Interesting nothing," I said. "You need to do all those caring things for yourself, like laundry and dishes. Get one of those compact washer/dryer units like they have in apartments."

"Mom'll fight it all the way. I know her. She's convinced my rebellion's going to send me to hell, but she's going to make my life here as comfortable as possible."

I watched him as he wiped the table, missing a half dozen spots in the process. "How do you like college?"

He looked up in surprise. "I was sure you'd jump on my send-me-to-hell comment."

"Another time. Right now I want to know how you like college."

He grinned, his black eyes sparkling. "I do. I like it very much. I like the learning. I like the questions everyone asks. I like the lectures and the library. I even like the quizzes. Now is that nuts or what!"

"It's nuts." But I understood. I'd always loved learning things, too. "What made you decide to go? I mean, why are you going?"

He shrugged. "Because I want to learn things. Because it passes time. Because I want to have a better life, though I haven't figured out yet what I'll be doing in that better life."

I rinsed out the sink and dried my hands. "I guess that's better than saying, 'I have no idea,' but not much."

"It's the best I can do at the moment."

"You should have some specific goals, some plans."

"I know."

"But you don't."

He shrugged. "Eventually."

"How old are you?" I asked.

"Twenty-six."

I looked at him for a few minutes. "And you don't know why you're spending all this money to go to school?" I tried not to sound accusatory, but I wasn't completely successful. I noticed my fisted hands were planted on my hips. I lowered them and took a deep breath. At least I didn't have my finger shaking under his nose.

He tightened his jaw. "No, I don't know why I'm spending all this money." He balled the cloth he'd wiped the table with and threw it in the sink. "I'm reinventing my life here, Rose, in case you haven't noticed, and I haven't got it all figured out yet." His voice was cold. "Is that okay with you?"

"Only if you truly are trying to figure it out."

"Hey!" He was quietly and justifiably angry. "A year ago I was a junior high dropout, a product of the Amish school system. Now I have a GED, I've proven myself at Millersville on a conditional acceptance, and I'm a full-time college student. I'd say that wasn't bad in one year."

I held up my hand, feeling somewhat embarrassed. What he did with his life wasn't mine to argue, I thought with chagrin. "You're absolutely right. In fact it's quite commendable for one year. I apologize."

"I'll get there, Rose. I will."

"I'm sure you will." I looked at him and prayed that was so.

"I've gotten a taste of using my mind, and I like it. It sure beats riveting together trailer shells."

"Trailer shells?" I repeated.

He nodded. "That's what I used to do. My only complaint is that I had to lose my legs to learn about learning."

I winced. There was no denying that he'd paid a very heavy price for his new direction.

He looked me right in the eye. "Not everyone's as driven to prove things as you, Rose."

I swallowed hard.

"And prove them today." His voice was quiet but it echoed wildly inside my head.

I sat down in Mary's rocker and stared at my knees. When Jake wheeled beside me, I didn't look up. I couldn't. I was ashamed of myself. I'd done it again, taking something that was precious from someone who was special. It wasn't my mother's husband and daughter I took today. It was Jake's self-respect and sense of accomplishment. And in the process, I had been cruel.

It was time to collect my duffel and go home.

I got up and started for the stairs

Jake caught my hand as I walked past. "Where are you going?"

"To get my things. It's time to go home. I've overstayed my welcome."

"No, no, Tiger." He pointed to his mother's chair. "Sit back down a minute. I have something to talk to you about."

Short of making a scene by pulling my arm from his grasp, I had no choice. I sat.

"Do you like your apartment?" he asked.

I looked at him, disconcerted by the subject change. I was still wallowing in self-inflicted guilt over my inappropriate accusations.

"It's okay, I guess. Small and dark but sufficient." I shrugged. "It came furnished, ugly stuff, but at least I didn't have to buy much when I moved in. I always planned to replace all the depressing things, but I seem to get a call every time I'm leaving to shop."

"Would you miss the place if you left it?"

I frowned. "No. It's biggest plus is that it's close to the Bird-in-Hand firehouse where the ambulance squad runs."

Jake grinned. "Then how about renting these rooms?" He waved his hand toward the upstairs apartment.

"Move here?" An emotion I couldn't define unfurled painfully in my chest at the suggestion. "Here?"

He nodded. "You do like the rooms, don't you?"

I did. I felt cozy up there, comfortable, at ease in spite of my nightmare. And I felt included down here. I felt that the family liked me and was glad I was around, but that they were also willing to let me be alone if that's what I wanted.

I was appalled at the piercing shaft of agony and desire that exploded in my chest at the thought of living here. I hadn't known that I was that lonely. I had always prided myself on my independence, my ability to cope in spite of the hard things in my life. But let a family show me a little affection, and I wanted to wallow in it like a pig in slops. I wanted Mary to hover and Esther to make me tea and Jake to—I stopped that thought before it got away from me.

And if this craving to be part of the Zooks was this strong after only two days, what would it become over a longer period of time?

Jake was still trying to sell me on the apartment. "Just think. You could talk with Mom and Esther all you wanted. They'd like you to stay."

My heart warmed. "Really? Are you sure?"

"And you'd be close enough to keep an eye on Becky and the baby. You know how concerned you are about them."

The emotion in my chest kept expanding, pressing against my ribs, my lungs, my spine until I could barely stand the anguished pleasure. I recognized it with a jolt as hope, hope that these people actually liked me, actually cared about me even when I acted foolishly and was unlovely.

And I was sore afraid. I swallowed hard, trying to curb my disproportionate reaction to a conversation about an apartment. And that's all it was about, nothing more. Certainly it wasn't about Jake and me. Right?

How could I move from my safe place just because of people? I'd always done things for sound reasons like getting better trained or preventing someone's death. But to do something based on emotion—how foolish was that! It was terrifying and so very attractive all at the same time. I began rubbing the ache in my chest.

"Besides," Jake finished with a smile, "I need the rent money."

Rent money! I grabbed at the idea. I could deal with

something so practical, so real, so unhopeish.

"You need the money, huh?" I eyed him like the money was the only reason I'd consider his apartment.

He nodded, looking hopeful. He must have seen something in my face that gave him reason to expect an affirmative answer.

"Then I'll take the rooms. I do like it here, and I like your family. And I certainly want you to have the money for next semester's tuition. I just hadn't been expecting to make such a large contribution."

"Good!" He seemed to release some pent-up tension and relax. "Mom and Esther will be delighted."

And you? I wondered. Are you pleased for any reason other than the rent?

"So let's go get your stuff."

"Now? This very minute?"

"Sure. Why not? Why should you go back there to sleep if you like it here?"

Why indeed.

"You're going to help me?"

He nodded. "I'll drive."

"That's it?"

He looked at me blankly.

"You don't get off that easily," I said. "I'll bring everything down to the porch, and you'll take it to the van. It's called cooperation."

He looked at me, his black eyes thoughtful. "You're good for me, you know that?"

It was my turn to be pleased, very pleased. Too

pleased? I ran upstairs for my coat before I could reconsider my decision.

Jake and I were out front when Esther walked into the drive. Her eyes were fixed on the ground.

"Hey, Esther," I called. "Guess what? I'm moving in for good. I'm renting the apartment."

She jumped and looked up. "That's wonderful," she said without enthusiasm. She had her arms wrapped tightly across her body as if she were in pain. It would be hard to imagine an Esther more unlike the spirited competitor of last night.

"Are you all right?" I moved to her side. I was surprised to see tears in her eyes.

"Is Elam here?" She looked at the house.

"In his room," Jake said.

Her eyes shifted to the window in the far right corner. "He left right after service without eating or anything."

"Mary Clare?" Jake asked softly.

A tear fell onto Esther's lovely cheek. "Yes. And Young Joe Lapp. They marry in two weeks."

"Go talk with him," Jake said. "Maybe he'll finally see what's right in front of his nose."

"I don't know," Esther said. "I've been talking to myself the whole way up the street. Should I? Shouldn't I? What is right? And I don't know. I've prayed and prayed and I still don't know."

"I wish I knew what to tell you," I said, my heart aching for her.

"I wish I knew what to tell him." Esther turned her bleak eyes on me. "But what can I say to a man whose heart has just been broken?"

Neither Jake nor I spoke. Finally Esther sighed.

"I can say nothing." And she turned and began to walk disconsolately back toward the Stoltzfus farm. Suddenly she turned, broke into a run, and rushed into the barn.

I started to go after her, but Jake caught my arm. "Let her alone. She needs to cry, and she needs to do it in private."

I nodded. "Can I go kick Elam in the shins?"

Jake smiled but his eyes were sad. "I think he's as distraught as she is. Maybe you should have a bit of sympathy for him, too."

"Probably. But she's such a wonderful girl!"

"You can't control who people love. Come on. Let's go."

As I watched him lock his chair onto the lift, I thought, you sure can't.

Seven

WHEN I OPENED THE DOOR TO MY APARTMENT, I WAS GREETED with the stale smell that comes from a house being closed up too long. Not that this odor was new to me. It greeted me every day when I returned from work or even if I just walked downstairs to check the mailbox.

I had decided it was the nasty orange shag rug left over from the sixties. It looked like it hadn't been cleaned in years, though I rented one of those rug machines at the grocery store not long after I moved in. I discovered that a wet rug smells much worse than a dry rug, whatever's hidden in it. I gave up trying to clean the thing and made a point never to go barefoot anywhere in the place, not even in the shower. It had so much grouting stained black with mildew that I anticipated disease every time I stepped in.

I wrinkled my nose as I walked to my desk. I would

not miss that odor any more than I'd miss the rusting refrigerator, the avocado green sink, the unbelievably ugly kitchen linoleum, and the lumpy sofa.

In fact, I wouldn't miss anything but the proximity to the firehouse. And the rent. It was by far the cheapest place I'd ever looked at, including the farm. But enough was enough. It was time to move on. The farm wasn't all that far from the firehouse, maybe three minutes farther. I bet I'd still beat Harry. And my rooms there were light and open and clean. The rug there was a lovely hand-braided oval, and there wasn't an avocado appliance on the premises.

I glanced at my answering machine, which sat on the corner of the desk, and saw the message light blinking. I had ten messages. As I reached to hit the play button, I tried to imagine ten people who wanted to talk to me. I couldn't.

The first message was from Lem Huber, the Lancaster cop. "Please call." He gave his number, and I wrote it down. As I stuffed the paper in my pocket, my mother's voice broke the silence with all the gentleness of a pneumatic drill.

"Rose Grayson Martin! What have you done now? Call me immediately."

What have I done now? I hadn't the vaguest idea. I waited for the third message.

"Rose, call me immediately." Mom again, her voice tense but not quite as angry. "If you need a lawyer, I know who to call."

I blinked. Why would I need a lawyer? My lease wasn't that tight. And she didn't know I was moving.

"Rose, you're upsetting me! How could you get involved in something so, so... Well, how could you?"

How could I indeed. I had no idea what she was talking about.

"Have you skipped town, Rose? Is that it? You've run away without even telling your mother you were leaving?"

That message gave me pause. I hadn't told her I was staying the weekend at the Zooks. But literally speaking, that wasn't skipping town. It was still Bird-in-Hand. Somehow I didn't think that's what she was referring to.

"Rose, I'm getting scared now." I could hear a distinct tremor in her voice. "They were here looking for you. I didn't know what to tell them. I don't want to make things worse for you. Rose, if you hear me, please, please call."

I blinked. Mom had abandoned her general-commanding-the-troops persona of the first message for that of a very upset—no, distraught mother hen, certain the sky has fallen on her baby. Was she upset about me and whatever she thought was my problem? The thought warmed me. Or about them, whoever they were?

"Rose, it's me." Mom literally sobbed in her next message. "Please call. I'm dying here." I stared at the answering machine. My mother? Crying?

There were two more frantic messages from my mom and another from Lem.

I decided to call my mother first.

"Rose, oh, Rose!" She started to cry when she heard my voice. "Where have you been? I've been so worried!"

"Mom, I'm fine." I tried not to let exasperation sound in my voice even though I thought she was over-reacting a tad to the absence of a return telephone call. "Truly I am."

"No," she said. "You're just saying that so I won't worry. I know you are." She lowered her voice to a whisper. "They're looking for you. I heard it on the radio and saw it on TV. And they were here."

"They?" I'd never worried about my mother's mental stability before, but I did now. She made it sound like a posse of extraterrestrials was after me. "At your house?"

"The police. They were here looking for you."

"Oh, that. I know. I just got a message to call them."

"Don't do it without a lawyer," Mom said. "I've seen enough cop shows to know you need a lawyer. And make sure they read you your rights."

"Mom! What are you thinking! I'm not under arrest."

"I don't know, Rose. The TV even showed your picture and said they were searching for you. They probably have an APB out. You know what that means."

"All points bulletin?"

"Guns," she said. "Lots of them! Shoot-outs. High-speed car chases. Oh, Rose. They're going to shoot you!"

I actually pulled the phone away from my ear and stared at it in disbelief. "Mom, calm down and think for a minute. Ask yourself if that conclusion is at all logical. Why in the world would they shoot me?"

"Because of the bombs!"

When she said *bombs,* all I could think of was Iran or Hiroshima and Nagasaki or Dresden. I had a great-uncle who flew the Dresden bombing raids in World War II and always talked about them whenever he felt morose, which for Uncle Mikey was often, maybe because of the terrible destruction he helped inflict during the Dresden raids.

"Because of that family that got blown up," Mom said. "And you were there!"

"Because of the Hostetters?"

"That's the name!"

"It was a bomb?" I felt dazed. A bomb? It couldn't have been a bomb. Bombs were set on purpose. Bombs were evil and ugly.

Bombs were murder.

Suddenly I was sitting on the floor, my hand over my heart. Sophie and Ammon hadn't been killed in a freak explosion. Someone had premeditated their deaths.

I think on some deep level I always knew it was a bomb that exploded. Cars didn't just go boom! I knew that. But the truth was so devastating that I hadn't wanted to acknowledge it. Now I had no choice. My stomach curdled and I swallowed several times to keep from being ill.

Another thought struck me between the eyes. I was

the closest thing they had to a witness!

"Look, Mom," I managed. "I've got to call the police. I'm sorry you've been worried about me. If I had known about the TV and radio announcements, I'd have called right away. But I truly am fine."

"But where have you been?"

"I spent the weekend with friends on their farm because I didn't want to be alone after all the emotion of the explosions." I noted that I couldn't bring myself to say *bomb*.

"You should have come here," she said.

"They were closer. In fact, I'm moving there permanently even as we speak. They have an apartment I'm renting."

"An apartment on a farm. That sounds nice," Mom said, approving. "What's their phone number?"

"They don't have a number. They're Amish. But here's my cell phone number until I get my regular one connected. I think there's a line into my apartment."

"You're not becoming Amish, are you, Rose?" She spoke with hushed horror.

"Of course not, Mom."

"I've worried about you doing something like that for years, ever since your father and sister died. Sort of like penance, you know?"

The thought of my mother worrying about me like that was so beyond my comprehension that I had no response. Equally strange was the idea of joining a sect as penance, no matter how nice the people might be.

"Look, I've got to go," I said.

"Call me, Rose," she pleaded. "As soon as you're finished with the police, call me. I'll just worry myself sick until I hear from you."

As I put the phone back in its cradle, I heard Jake calling for me.

"Rose! Rose! Come down here a minute. I need to talk with you!"

I picked myself up off the floor and went down to him.

"You're on the radio," he said. "The police are looking for you."

I nodded. "I just spoke to my mother and she told me. There was also a message to call the police. I was just getting ready to do so."

Jake looked at me in a way that made me nervous.

"What?" I asked apprehensively.

"You need to know there's been another bombing."

My heart stopped. "What? Who?"

"Peter Hostetter's car."

I stared at him in disbelief.

"But Peter wasn't in it at the time," Jake hurried to say.

I sagged in relief against the porch post.

"What is going on here?" I whispered. "Evil Ernie?"

Jake took my hand and began patting it. "Who in the world is Evil Ernie?"

"Peter's uncle. Sophie's brother-in-law. And he wants the company." I straightened. "I've got to tell Lem!"

Jake held out my cell phone to me. I took it, pulled the paper with the number from my pocket, and dialed.

"Well, Rose," Lem said when we were finally connected. "I've been looking for you."

"So I hear." I cleared my throat nervously. "I'm sorry. I've been visiting friends for the weekend and haven't listened to the radio or seen a TV."

"Yeah, well, I'm sorry it ever got into the news. It never should have. They made you sound like you were a suspect or something."

"But I'm not, right?"

"But you're not. Unless you've got some deep, dark secrets we haven't discovered yet?"

I thought of Dad and Rhoda, but I knew that wasn't what he meant.

"I originally called to make certain you came in and signed your statement," Lem said. "Then when we couldn't find you, we began to get concerned for your safety, especially after the second incident."

Incident. Somehow that sounded so unemotional, so routine.

"You mean Peter's car?"

"Um."

"But Peter wasn't hurt?"

"Not at all. He was in the house, and the car was in the garage. Or I should say, the former garage."

"How come his car blew up empty and Sophie's car had people in it?"

"The lab's working on that as we speak."

"Come on, Lem. You must have some idea."

"All I know is that we're dealing with a murderer here, and a nasty one."

"Do you know about Ernie Hostetter?"

Lem answered carefully. "I know the name."

"Did you know he tried to get Hostetter, Inc. away from Sophie unethically?"

"How?"

"By buying her out at well under the value of her stock. He apparently thought she was unaware of its value."

"Unethical, as you said," Lem said. "But hardly illegal."

"Well, keep an eye on him," I said. "And I'll stop in sometime tomorrow to sign my statement."

I punched off the phone and turned to Jake. "It's so hard to believe. Who would want to kill nice people like Sophie and Ammon and Peter? If it wasn't Evil Ernie, I mean."

"They were rich, weren't they?"

I ran my hand through my hair. "Sure, but..."

"But nothing," Jake said. "Money's one of the biggest motives for murder. Who in the family would benefit most? Besides Evil Ernie?"

"I don't know. I never met any of their extended family."

"So there was just the mother and the two sons in the immediate family?"

I nodded. "And Sophie and Ammon are dead, and

139

someone just tried to kill Peter."

"I bet he was supposed to be killed the first time," Jake said. "He just got lucky."

"Because he went back in the house for his sunglasses." I sighed. "He and I waited together for help to arrive. I felt so bad for him."

We sat quietly for a few minutes, pondering the fact that something as innocuous as sunglasses spelled the difference between life and death.

Then we got to work. I went up to my apartment, accessible only by stairs, grabbed a box or suitcase full of things, brought it down, and gave it to Jake. He took it to the van and loaded it. In no time we developed a good rhythm. We finished much more quickly that I expected.

I was bringing down one of my last loads when a loud voice said, "And just what do you think you're doing, young woman?"

I looked up to see my landlord, a round, cherry-cheeked man who looked like St. Nick and had the disposition of a shrew.

"Hello, Mr. Metz." I smiled warmly at him, hoping to thaw his demeanor some. No such luck.

"Are you moving, Miss Martin? Or are you officially running from the police?"

"Mr. Metz!" I looked at him in astonishment. "What a terrible thing to say."

"Don't give me your wide-eyed innocent stare, Rose Martin." He glared at me as he shook his forefinger under my nose. "I heard all about you on the radio."

"An inaccurate report," I said quietly.

He either didn't hear me or made believe he didn't. He continued without taking a breath, "And I had the cops here all weekend looking for you."

"I'm so sorry, Mr. Metz. I've been staying with friends." I indicated Jake, who returned from the van for another load.

Mr. Metz glanced at Jake, then rounded on me. "Visiting friends? So that's what they call it these days."

It took a minute for his implications to sink in. Then I was so furious that my voice shook. "Be careful what you say, Mr. Metz, because you are very wrong."

"Riiiight."

"Mr. Metz." Jake's voice could have frozen the Caribbean. "My name is Jake Zook. My family and I have been pleased to have Rose as our guest this weekend. We are delighted that she has decided to move to an apartment that we rent, though why she would want to leave such a considerate and kind landlord as you is hard to imagine." He smiled with such disdain that even Mr. Metz felt the insult.

"Now wait a minute," he said. "You can't talk to me that way."

"And you can't talk to Rose unkindly, either." Jake's black eyes snapped with anger.

Mr. Metz looked down at Jake, sniffed, and swung to me. "You've got a lease. You can't break your lease."

"I'm afraid you're hoist by your own petard, Mr. Metz," I said, trying not to be petty enough to enjoy pointing out his self-made trap. "You've never been willing to give me a lease for longer than a month at a time, just in case you wanted to evict me for unseemly behavior."

"And wasn't I just right about that!" He puffed out his chest self-righteously as he glanced at Jake.

"Well, no, not in the least," I said, knowing he wouldn't believe me. "But that's not the point. The point is that I can leave. As you know, I've paid you through the end of November. As of the first of December, you can rent this place to someone else."

"And I'm not giving you any money back even though there's more than a week of November left, if that's what you're hinting at." He glared at me like a kindergartener trying to start a fight over whose father was bigger.

I refused to rise to his bait. "I'm not asking for anything back."

"And don't give me your forwarding address," he hissed, "because I'm not forwarding nothing!"

"Don't worry," I said. "I'll contact the post office."

"And I'm coming up to make sure you're not running off with what's not yours."

I looked at Mr. Metz and wondered, not for the first time, how someone who looked so cuddly and Santa Clausy could be so vile and judgmental. "Be my guest."

"And I'm calling the police!" He leaned toward me, his plump, rosy cheeks shaking with the intensity of his venom.

"You needn't bother. I already called."

"Like I can believe that!" He turned away in a huff, but he didn't go upstairs. He went inside the front door of the first floor that he shared with his little wife who always reminded me of a kitten who had been abused so long that she ducked even when there was no threat. In a minute he came to stand in the doorway, a phone in his hand.

"Nine-one-one," he said very loudly as he depressed the numbers so we'd be certain to know he was indeed calling the cops.

Jake and I looked at each other and rolled our eyes.

"Is there much more?" Jake asked as he set a box on his knees.

"About two more loads."

An hour later I surveyed the mess in my living room at the farm and shuddered. I glanced at my watch. Almost time for the TV news. Quickly I set my small TV on the battered old desk and plugged it in. I turned to WGAL to hear what, if anything, they were still saying about me.

"Another bomb," Matt Dolman, the anchor, said as he looked seriously at the camera. He was the picture of pained disbelief. "And another death." He paused as if giving his audience time to give a mental tsk-tsk. "Our Patty Carlson is at the scene with the latest report on what has become a story of tragic proportions."

I sank into a chair to hear what they said about Peter's car bomb.

Then the face of reporter Patty Carlson filled the screen. I stared in disbelief as I realized she was standing in front of my old apartment. It was easy to see flames ripping through the roof of the house, smoke billowing into the night sky, and emergency vehicles littering the street.

"Yes, Matt," Patty said earnestly to the camera, "this is a tragic story. Just thirty minutes ago, a bomb ripped through the apartment of Rose Martin on the second floor of that house behind me. Martin is the home health nurse police have been looking for all weekend. Martin was present on Friday when Pockets CEO Ammon Hostetter and his mother Sophie died in another bombing outside their Lancaster home. It was just late this morning that another bomb exploded at the Hostetter home, destroying the car of Peter Hostetter but leaving him unscathed."

The cameras moved away from Patty and focused on the firemen showering the blaze with their hoses. Also shown were two uniformed policemen standing by an unmarked car and two other men in plain clothes standing near them. One of these two was Lem Huber. All four were staring up at the flames still licking the edges of the roof.

I listened, paralyzed, as Patty's voice continued over the pictures.

"At this time authorities do not know any particulars about the bomb, but they do acknowledge that they have discovered a body just inside the door of the second floor apartment where Martin lived."

Matt Dolman's voice was heard from the studio. "Excuse me, Patty. Have they identified the body as Rose Martin?"

"Not at this point, Matt. But it is certainly a strong possibility, isn't it?"

They thought I was dead? The idea was appalling! I shivered and remembered my grandfather, Joseph Phineas Martin, who opened the paper one day and read his own obituary. It turned out that someone with the same name had died, and they'd run a write-up on Grandpop, an ex-mayor of Honey Brook.

Then my blood chilled as I thought of my mother. What if she were watching? She'd been close to hysterical this afternoon. How would she react to my presumed death?

I grabbed my cell phone and began to dial when Jake bellowed, "Rose! We've got trouble!"

I rushed to the top of my steps and looked down at him. He was forcing his arms into the sleeves of his jacket.

"I know! I saw it too."

"Get your coat and let's go over there and see what happened. While we're at it, we can tell them you're okay."

I clicked off the phone and ran for my jacket and purse.

"I've got to call my mom," I said as I thundered down the steps.

"I'll drive," Jake said. "You make the calls you need to."

We hurried out through Jake's apartment with its ramp and over to the van. I climbed quickly into the passenger seat, my mind a sea of conflicting emotions. I wasn't dead. Thank You, Lord. But someone was. Who? Did I feel guilty because it wasn't me? Was it really a bomb like Patty Carlson said? Or did Mr. Metz's heating system finally explode? Was he hurt? Was mousey Mrs. Metz hurt? Who was the body?

Suddenly I realized I was jiggling my foot with impatience. It felt like it took Jake so long to lower his lift, to lock his chair on it and lift to the van, to unlock, roll to the driver's seat, and lock his wheels again. I was biting my nails by the time he turned the key in the ignition.

He glanced at me with that uncanny understanding of his. "Everything you do with me will take you ten times longer," he said. "Fact of life for a paraplegic."

"You're much too perceptive," I said. "And I don't mean to be impatient."

"You'd be superhuman if you weren't in a situation like this." He put the van in reverse. "Now calm down and make your calls."

I spit a final piece of fingernail out of my mouth and dialed my mother.

"Mom!" I all but screamed when she answered the phone. "I'm okay. You don't have to believe the TV. They're wrong!"

"I'm glad you're fine, dear," she said, obviously not

upset, also obviously not watching TV. "But what are they saying now?"

"There was someone killed in a fire in Bird-in-Hand, and they thought it might be me."

She caught her breath. "Why would anyone think it was you?"

"Because the fire was in my old apartment."

"The one you lived in before you decided to become Amish?"

"Mom, I haven't decided to become Amish, but yes, that's the place."

"Well, I guess it's a good thing you decided to move, isn't it? Even if you do have strange plans."

I closed my eyes and took a deep breath. "Mom, I don't have strange plans. I just decided to live somewhere else."

"Certainly, dear."

I shook my head, ignoring Jake's soft laugh, and said, "Well, I'll call you later."

"Good, dear. And don't forget Thursday is Thanksgiving. We'll put up the tree."

I hung up and turned to Jake. "My apartment is bombed and we were talking about the Christmas tree?"

Every year for as long as I could remember, Mom put up the Christmas tree on Thanksgiving Day. Every year for as long as I could remember, she encouraged me to decorate it as I pleased. And every year for as long as I could remember, she rearranged everything the first time I left the room.

I rubbed my forehead, concentrating on the vein in the center of my forehead, the one that throbbed with pain.

Jake glanced at me. "Don't let her upset you, Tiger. She doesn't mean any harm."

I nodded. "I know. She's just so ditzy sometimes. Now you know why I live in Bird-in-Hand instead of Honey Brook."

I put Mom out of my mind and phoned Lem Huber.

"Well, well," he said when my call was forwarded to him. "So you're all in one piece. I've got to say I'm relieved. Though now I've got an unknown here." He sounded pleased that I was among the living in spite of now having an unknown. I could hear the noises of the fire scene in the background.

"We left the house before anything happened," I said. "I was back at the farm unpacking." I paused. "Uh, what did happen?"

He didn't answer my question. Instead he said, "So where are you now?"

"In a van about two miles from where you are and closing fast."

Lem was silent for a minute. "Rose, don't come to the scene."

"What?" I said, taken by surprise at the request.

"Don't come. Let them think that it was you we found."

Jake made a turn and the glow of the flames in the night leaped all rose and red, undulating along the sky like an active Northern Lights.

"Jake, stop." I grabbed his arm. "Don't go to the scene."

Jake immediately slowed and looked at me.

"The police don't want me to be seen."

"Pull over a block before you get here," Lem said in my ear. "I'll find you. Make sure you turn off the inside light. Our bomber may be here watching the fun, and I don't want him to see you when the van door is opened."

"We're in a dark green modified Caravan," I said and clicked off.

As we approached the scene, Jake had to drive carefully because of the usual gawkers paying more attention to the fire than the road. A little over a block before we reached my old apartment, he pulled over. We sat in silence and stared.

The flames shimmering along the roofline slowly diminished as the firemen played their hoses with great skill. There was lots of smoke pouring from the shattered living room windows on the second floor. The flames flickered with one last effort to control the night, then were doused. The sky was once again an opaque black. Other than the smoke, there was nothing to see of the catastrophe, at least from this distance. Rather, it was a matter of smelling it. The stench of wet burned wood hung thick and rank over the neighborhood.

"I wonder if the Metzes are all right," I said. "Or if he was the body."

"He did say he was going up to check that you didn't take any of his things."

"Like I wanted any of his things."

As I spoke, the back door slid open and Lem quickly climbed in. He brought with him a great, reeking wave of smoky fumes.

"I'll never get that smell out of these clothes," he groused. "I ought to know better than to wear anything good to work."

"There's a lot to be said for uniforms," I said.

He looked at me and smiled. "We knew it wasn't you up there, but it's still good to see you in person. Congratulations on being alive."

I shivered. "Last week at this time, I would have been there."

"Last week at this time, you weren't in danger."

"And she is now?" Jake asked.

"I'm afraid so." Lem studied Jake with interest. "Are you her new landlord?"

Jake nodded. "She's taken rooms at our family farm." Jake introduced himself, and Lem wrote down his phone number and the farm's address.

Then Lem turned his attention to me. "Who knows you're living at the farm?

"Only my mother," I said. "I was afraid she might have heard something on TV and would think I was dead."

"No one else?" Lem was very intense. "Think carefully."

"No one." I was definite.

"Then I think you can continue to live there. But

you can't go to work. You can't go into Bird-in-Hand or Lancaster. You have to stay hidden for your own safety."

"But I have to go to work! What about my cases?"

Lem shook his head. "No."

"What you're saying," Jake said, "is that you think that the bomb that exploded here tonight was meant for Rose, and you're afraid that if whoever sent it knows she's alive, he'll try again."

"That's it," Lem said.

"But why should anyone want to kill me? I don't know anything. I didn't see anything."

"Someone thinks you're dangerous in some way." Lem was very emphatic. "I don't know why any more than you do, but there's no avoiding that conclusion."

"So I stay hidden until you solve the case?"

Lem nodded.

"How long will that take?" I tried not to whine. Much as I liked the farm, the thought of being cooped up there was upsetting.

"I don't know," Lem said. "But until the bomber is apprehended…"

I nodded. "Okay. So who let's them know at work? You or me?"

"Neither," he said. "You're dead. They're hearing it on the news tonight just like the rest of Lancaster County."

I thought of Madylyn, my whiny office manager. I thought of the rest of the nurses I worked with and the people I ran with on the ambulance squad, especially

Harry. "It seems cruel," I said. "Believe it or not, some of them like me."

"In a way it *is* cruel," Lem said. "But it'll keep you alive."

I looked at Jake to see what he thought, and he gave a slight shrug that I heard in the movement of material more than saw. "That is the main goal, right? To keep you alive. I think you do whatever it takes."

"What about my mother?" I asked. "What if the papers or TV comes to interview her? She knows I'm alive."

"It would be wonderful to have a policewoman live there and pretend she's your aunt. She could deal with the media, saying your mother is too distraught to talk with them. Which would be true in a way. She couldn't handle the pretense. No one could if they knew the truth."

"You actually have a spare policewoman who can go live with my mom for the duration?"

Lem shook his head. "Probably not. I'll ask for one, but realistically we'll just have to hope no one goes to see your mother."

We were silent a minute, digesting this thought.

"For your information, Huber," Jake said suddenly, "I have a gun, and I know how to use it."

I gulped and stared. "You have a gun?"

"Several, in fact. And not just hunting rifles, either." Jake grinned. "Can you think of a better way for a son of nonviolence to rebel?"

Lem laughed. "But are you any good?"

"I target practice frequently. You can check me out anytime you want."

Lem grunted.

Jake's mouth thinned. "I know what you're thinking. With no legs, what use am I, right?"

Lem looked him straight in the eye. "Can you blame me?"

"No. But I'll see to it that she's never in a dangerous place alone."

Just then I saw a familiar car fly by. It came to a stop by the ambulance. Harry Mast climbed out. He walked to the front of the vehicle and leaned against the grillwork. He stared, shoulders slumped, at the damaged house.

"That's my partner," I said, appalled at the sight of him, obviously upset. "We have to tell him I'm all right!"

Lem grabbed my arm as I reached for the door handle. "No, Rose. You're dead."

"He's right, Tiger," Jake said. "You're dead."

I shrank into my seat. "I hate this."

We sat in silence for a few minutes, me with tears running down my cheeks as I watched Harry.

"I'll be in contact," Lem finally said and let himself out. He walked past Harry as if he didn't see him.

"Let's go," I whispered to Jake. "I've got to get out of here before I rush up to Harry and hug him."

When we reached the farm, I climbed out of the van on my side and waited morosely for Jake. I heard the motor as he was lowered to the ground and again as the lift went back into the van. I heard the door slam.

Then I heard a sound that made my blood run cold. I heard Jake gasp, curse, and then I heard the unmistakable sound of a body and a wheelchair hitting the ground.

"Jake!" I ran around the van and knelt beside him as he lay on his side, trapped in the chair by the straps that were supposed to protect him. A large rock lay beside the still-spinning wheel. I pushed it out of the way.

"Are you all right?" I asked, automatically feeling for damage. I was most concerned about his left shoulder that had taken the brunt of the fall.

"I'm fine," he muttered, wincing as I palpated the shoulder. "Just fine."

When I was satisfied that nothing was broken, I pulled his right arm across my shoulder, braced my foot against the wheel of the chair, and pulled.

"What do you think you're doing?" Jake asked.

"Isn't it obvious?" I panted as I heaved again.

He slapped at my arm. "Let go, Rose. Go get help."

I stood and looked at the dark house. "I don't think anyone's home."

Jake tried to see over his shoulder, but he couldn't. With an exasperated sigh, he rested his head on the ground. "Elam's probably still here, either mooning over Mary Clare in the dark or sleeping. Just go get him."

"Elam, Elam!" I screamed as I rushed inside and started up the steps to the family quarters. "Help! Jake's fallen."

I was almost to the top of the stairs when a giant shadow loomed out of the dark, scaring me so much that I screamed.

The shadow screamed back, and I recognized Elam's voice.

"Help, Elam! Jake's fallen."

We rushed outside, and it wasn't until Elam stubbed his toe on the rock that had upended Jake that I realized he was in his stocking feet.

From his unpleasant position on the ground Jake grunted in satisfaction.

"Like sharing the pain?" Elam said as he limped to his brother's side.

"Like sharing the indignity," Jake retorted.

In no time Elam had the wheelchair righted, and we both went with Jake to his apartment in spite of his frequent requests that we just leave him alone. On the way I took a short detour to my car for my first aid kit.

Jake was stoic as I cleaned and disinfected the scrapes on his palms and his left cheek.

"You need some of that orange stuff like you had on your forehead," Elam said as he watched. "It hurts a lot when you put it on, doesn't it? He'd look so cute painted like a fruit."

"Go away," Jake said as he jumped from the sting of the disinfectant. I wasn't sure whether he meant me or Elam, but since I wasn't finished yet, I ignored him.

"You're in a sour mood." Elam scowled at his brother.

"Look who's talking."

"Boys, boys," I said. "Enough. We've all had a hard day."

"Say good night, Elam," Jake said.

"Ingrate," muttered Elam as he left. We could hear him limping upstairs.

When I attacked the remaining cinders in his left palm, Jake grabbed my arm. "Stop, Rose. You need to go, too."

I looked into his black eyes. "I can't go yet. You'll get an infection."

"I can take care of myself." His voice was like the lick of a whip.

I flinched and dropped his hand as if it burned. "You're right. You can." I set the disinfectant on an end table beside the little blue Pockets car. I heard him sigh as I picked up my purse and started for the door. I told myself I wasn't hurt by his attitude, that he had more right to be distressed than I, that it was just his pride kicking in.

Well, I had pride too.

"Rose."

I ignored him.

He muttered under his breath and followed me through the door and to the bottom of my stairs. As I started to ascend, he grabbed my arm again.

"Rose, I—" He looked up at me, but I couldn't read his expression in the dim light that escaped from his apartment. He sighed again. "Thank you."

I stepped back down and turned to him. "Don't take

your frustration out on Elam and me, Jake. It's not our fault." I laid my hand on top of his as it rested on my arm.

He nodded. "I know."

I tried to smile at him. "You've been there for me these last few days in the most unbelievable way. I want to be there for you. Friendship and caring go both ways, guy. You've got to let me help you. As Esther would say, you don't want to take my blessing, do you?"

He stared at me, his face grim. "Some blessing." Then he looked away, his mouth tight with frustration and pain. Slowly he turned the hand gripping my arm palm up until he clasped my hand in his. In a choked voice he said, "Thank you, Tiger. For being you. For putting up with me."

He squeezed my hand hard and was gone.

Eight

"GOOD MORNING, MARY," I SAID AS I WALKED INTO THE kitchen the next morning.

Mary smiled sweetly at me, though I thought she seemed a bit less serene than usual.

Jake, on the other hand, didn't even look at me. He continued drinking his coffee as if I weren't in the room.

"Good morning to you, too, Jake," I said brightly.

He grunted but didn't look up. I decided he was still upset over last night.

Mary slipped another egg into the pan with Jake's and continued the conversation she was having with her son.

"I'll pack a sandwich and a piece of apple pie and some chips for you to take to school. Will cold meatloaf be all right?"

"Whatever."

"It's no bother. I want to do it. And your laundry. I'll get it later this morning. Esther and I are washing all day. That is, she's washing and hanging out to dry, and I'll fold and iron when I get back from Annie's."

"I don't want you to do my laundry, Mom." While the words sounded considerate, his tone didn't. It was downright belligerent. "I'm going to get one of those little washer/dryer combinations."

I smiled, thinking of our earlier conversation about his doing more for himself. I poured hot water over my tea bag.

"No, no," Mary said as she pulled toast from a wire rack over an open burner on the small propane stove. "I'll do it."

"Mom, I said no." Jake's voice was as cold and abrupt as his stare.

Mary lifted her chin like she had received a blow to it, but she said nothing. She slid our eggs onto plates and put them on the table in front of us along with the toast and homemade strawberry jam.

After a minute or two during which Jake and I buttered our toast without his once looking in my direction, Mary said, "I think we'll have pork and sauerkraut this evening. Do you like that, Rose? Some people don't like sauerkraut, but our family always has."

I nodded around a mouthful of food, and she kept on talking. I looked at her with interest. Such volubility was not common for her.

"I can't decide on the sauerkraut with caraway seed

in it or not. What do you think, Jake? Rose?"

I shrugged. I had no opinion. I'd never eaten it with caraway seeds. Jake ignored the question, though I noticed his eyebrows drawing ever closer together the longer Mary talked.

"And we'll have mashed potatoes and that wonderful applesauce Esther made. She put just a bit of cinnamon in it, and it is delicious. Don't you think iss goot, Jake? You'll love it, Rose. You really will. Chust the tiniest taste of cinnamon. She's such a goot girl, our Esther, such a nice girl. And she can cook so goot. If I've told her once, I've told her a hundred times, you will a goot wife be to some man. Don't you think so, Rose? Don't you—"

"Mom, please!" Jake skewered his mother with a ferocious gaze. He'd obviously reached and surpassed his tolerance level for chitchat "Be quiet, will you? I'm trying to eat here."

"Jake!" I looked at him with censure.

In response he drained his coffee mug—this one read New Holland Farm Machinery—and turned abruptly away. He rolled out of the room without a look or word.

I stared after him. Where had the gentle and helpful man of the weekend gone? Something was wrong, something more than the accident. The question was, could I get him to tell me what it was before he hurt anyone else?

I turned to Mary. "Are you all right? I'm so sorry he spoke to you like that."

She smiled sadly. "He was like that a lot when he first came home from rehab," she said. "But he hasn't been in one of his black moods for quite some time."

"Black mood or not, there's no excuse for talking to anyone, let alone your mother, in that tone of voice."

"It's all right," she said. "Things is hard for him."

"So what? Things are hard for a lot of people. Look at me. I'm dead. But I'm polite."

Mary blinked. "What?"

I remembered that she didn't know about my recent demise. "Nothing," I mumbled. "A poor joke."

She looked at me, confused, then turned and walked into the shedlike addition that housed the wringer washing machine that Elam had rigged to work on a twelve-volt battery.

I finished my breakfast thoughtfully. There was a bomber out there who seemed to want me dead. I was pretending to be dead and hurting and/or confusing lots of people by doing so, and all I could think of was Jake and his inexplicable anger.

Or was it all I could think about was Jake, period? I thought of him before I fell asleep and first thing when I awoke. I thought about seeing him as I came down the stairs.

Now I thought about him as I waited at the window for him to roll down the sidewalk on his way to the van and school. As soon as I saw him, I threw open the front door and met him where the front walk met the walk that circled the house to his front door.

It was obvious he planned to ignore me, so I planted myself in the middle of the walk, blocking his movement.

"Jake, what's wrong?" My voice shook a bit with anger and distress in spite of my best efforts. I looked at his impassive face and thought I'd never before cared about anyone the way I cared about him.

"You're in my way, Rose."

I looked at him, overwhelmed with the need to hear him call me Tiger. Instead his voice was cool, disinterested.

"Please move," he told my belt buckle "or I'll be late for class."

"Not until you talk to me," I said. "Or look at me."

"We've got nothing to talk about." He rolled forward until his foot plate rested against my shin. Then he looked up pointedly.

His eyes were black holes in his unhappy face. His hands were clenched fists. Hawk ambled over just then and nudged Jake's knee. Automatically he reached out and petted the animal, but his other hand remained in a white-knuckled fist.

"Jake, what's wrong?" I repeated. "Please tell me. Is it last night? If so, don't worry. The accident meant nothing to me. You know that. I'm a nurse, for heaven's sake. I've seen far worse."

He snorted. "Last night was but one more reminder that I am not what I was."

I smiled, though I imagined it looked a bit forced

and artificial. What I said was absolutely true. "I happen to like what you are."

He looked at me with something like pity. "Give it a rest, Rose. I will not be one more of your charity cases. Rose the Resourceful helping poor Jake the Judged-and-Found-Wanting."

For some reason his snideness angered me. "Oh, grow up," I said, the picture of maturity myself. "So life isn't perfect."

He made his deep-in-the-throat noise. "I'm going to be late for school. Move." He put pressure on my shins by rolling his chair a wee bit forward.

"You can give me black and blue shins, but I'm not moving. I can't. Not until you tell me what's wrong. Have I done something? If so, tell me." I hated the pleading note that had crept into my voice. I cleared my throat and tried for authority. "Tell me!"

"My problems are none of your business, Rose." He spit the words like lethal darts from a blowgun. "If your living here means you're going to probe where you're not wanted, maybe we'd better reconsider."

His words were so unexpected and painful that I actually took a step backward. "Jake! You don't mean that!"

He didn't answer but stared over my left shoulder in the general direction of the great barn. I tried to think of some smart remark to cover my hurt, but none came. Without thinking I reached out and brushed a lock of silky, dark hair off his forehead. He jerked as if I'd burned him.

"Rose," he said through clenched teeth, "I'd appreciate it if you kept your hands to yourself. And while we're talking so nicely here, don't ever, ever apologize for me again." His voice shook with rage.

"Why not?" I blazed back. "Someone had to. You were absolutely terrible to your mother."

He shrugged. "She's used to it."

"And that's an excuse?"

"Rose." He skewered me with the same gaze he'd used on Mary. "Leave. Me. Alone. This is not a request."

I actually felt the blood drain from my face. "That's really what you want?" The words were a mere whisper.

"Yes," he said, his voice steady. "That's what I want."

I thought I'd rarely seen such pain and resignation in anyone's eyes as I saw in his. I also saw strong resolve. Whatever was making him so hateful and hurtful this morning was causing him much more pain than he was meting out, but he was determined not to bend no matter how great his inner anguish. I stepped off the path and let him pass. Hawk padded after him to the van, then returned to stand by me.

"Talk to him for me, boy." I whispered as I watched the van disappear down the road. "Tell him it's okay. He's okay."

Hawk answered by pushing his wet nose against my palm.

I went up to my rooms and cried as I emptied my suitcases into the drawers and hung my clothes on the wall pegs.

In spite of my tears, I knew one thing: I was not leaving the farm, especially when I had no idea what was wrong. Besides, I had no apartment left to go back to, and the police wanted me to be dead and hide here.

Ha! I said to an imaginary Jake. You're stuck with me, boyo.

It was midmorning when Lem Huber called me.

"I think we've established quite credibly that you're dead," he began, "but I need to know that you are truly safe where you are."

"I can't imagine a safer place," I said. "The lives of the people here and the people in the rest of my life don't intersect. Also, no one knows I was thinking of moving from my old place, let alone moving to a farm."

"How did you meet these people in the first place?" Lem asked.

"I came here in the summer on an emergency run, and then I was assigned as home health nurse for Mary, the one who fell. I became friends with the family."

"Especially Jake?"

I laughed shortly. "That's a moot point at the moment."

He waited but I chose not to explain.

"Well," he finally said. "I'll check-in every couple of days."

"Sounds good. Do you have any leads? Any idea how long I'll have to be dead? What does Evil Ernie say?"

"We've leads, but no evidence that would allow an arrest and conviction."

I jumped on his comment. "What leads? What do you know?"

He was quiet, considering what he should or could tell me. "Well, we know they were homemade bombs way too powerful for their purposes, a sign of an amateur, and they were made with materials anyone could buy. We're talking with hardware stores and building supply stores, looking for someone who bought certain items recently."

"Do you know why Sophie's bomb detonated with people in the car and Peter's didn't?"

"Sophie's detonated when the engine turned over. Peter's was a remote control setup that detonated prematurely—at least from the bomber's perspective."

"Yeah," I said dryly. "I'm sure Peter views it differently. What about the one at my apartment?"

"It's too early to know much. Men are going through the ruins as we speak."

The ruins. I shivered. It could so easily have been me.

"Don't worry, Rose. It's just a matter of time and detail work. We'll get the guy."

I swallowed the desire to say, "You'd better." We said our farewells and disconnected. It took me a while to realize he'd not said anything about Ernie.

I went downstairs in time to see Esther come in the front door with an empty laundry basket under her arm. She smiled at me wanly as she pulled off her black hip-length coat and hung it by the door.

"That looks like a castoff of Elam's," I said, indicating the jacket.

She reached out and brushed a hand down the sleeve. She nodded, then actually punched the sleeve. She made a comment in Pennsylvania Dutch that I gathered was addressed to Elam and wasn't complimentary. Some things translate across language barriers.

"Where's Mary?" I asked, hiding a smile.

"She's at Annie's. I baked a pie this morning, and she took it and some of her chicken bot boi for eating."

She picked up her laundry basket, a blue plastic number, and headed for the shed. I always found a fascination in watching the Amish, so at odds with the modern world in so many ways, use petroleum products like plastic laundry baskets, in-line skates, and polyester material with impunity. Practicality. Accommodation. And a lack of information about plastic and petroleum, hydrocrackers and high technology.

As Esther walked by, I noticed her slumped shoulders. She was hurting over Elam and his obvious distress at Mary Clare's engagement. I wished there were something I could do to help her, but I had no idea what.

"Come sit with me a minute," I said. "I need company."

I poured us cups of spearmint tea and she put a plate of her homemade gingersnaps on the table. We drank in companionable silence for a few minutes.

"I'm surprised you didn't go with Mary to visit Annie," I finally said.

"No. Not today." She stared at the floor. "Too many people."

"Too many busybodies?" I asked.

She looked at me and smiled sadly. "I don't think I'd use those words, but the last thing I want is pity. Or people staring at me."

There was a knock on the door. I went over and let Becky and Trevor Stoltzfus in.

Esther's eyes brightened some when she saw who was visiting. "Can I have Trevor?" she asked immediately, her arms open and reaching.

Becky nodded as she draped her black shawl over a peg. "I just fed him and he's asleep." She passed him to Esther who kissed his wan little cheek.

Becky looked at us grimly. "I had to get out of the house for a few minutes."

"That bad?" I asked as I got her a mug from the cupboard.

"They stare," she said. "I can feel their eyes on me wherever I move. I feel like they're looking for the scarlet A on my chest."

I looked at her, amazed that she knew of the Nathaniel Hawthorne classic but she hadn't known where Texas was. "You read a lot, don't you, Becky."

She nodded. "It's my contact with what I've come to think of as the real world."

I understood exactly what she was saying, but Esther looked shocked.

"Becky, what are you saying?" She looked almost scared.

Becky sat straight and looked at Esther as if she expected a blow. "I'm not staying Plain."

"Because of Trevor's father," Esther whispered. "Oh, Becky, you can't! He's meidung."

"I don't care," Becky said. "I love him."

"But you'll be under the ban, too."

Becky shook her head. "I never took my vows. I will be fine. I'll be an outcast, but not like Samuel. My family will be able to talk with me—if they want to."

"Are you sure?" Esther's face was a mask of concern. "You will be giving up everything!"

"No," Becky said. "I will have Samuel and Herr Gott."

"It'll be okay, Esther," I said, putting a hand on hers and squeezing gently. "Becky'll be fine. Millions of people are fancy, and we manage. We love and follow God with as much dedication as you do."

"But the Ordnung," Esther whispered.

"I will reject the Ordnung," Becky said. There was about her much of the same fear and trembling I imagined infused early believers who declared their rejection of the Law. "But I will love Herr Gott with all my heart. And Samuel."

"Samuel!" Esther had something she could grab onto. "What kind of a man is he that he would break the Ordnung and take you away too?"

"He is a wonderful man, Esther. A kind man. A practical man. I love him with all my heart." Becky looked intently at Esther. "Certainly you understand that."

170

A spasm of pain streaked across Esther's face. "Did you know I'm leaving here?"

"No, I didn't," I said, surprised. Esther was such a part of the Zook household that it was hard to imagine the place without her.

"You can't," Becky said, distress written across her face. "You're my only friend here."

"Thank you, but I can't stay any longer." Esther stared into her mug, Trevor all but forgotten in her arms. "Mary doesn't need me now. She's feeling well and hardly limps unless she's very tired." She looked up and tried to be enthusiastic. "I've been asked to come and be maud for a family with five children. The mother is having a very difficult pregnancy. It's a fine opportunity." She failed miserably.

"Elam," I said, saying out loud what Esther couldn't bring herself to say. "You're leaving because of Elam."

"Why leave?" Becky asked. "Why not marry him? It's obvious to anyone who watches that you love him."

Esther put a hand over her mouth like she was trying to hold the pain inside. Her beautiful peat-colored eyes were awash in tears.

Becky looked at me, obviously confused.

"Were you at church yesterday?" I asked.

Becky nodded.

"Did you hear the banns read?"

Becky looked from me to Esther. "But it wasn't Elam. It was—I don't even remember their names."

"Mary Clare Epp and Young Joe Lapp," I supplied.

"Elam fancies himself in love with Mary Clare."

"Oh no!" Becky turned to Esther. "I didn't know that!"

"It's all right," Esther said. "I should be used to it by now."

Becky looked at Esther with pity. "I don't know what I'd do if Samuel didn't love me."

"You'd leave," Esther said. "Just like me."

"Maybe," I said. "Maybe not." I studied Esther, her head bent, her kapp covering the shining knot of her glorious hair. "Maybe you ought to bring out some of that competitive spirit I saw the other night when we played Parcheesi. Maybe you need to fight for him as keenly as you fought for that victory."

"Oh, Rose." Esther looked appalled and blushed furiously. "That is such a bad way to be! I want to stop acting like that, not act that way more. Besides, I saw Elam's face when they read the banns." Her eyes grew cloudy with pain. "I have no chance against sorrow like that."

We fell silent, and I got up and poured us all a fresh cup of tea.

"Is it better to be rejected for a real person like Mary Clare or for no one?" I asked, thinking of Jake.

"What?" Both Esther and Becky looked at me.

"The man who seems to be taking over my heart wants me to go away, but not because he wants someone else. He just doesn't want me." I felt the tears building again.

"Is that why you were crying upstairs?" Esther asked.

"You heard me?" I was mortified.

"No. I knew when you came down. Your eyes looked like mine felt."

"Who is this man?" Becky asked. "I want to tell him a thing or two, right after I finish telling Elam."

"Becky, you'll make a feisty fancy lady," I said with a half smile, which was all I could manage.

"It's Jake, isn't it?" asked Esther.

I shrugged.

Becky looked at me wide eyed. "But he's in a wheel-chair!"

I bridled. "So what? He's still wonderful."

Esther nodded to Becky. "They are easy together, Jake and Rose. They talk and laugh, and Jake is lighter."

"Jake is not interested," I said, my voice bleak.

Esther patted my hand in sympathy. "Are you sure?"

"Unfortunately, yes."

We drank our tea, lost in thought.

"You know," I said after a few minutes. "Here we are, three women, one Amish, one about to be fancy, and one fancy, and we've all got the same problem—men. That must mean something, though I haven't the vaguest idea what."

Esther opened her mouth to comment, but the words died when the door opened and Elam walked in.

The three of us stared at him. I'm sure our faces reflected different levels of emotion, everything from anger to loss. He frowned and quickly looked away.

Esther cleared her throat. "I thought you were at the *Graabhof* digging Old Nate's grave with John and Big Joe Lapp."

"We finished," Elam said as he pulled his arms from his jacket and hung it on a peg. "Isn't there dinner?"

Esther shook her head. "I didn't expect you. I thought you would go from the digging to sit with Annie."

"I stopped there with Father, but they do not need me."

Esther nodded as she and Elam continued to stare at each other.

"Mom says you're leaving." Elam's expression was almost belligerent.

Esther nodded.

"You can't leave."

Esther leaned her head forward expectantly, but he had said all he meant to. "I can't stay," she said softly.

"Becky," I said, getting to my feet. "Why don't I walk you home?"

Becky blinked, then nodded. "Good idea." She turned to Esther and took the baby from her.

Esther broke her stare long enough to kiss Trevor's little nose and smile a farewell. "Maybe I will see you again," she whispered. "Before I leave."

Becky took her shawl from the peg as I ran upstairs to grab my jacket. I had my hand on the doorknob when Esther looked at me in something like panic.

"Don't go," she said.

I smiled and nodded. "I won't be long."

Becky and I walked down the road toward her grandparents' farm, Hawk loping along beside us. It was a crisp day, bright with sunshine and unseasonably warm.

"I think tomorrow is supposed to be even warmer than today," I said. "It'll be nice for the funeral."

Becky stopped and looked at me, excitement flashing across her face. "I've got to tell you what happened. I didn't want to say in front of Esther because I wasn't sure how she would feel."

"You got in touch with Samuel?" I grabbed onto the most exciting possibility I could think of.

Becky shook her head. "But it's almost as wonderful."

I watched a cardinal flash by. "So tell me."

"Last night after everyone left and Grandmother Annie and I were ready for bed, she came to my room. 'Tomorrow I want you to move into one of the front rooms,' she said. 'You pick the one you and Trevor will like most.'"

I looked at Becky's glowing face and knew how much this gesture meant to her.

"And," Becky continued, "she said, 'Can I hold my great-grandson? My arms have been aching for him.'"

"Oh, Becky!" I hugged the girl.

"She sat on the bed and held him for a long time, talking to him and playing with him. And this morning she held him in her rocking chair downstairs until people started to come."

She saw the question on my face and answered before I even asked. "She didn't hold him in front of people because she didn't want to seem disrespectful to Grandfather Nate."

I nodded. "That's very wise of her and understanding of you."

She shrugged. "Trevor and I moved into the yellow and blue room this morning before anyone came. It is so light and pretty. We love it, don't we, mein bubbli?"

"Do you have an appointment with the doctor?" I asked, holding my arms out for Trevor. He was so light, so small it scared me.

"Wednesday morning," Becky assured me. "We already have the taxi reserved."

Another interesting Amish custom, the taxis. Because they won't drive but want to go places farther and faster, they rent vehicles and drivers to take them.

"Good girl," I said. "We need to take care of this little boy."

We walked past the farm pond on which several Canada geese swam gracefully. Suddenly one near the edge of the pond turned bottoms up, his white rump pointing to the sky as he searched the bottom for food. Hawk barked at him for form's sake, but he didn't leave our side.

"You're a good boy, Hawk." I petted his great head. "It's not nice to chase the birds."

"Do you want to come in and see my grandmother?" Becky asked when we reached the Stoltzfus farm. "I think she looks better today."

I shook my head. "I don't think I'll come in. You've got lots of company." I indicated the drive full of buggies.

I also didn't want to go in and risk being seen and recognized. Several Amishmen served in the Bird-in-Hand fire company, and with my luck, one of them would be here.

"But I'll tell you what," I said. "I'll watch Trevor for you tomorrow if you'd like. That way you can be with your grandmother and help hostess the postfuneral meal."

Becky looked interested. "Don't you have to go to work?"

"I'm on a vacation of sorts."

She hesitated, then nodded. "I'll bring him down early. Is that all right? And I'll bring bottles and my milk."

I nodded and walked slowly back home, Hawk still my companion. He and I watched a red-tailed hawk wheel and float on the air currents, then dive suddenly after a poor sparrow who was innocently flying towards a tree. A large horde of a hundred or so seagulls squawked and complained as they waddled over a field looking for fallen kernels of corn.

Lord, I love it here. I thank You for this beauty, this peace, and for these people. Be with Peter Hostetter and comfort him. Be with Annie Stoltzfus, too. Help Jake find peace in

You. Help him understand Your grace and forgiveness. And help me sort through my feelings for him and his for me— that is, if he has any for me.

I came downstairs for supper just in time to overhear Jake talking to Mary.

"Mom, I have to apologize for my attitude this morning." He sounded genuinely penitent. "I was upset about something that had nothing to do with you, but I took it out on you. I'm sorry."

I studied his strong shoulders as I hesitated in the doorway, his wonderful dark hair, his strong arms. I knew his black eyes would be looking at Mary with a sincerity that would make her mother's heart melt. It'd make mine melt, too.

Mary looked at her son, imprisoned in a chair he hated, forced to live a life he would never have chosen. I could see her pain for him from across the room.

"Thank you, Chake." She touched his cheek with uncharacteristic emotion. "I understand."

He gave a half smile. "I know you do, but that doesn't make me any less wrong." He paused for a beat, then said, "Right, Rose?"

I hadn't realized he even knew I was in the room. "Right," I said softly, proud of him for seeking her out.

He turned toward me. "Now I need to talk with you a minute."

"Sure," I said, hoping my eyes didn't reveal quite

how much those words meant to me. After this morning's parting, I hadn't been sure he'd ever want to talk again.

"Come into my living room." He smiled over his shoulder at his mother who was trying not to appear too interested. "How much time until supper?"

"Fifteen to twenty minutes."

"Time enough," Jake said.

I followed him into his apartment. His living room was clutter-free, the center of the room open to allow the chair easy movement. A deep navy leather sofa rested against one wall, a glider/rocker at right angles to it. A TV sat across the room from the furniture. A desk and bookcase filled the wall under one window, his school texts piled beside a notebook and a laptop computer. A set of free weights filled a corner and a large machine that exercised his legs for him filled another. There was no rug, and his chair glided easily to the sofa.

"Sit," he said. "We need to talk."

He looked cool and unflappable while my stomach was looping about my insides, churning up enough acid to etch a whole collection of questionable engravings. I dried my damp palms on my thighs and sat. I was immediately distracted by how comfortable the couch was even if it was so deep that I couldn't sit back and still have my feet touch the floor. I perched on the edge and gave Jake my attention.

"Rose, I owe you an apology too," he began earnestly. "I was unconscionably rude this morning."

I nodded. I wasn't going to be quite the easy mark his mother was. "You were."

"I'm sorry. I didn't mean to hurt you." There was that earnest stare, softening me just as I had known it would.

A touch of pride stiffened my backbone before total meltdown and made me ask, "What makes you think you hurt me?"

"I saw you and Hawk standing there as I drove away." He smiled gently. "I've rarely seen a more dejected-looking pair."

"That'll teach me to hang around after a confrontation," I muttered, feeling as exposed as the emperor when he found out the secret of his new clothes.

Jake cleared his throat, and suddenly he became very nervous. I watched him with interest and apprehension, wondering what in the world was coming next.

"I was struggling with some things," he said, "and I didn't know how to come to terms with them, so I took my frustration out on you and Mom."

"Nothing excuses hurting people, Jake." I sounded so pompous that I shuddered, but I was right. I lifted my chin and looked steadily at him.

He looked pained and a bit peeved. "I know. I said I was sorry."

After a beat I said graciously, "Apology accepted." I nodded my head in a dignified and queenly manner.

Then I made the mistake of leaning back on the sofa.

I found myself almost lying down, the thing was so deep. So much for grace and dignity. I struggled upright, trying to look casual, like sprawling awkwardly was my intended purpose. It's bad enough having to force a collected manner when your insides are rioting with nerves. When your outsides fall on their faces too, it's an uphill battle.

I glanced at Jake just in time to see him swallow a smile at my turtle on its back flailings. I flushed.

"And I presume that now you've come to terms with these issues that were bothering you?" I said as composedly as I could manage.

He shrugged. "I guess. At least as much as I can come to terms with them."

"But what happened between last night and this morning to make you so distressed?" In spite of my pique and hurt, I wanted to understand.

He took a deep breath while he debated with himself.

He was sitting facing me, his hands resting on his knees. I reached out and touched a hand. "Tell me. Maybe I can help. Isn't that what friends are for?"

He turned his hand over and held mine. He stared at their joining for a minute. "You see, there's this woman."

I swallowed, trying to dislodge the lump that had suddenly risen in my throat. "A woman?" There's a woman?

He nodded, still studying our hands.

"And you like her?" I prompted, pleased I could still speak.

"I think I love her."

"What?" But what about me? You called me Tiger!

"That accident last night reminded me in crystal clarity that I can't love a woman, any woman, especially this woman."

"Nonsense," I said, amazed that a cotton mouth could still form words. "Of course you can love." Just not her!

"Easy for you to say." His tone was acerbic. His thumb ran back and forth over my knuckles. "Last night I had a dream. No, make that a nightmare. I was with this woman, and she was in terrible trouble, and I couldn't help her. She was running and screaming and someone was chasing her, and I could only sit and watch. I yelled at the man, I swore at the man, I asked God to strike the man dead. But I couldn't help her." He said the words slowly, his teeth clenched with the intensity of his feelings. "I watched as the man grabbed her. She looked at me, pleading for my help. Then she was dead on the floor, the man was gone, and I was still in my chair screaming." His voice was full of anguish.

I slid forward on the sofa until my knees were against his. "Jake, it was only a dream."

"I woke up in a cold sweat," he said, his eyes staring at some middle distance, seeing himself in the dream, feeling the agony and helplessness all over again. "And I realized two things. I had never before dreamed about myself in a wheelchair. I always dreamed about myself as I'd been my whole life, running, walking, riding my cycle. Last night I saw myself as I am: a man chained to a chair."

He ran a hand through his hair, a gesture of sheer frustration. He looked at me, his eyes bleak. "Which brings me to the second thing I realized." His hand gripped mine so hard it hurt. "I can't love this woman and I can't let her love me."

Suddenly I couldn't breathe because I knew as clearly as if he'd said my name that he was talking about me and how he felt about me. Our gazes held as he stared at me in utter desolation and I stared back in unabashed wonder.

Jake thought he loved me!

I looked away first, mainly because I had to start breathing again or I'd pass out from oxygen deprivation. I took a couple of deep breaths and told myself to be calm.

"You're saying you can't love m—this woman because you're a paraplegic?"

He nodded, back to studying our clasped hands. His thumb still rubbed softly across my knuckles, a soothing and wonderfully possessive thing.

"But what does she think, Jake? Doesn't she get to make a choice here?"

He looked up immediately and with a fierce glare practically shouted, "No!"

I jumped in surprise. I reached for his other hand.

"Jake, do you think that's fair to her?"

"Anything else is unfair." His stare was uncompromising.

I nodded as I heard a knock on the door between Jake's rooms and the main house.

Elam stuck his head around the corner. "Mom says it's time for supper."

I took one last look at our clasped hands. They looked right entwined like that, his large ones enveloping my smaller ones. Without forethought I lifted one of his hands to my lips and gently kissed his knuckles. He flinched.

Then I released him and stood. "I guess she'll have to pray a lot, won't she?"

He made that throaty sound of his. "A lot of good that'll do her."

I just smiled and knew I was about to develop a prayer life like I'd never known.

Nine

JAKE AND I WENT INTO SUPPER AND TOOK OUR PLACES AT THE table. John bowed his head and the rest of us followed suit. I peeked at one point, glancing over at Jake, still bemused by the knowledge that he loved me. That's when I noticed Elam.

He sat with his eyes focused on Esther's bent head. His face was impassive, and I wondered what he was thinking, feeling. After all that time wasted mooning over Mary Clare, was he realizing that he loved Esther? Now that she was leaving, did he realize what he was losing? Romantic that I was, I hoped so.

For her part, Esther kept her head bowed long after the rest of us had begun passing food. When she finally looked up, her eyes were bright with tears and her expression full of sadness. When I caught her eye, I smiled gently and winked. She smiled wanly back.

She would not look at Elam all through the silent meal.

After dinner things were no livelier. Jake announced he had to study and left us immediately. Esther went to her room as soon as she and I finished the supper cleanup. Elam sat in his chair in the living room, one hand absently gripping his suspender, and stared into space.

I went up to my rooms to get away from all the gloom. I sat in one of the overstuffed chairs with my legs hanging over the arm and thought about my conversation with Jake. What were the ramifications of his declaration? *"I can't love this woman, and I can't let her love me....Anything else is unfair."*

Jake was a strong man, a dynamic man whose legs happened not to work anymore. He was by turns caring and gentle, then nasty and moody. He had learned to function in spite of his losses though he insisted on going at his own pace. He had stepped beyond the scope of his family's heritage to find a way of life that suited him, first as a rebel and now as a student. He was a man not easily dissuaded when he reached a conclusion, and he knew how to stand on his convictions in the face of loving opposition.

I pictured our hands clasped as he told me he wouldn't love me. I pictured him holding me the night Sophie and Ammon died. I pictured him laughing with me over Allie's secondhand ring.

I heard him say, "You're good for me, you know that?"

Then, "I can't love this woman, and I can't let her love me."

And finally, "I can't believe God can forgive me."

And that conviction of his was a much greater problem to me than his legs ever would be. It was a problem that could keep us apart forever, love notwithstanding. No matter how much I might love Jake, I couldn't marry him if he remained an unbeliever. Even if he overcame his noble idea of sparing me because he was unfit, I couldn't marry him.

Suddenly I felt as depressed as everyone else in the house.

I was enjoying a good sulk when my cell phone rang.

"This is Davy Stoltzfus," a man's voice told me.

"Hello! I'm so glad to hear from you. I'm Rose Martin. I live at the Zooks, next door to your parents' farm."

"Ah. I was wondering who I was calling."

I laughed. "I can imagine. I rent a small apartment from Jake."

"Ah. Remind me to ask about him in a minute. How's my mother?"

"She seems to be doing well. I haven't seen her, but I've spoken with Becky a couple of times. If anything were wrong with Annie, she would have told me."

"What's Becky doing in Bird-in-Hand? Has her family moved back to Pennsylvania? Ma mentioned in a letter that she was staying with them, but she never said why."

So Annie *was* writing to Davy behind Old Nate's back.

"She's here having a baby." I paused. "She's not married."

"And my father let her stay with them?" I could hear his surprise. And no wonder, after the way Old Nate had treated him.

"I think he felt he had no option. Your sister apparently felt she would taint the younger kids and sent her here."

"Poor Becky." There was genuine pity in his voice.

"Don't worry about Becky," I said. "She's doing fine. She'll leave here and marry her Samuel if she has anything to say about it."

"Have you met this guy? Is he nice?"

"He's in Ohio, so I've never seen him. He's meidung."

There was a minute of silence as he took that in. "Is Becky under the ban too?"

"Apparently she hadn't joined the church yet. Besides, she confessed before the congregation."

He laughed shortly. "I remember when they wanted me to do that. I wouldn't."

"I sort of guessed that." After all, he was still racing.

"Look, will you tell my mother that Lauren and I will be there Wednesday morning? We're arriving in Harrisburg tomorrow, and we'll spend the night there. We don't want to be present during the burial. It might be too distressing for her, dealing with my father's death, her friends, and Lauren and me, all at the same time."

Just how long was a person shunned? Forever, even when it was obvious he'd never return to the community?

"Sure, I'll tell her. I know your sister and family are due this evening. They're coming by bus as far as Harrisburg, then taxi. It'll be the first time they've seen Becky's baby. She's nervous."

"I don't think she has to worry," Davy said. "Rachel's strict but not cruel. And she's always loved babies."

"Well, this little guy needs her love. He's not well, Davy."

"What do you mean, not well?"

"He's going to die."

I heard a sigh of distress. "How's Becky with this?"

"Amazing. She knows and is prepared. She's got a real strong faith, and I mean in God, not the Ordnung. But it'll be hard. She loves Trevor fiercely."

"Trevor? She named him Trevor?" Amazement and disbelief zinged in my ear.

"She's about to jump the fence, Davy. She can't wait to wear lipstick." I laughed. "And there's Samuel waiting for her when she does jump."

"Speaking of jumping the fences, how's Jake?"

I smiled to myself, warmed by the thought of him. "He's fine. He's taking a full course load at Millersville this semester and loving it."

"When Ma told me about his accident, I was so upset. We were best friends for years."

"Stop by while you're here. He'll want to see you.

His apartment is the first floor of the grossdawdy haus. I'm on the second."

After promising to visit, Davy rang off. I felt better after talking with him. There was no concrete reason I should, but I did. I pulled out my Bible and turned to Psalm 66. It was a favorite of mine.

> Let the whole world bless our God
> > and sing aloud his praises.
> Our lives are in his hands,
> > and he keeps our feet from stumbling.
> You have tested us, O God;
> > you have purified us like silver melted in a crucible.
> You captured us in your net
> > and laid the burden of slavery on our backs.
> You sent troops to ride across our broken bodies.
> > We went through fire and flood.
> > But you brought us to a place of great abundance.

Many times when I felt overwhelmed with guilt about Dad and Rhoda or some other more mundane problem in life, I went to these verses. They acknowledged that God was God, life was sometimes difficult, but he always brought us through. I buried my face in my hands.

Oh, Father God, I feel like an emotional yo-yo. I love Jake. I do. And he loves me whether he'll ever admit it to me or not—but please, Lord, let him admit it!

I could break into a cold sweat at the thought of his

never acknowledging his love for me.

But he doesn't know You yet, Lord. What should I do? What should I say? Please help me. And help Annie with her meeting with Davy and Lauren. And be with Becky and Sam. Help them find each other. Protect Trevor, Lord. He's so tiny. And Elam and Esther. I know what I think is the best here, and I ask for that. I ask that they get together. But more than that, I ask for Your will for all of us, Father. That's the only way we'll find that place of great abundance You promised us.

When I glanced at the clock, I saw it was time for the news. I turned WGAL on and watched a report on Sophie and Ammon's double funeral. I saw Peter entering and leaving the church, his sunglasses firmly in place to hide his eyes. My heart ached for him, alone and under attack, his life in jeopardy.

The last item in the report was a clip of a short, slight man giving a eulogy. I wondered who he was when suddenly his name flashed across the bottom of the TV screen.

Ernest Hostetter.

I stared at the man. This was Evil Ernie? He looked like someone a gentle spring breeze could blow away, not someone who would blow away his family for the sake of little cars.

But then what did a man's appearance have to do with the evil that lurked in his heart?

Why did you go after me, Ernie? I silently asked his image. *What did I ever do to hurt you? How can I possibly be a threat? How can I possibly dissuade you or* stop you from doing more harm? And how long will it take Lem and the others to get rock-solid evidence against you?

When I finally went to bed, I expected to toss and turn all night, but to my amazement I slept the night through.

I was in the kitchen having a second cup of tea when Becky arrived with Trevor Tuesday morning. I rose to take him, but Esther beat me to it. She took him from Becky, smiled down at him, and held him close.

Becky looked at Trevor with doubtful eyes. It would be the first time she had ever been away from him, and she was having second thoughts.

"Go, Becky," I said. "Trevor will be fine. When I can pry him out of Esther's arms, I'll take good care of him for you. I promise."

Becky smiled. "I couldn't leave him with anyone else." She bent and kissed him good-bye.

"Oh," she said, pausing at the door. "My mother and father arrived last evening."

"Tell your grandmother that Davy and Lauren will be here tomorrow," I said. "He called last night."

She smiled broadly. "Grandmother Annie will be so glad!"

I glanced around to see if anyone was listening. Only Esther was near and she appeared absorbed with Trevor. I moved closer to Becky and whispered, "Annie's been writing to Davy and Lauren."

Becky grinned widely. "Good for her."

I agreed. I could see no reason for her to lose her son forever over a difference in beliefs. If the shunning had served its purpose, Davy would have returned to the church. Since he hadn't and never would, the time of shunning should cease. It separated families and caused great hurt. Maybe the closeness shared with those of mutual beliefs and community would be absent, but at least affection could live.

Becky reached for the door again just as Elam opened it and came into the room from the barn where he and John had been harnessing the horse to the buggy. They were treating this morning with the funeral services much like they would treat Sunday as far as workload went. They were only doing what was absolutely essential, things like milking and feeding the stock.

I thought Elam looked quite handsome in his black, split-tailed frock coat with its hooks and eyes, appropriate dress for Sundays and special events. His white shirt was buttoned to the collar, and his cleanly shaven face glowed with the ruddy health of a man who spent most of his time outdoors.

"Mom," he said as he pulled his hat off, "Father says he's ready—"

His words trailed off as he caught sight of Esther cradling Trevor. He stared, frozen, like he'd never seen her before, his face a mix of loss, resignation, and poleaxed wonder.

She must have heard him speak, but Esther never acknowledged him. *"Schloff, bubbli, schloff,"* she said quietly to Trevor. "Close those little eyes. *Ich lieb dich.*"

"Did you call, Elam?" Mary's voice drifted down from upstairs.

Elam started and cleared his throat. Suddenly he looked anywhere but at Esther.

"Father said it's time to go." He turned to the door, paused, and said, oh so casually, "You too, Esther."

She nodded without looking up. She turned to me and laid Trevor in my arms.

"I think I'll walk down with you, Becky," she said. "Iss all right?"

Becky nodded. "Yah."

Elam slapped his hat on his head and went out with a barely contained slamming of the front door.

Becky and I looked at each other and couldn't resist smiling. The course of true love.

Esther put on her black bonnet over her white organdy kapp and took her black shawl from a peg by the door. As she and Becky walked away down the road, they looked like twins in their matching dresses, though Becky's was navy blue and Esther's a rich brown. As a symbol of uniqueness and community, clothing was one of the big three, the others being horse and buggy travel and no electricity.

Trevor was a joy to baby-sit. He was good but not docile in spite of his ill health. I listened to his heartbeat with my stethoscope and found it steady. Still I didn't like the cyanosis all too readily visible about his lips, nails, and little feet. I kissed his tiny toes, then put him on my bed to sleep. I sat down to read and promptly fell asleep myself. Trevor and I both woke up over an hour later when he demanded some food.

We went downstairs and I gave him a bottle. At first he wasn't happy with the strange feel of the nipple, but after he got a few tastes of his mother's milk, he settled down like a trooper. He even gave me a glorious burp.

I wrapped him in a blanket, and he and I went outside. The day was beautiful, much warmer than it had been when Esther and Becky walked off in their shawls. Reveling in the unseasonably high temperatures, I took Trevor for a stroll, walking down the road away from the Stoltzfus farm. I didn't want to seem like a typical nosey or curious Englisher spying on the funeral.

We hadn't gone far when a flock of farm geese waddled across the street in front of us, their little rumps twitching back and forth with every step. They glanced at me for a brief moment and decided I wasn't a threat. They went back to their conversation, quacking and honking to each other as they moved with absolutely no hurry.

A blue pickup truck approached from the opposite direction and came to a halt on the other side of the parade of geese. To be polite I smiled at the handsome young man behind the wheel. After all, we were both caught in a major traffic snarl, Bird-in-Hand style. He smiled vaguely back.

I held up Trevor and said, "See the geese, sweetheart? Aren't they pretty?"

Trevor looked completely unimpressed.

Finally the geese were safely across the road. The pickup drove by and Trevor and I continued our stroll. When I began wishing for one of those Snuggli things that strap a baby to your chest, I knew it was time to turn around. We were almost back to the house when the pickup truck came by again, now from the opposite direction. It stopped beside us.

The young man leaned out his cab window and said, "I'm looking for the Stoltzfus farm."

I smiled, thinking of the multitude of Stoltzfuses in the area. "Which Stoltzfus?"

He shook his head. "That's my problem. I don't know. I'm looking for a girl named Becky Stoltzfus."

I stared at him, transfixed. Samuel?

He misinterpreted my silence as my not knowing enough. "Her grandfather died recently, and I think the funeral's today."

I nodded. "It is."

He broke into a great smile and his whole face lit up, igniting with hope like a recently lit torch. "You know her?"

I nodded again. "I do."

"I've been trying to find her for four months. I can't believe I've finally done it!"

Suddenly I became aware of a procession of buggies bearing down on us from the Stoltzfus farm.

"Uh-oh. Here comes Old Nate's funeral procession now. See that drive right there?" I pointed to our drive. "Pull in there, but don't get out of the truck."

He turned quickly and drove toward the procession until he reached our drive. Then he turned in as instructed. He started to get out of the cab.

I hurried to reach him before the first buggy passed. It wouldn't do for anyone who might recognize him to see him right now. Becky, Rachel and her family, and Annie all had more than enough to handle at the moment.

But Samuel understood my concern. He walked around to the front of his truck and stood by the bumper. From here he could see but not be seen, especially since no one was looking for him.

Trevor and I joined him, and we watched as buggy after buggy passed on the way to the Graabhof, the horses walking at a slow but steady pace. It crossed my mind that burial was at the same sane, slow pace that dictated all of Amish life.

When the last buggy had passed and driven on, I turned to Samuel. He wasn't a tall man, but he had a rugged physique, probably from his early farming experience and present construction work. He had sun-streaked light brown hair, the gold, amber, and gilt strands of his head mirrored in the bushy mustache that sat on his upper lip.

I stared at his mustache in fascination. Here was a definite challenge to the community that had ostracized him because of the vehicle that Trevor and I were leaning against. Amish men wore their beards without mustaches. It went back to the Reformation and the beginnings of the Anabaptist movement. Mustaches were an affectation of military men, so the nonviolent Anabaptists refused to wear them. To this day, hair on the upper lip is shaved.

"What's taken you so long?" I asked Samuel without preamble. I didn't mean to sound accusatory, but my tone of voice wasn't exactly warm.

He raised both hands shoulder height as if in surrender. "I know. It's been four months too long." He shook his head in a sort of dazed disbelief. "No one—and I mean no one—would tell me where she was. I talked to her parents, her brothers and sisters, her neighbors. I talked to everyone. Or I tried to. No one would talk to me. They'd just shake their heads and turn their backs. Or they wouldn't open their doors."

I nodded. "So how did you find her now?"

"I've been watching her family for weeks now, thinking that soon someone would want to go see the baby or bring her home or something. I saw them leaving with suitcases Monday morning. I followed. The van driver who took them to the bus depot had a loud voice. 'I hope your father's funeral goes well,' he said as the family got out of his van and headed for the bus. Rachel nodded and gave a sad smile."

He glanced at Trevor and back to me. His brown eyes were warm and shining. It was obvious he was pleased that his quest might soon be at an end.

"They took a bus east," he said, "and I continued to follow all across Pennsylvania. I knew they must be going to Lancaster County. When they got off the bus in

Harrisburg, a taxi picked them up. I followed it here, but we got separated when a milk tanker turning into a farm lane on Route 340, misjudged the turn, and had to maneuver back and forth for a few minutes. When I could finally get around him, the taxi was long gone."

"So you've been driving around all morning looking for the right farm?"

He nodded. "I knew I was in the right area, and how many funerals could there be today?"

As we talked, I wondered what I should do with Samuel. I thought it was probably politically incorrect to invite a man under the ban into Mary and John's living room, and I certainly didn't want to ask a man I didn't know into mine. On the other hand, it seemed rude not to offer him some hospitality until the funeral was over and he could do whatever it was he'd come to do.

Just then Jake pulled into the drive like an answer to prayer.

Samuel watched with interest as Jake got himself out of the van.

"I thought you had classes until midafternoon," I said as I enjoyed the sight of his handsome face. *Oh, Lord, he's got to admit he loves me. He's got to!*

He nodded. "One of my professors called in sick and class was canceled, so here I am." He held out a hand to Samuel. "I'm Jake Zook."

"Sam Hershberger."

Jake raised an eyebrow and looked at me. "Becky's Samuel?"

"One and the same."

"What took you so long?" Jake asked.

Trevor started to cry just then. He was undoubtedly hungry and probably wet.

"Jake, why don't you entertain Sam while I take care of the baby."

"Good idea." Jake began wheeling toward the walk. "Follow me, Sam."

Sam fell in beside him and I heard him say, "I've got to thank you and your wife for being so kind. I had no idea what to expect when I got here."

Jake's hands stilled on the wheels at the word *wife*, and I wondered what was going through his mind. I listened with interest for his response.

"We're glad to be of help. It's little short of a miracle that I'm not meidung myself, so I understand what you're going through."

"How did you escape?" Sam asked as they turned the corner of the house.

Jake's voice floated back. "Never took my vows."

I went into the main room of the house, going to the refrigerator for the last of the milk for Trevor. Becky had better show in the next couple of hours or we would have a very unhappy baby on our hands. While the bottle warmed in a pan of water on the cookstove, I changed Trevor's diaper. He definitely needed a dry, clean one.

"That's your daddy in there with Jake, Trev," I told him as I bent over him. "But he doesn't know that. He thinks you belong to Jake and me."

I got a funny little choke in my throat and a great fluttering in my stomach at the thought of Jake and me and a baby. I'd always assumed I'd have two or three kids just like every other girl child did, but I'd never before thought about it in terms of a specific father, not even when I was engaged to Ben—which undoubtedly said much about my depth of affection for him.

I closed my eyes. *Maybe someday, Lord? Please?* I promptly stuck myself with a diaper pin.

Still sucking on my finger, I carried Trevor and his bottle over to Jake's. I found the men talking like old friends, Sam on the sofa, Jake beside it. I noted with jealousy that Sam sat all the way back on the sofa and his feet still touched the floor. I took the rocker and began feeding the baby.

"How old?" Sam asked, looking at the baby with interest.

"Two months." I shot Jake a look that meant *don't tell*. It seemed to me that Becky should be the one to introduce Sam to his son.

"That's about how old our baby is," Sam said. "And I haven't even seen him yet." His eyes were full of sorrow.

"What happened to you, Sam?" I asked. "Becky tried to call you when she could escape long enough to get to the phone shanty. Your phone was disconnected."

He nodded. "When she disappeared, I went crazy trying to find out where she was. I missed work and got myself fired. Then I couldn't pay my rent and got evicted. If it hadn't been for Mr. and Mrs. Trowbridge, I don't know what I would have done. They took me in and treated me like their son."

"Who are the Trowbridges?" Jake asked.

"Becky used to clean for Mrs. Trowbridge. She—"

"She's the one who told Becky about grace!" I interrupted.

Sam blinked, startled by my outburst. Jake merely smiled.

"Don't let her bother you, Sam," he said. "She's like that. That's why I call her Tiger."

I looked at Jake, surprised and delighted at his words. He admitted to calling me Tiger! He glanced at me, grinning. The grin faded when he saw my expression, full of love and joy as it undoubtedly was. Our gazes held until Sam cleared his throat, a goofy smile on his face as he glanced from one of us to the other.

Jake looked away from me and quickly said, "So the Trowbridges helped you?"

Sam returned to his story. "When Becky disappeared, I didn't know anyone else who knew her, at least anyone who would talk to me, so I went to see them. They took one look at me and invited me for supper. I told them my sad tale, and Mrs. Trowbridge said as quick as you please, 'You just move in with us for a while, Sam. You stay here while you hunt for that dear girl. All we ask is that you have a Bible study with us for fifteen minutes each evening. No rent. All meals included. Just a Bible study.' Then she smiled at me and said, 'I think Becky would like that.'"

He ran his finger over his mustache. "They accepted me just as I was, rebel heart and all."

"How rebellious were you?" I asked. "Becky keeps saying you're just practical."

"I might have been just practical and fed up with regulations when this all started, but when they hid Becky, my whole spirit went wild." He stopped, trying to find words to tell us how he felt.

"I had a horse once when I was about fourteen. He was wonderful and I was so proud of him. I took him for a ride one summer afternoon, just him and me. It was hot, and after a while I decided he wanted a drink. I took him to a stream. He lowered his head and began to drink, the stream lapping over his nostrils. His reins got caught around some rocks in the water and he couldn't raise his head. He panicked and began kicking and flailing. I couldn't get near him, no matter how much I tried. He was wild with fear. He drowned right there."

Sam was stroking his mustache rapidly, his reaction to the accident still very pronounced. He looked at Jake and me. "When Becky disappeared, I felt like that panicky horse inside. I was terrified, furious, unable to help myself or her. It was terrible! I wanted to kill someone. I wanted to beat her father and scream at her mother." He shook his head. "I was absolutely full of hate."

Trevor stirred in my arms and I held him to my shoulder. I rubbed my hand over his little back, feeling the bones of his spine with much too much clarity. He quieted under the rubbing.

"But the Trowbridges loved me just as I was, all ugly. They told me they loved me because of Jesus. They listened to me shout and carry on. They listened to me whine about missing Becky without ever once telling me it was my fault she was missing to begin with because I got her pregnant. But they closed every conversation by telling me God loved me and wanted me to forgive the Stoltzfuses as He had forgiven me."

"And once you got the worst of the venom out of your system, you told them you didn't deserve forgiveness, didn't you?" I asked.

Again Sam looked at me in surprise. "How did you know?"

"I've had similar conversations with another rebel." I smiled at Jake who glared at me.

"Well, when you think of it," Sam said, "why should God forgive me? I broke the Ordnung, I sinned with Becky, and I held hatred of the vilest kind in my heart."

"So why should He forgive you?" Jake repeated, interested in spite of himself.

"No reason," Sam said. "That's what took me so long to see. He forgives because He wants to, and that's it."

I don't think Jake realized that he was shaking his head, unable or unwilling to accept Sam's words.

"Being raised Amish makes you think you have to be good enough for salvation," Sam said. "Right? You have to keep the Ordnung and live pure lives and then maybe, just maybe—"

Jake lifted himself to redistribute his weight. "You've

got to earn God's forgiveness."

"But that's not what the Bible says." Sam had his index finger in the air, waving it for emphasis. "'God saved you by his special favor when you believed. And you can't take credit for this; it is a gift from God. Salvation is not a reward for the good things we have done, so none of us can boast about it.'"

I wondered if Jake recognized those verses as ones I'd quoted to him before. I didn't dare look at him. I sensed he'd resent my checking up on his thought patterns by even so small a gesture. I kept my eyes fixed either on Sam or Trevor.

"'Salvation is not a reward for the good things we have done,'" Sam said again. "That's a hard truth for an Amish boy to understand."

"It is," Jake agreed. "It is."

As Sam spoke, I watched over his shoulder as the long line of buggies passed again, returning from the Graabhof. I knew Becky would be here very soon.

Jake gave me a look I couldn't decipher. "Tell me, Sam. What do you think of a Christian woman who says she believes in God's forgiveness, but she can't forgive herself?"

Sam thought for a minute. "Why do we need to forgive ourselves if God's already forgiven us in Christ?"

"Isn't not forgiving yourself saying you're more important than God?" Jake asked. "Or as important as God?"

"What?" I was scandalized at such a thought.

"I've been thinking about this, Rose, because I know it bothers you," Jake said. "If God forgave you and God is

205

really God, shouldn't that be enough? Doesn't insisting that you have to forgive yourself, too, raise you to His level? He did you a favor but it's not enough?"

My heart beat fast as I listened. Was he right? Was I slapping God in the face and saying Jesus' death wasn't sufficient? I certainly never meant to.

"The Amish add the Ordnung to grace and forgiveness," Jake said. "Are you adding something too?"

I stared at him. My mouth was probably hanging open in shock. My thoughts whirled as I tried to grab hold of this new and potentially freeing concept.

"Christ's forgiveness is enough," Sam said with the enthusiasm of a new believer who has found unexpected joy in his salvation. "Enough for everything."

Oh, dear God, it hasn't been enough for me, has it? All these years, it hasn't been enough!

As I struggled to understand the implications of Jake's insight, Becky arrived. "Rose?" she called from the front room. "Rose? Trevor?"

Sam jumped as though shocked. "Becky," he said, his voice a mere whisper.

"In Jake's rooms, Beck," I called. "Come on in."

Sam got to his feet and started toward the door to the main house. "Becky?" His voice had volume this time. "Becky, sweetheart?"

"Samuel? Samuel?" Becky burst through Jake's doorway, hope alight in her face. "Samuel!"

She threw herself at him and they met in the middle of the room, clinging like they'd never part.

Ten

JAKE AND I SAT IN THE MAIN LIVING ROOM, LETTING BECKY and Sam have some privacy. I kept sniffing and tearing, remembering the look on Becky's face when she saw Sam. Jake just looked at me, eyebrow raised.

"You have a cold heart," I accused.

He raised his eyebrow higher and gave me a smoldering look that took my breath.

"Jake," I sighed, my heart tripping over itself.

Immediately his face altered. "Yes, Rose?" he said very matter-of-factly.

I stared at him, so cool and in control. The man was going to make me crazy.

"A cold heart," I repeated.

Again he smiled with enough heat to scorch paper. "Me?" he asked, all innocent.

I had to clear my throat before I could answer. This

time I was unemotional enough to please him at his most persnickity, at least on the surface. "Yes, you. You have no sense of the romantic."

He turned and looked out the window for a few seconds. When he looked back at me, his eyes were dark with longing. He said gently, "You know that's not true."

As I searched for some way to respond that wouldn't make him withdraw, the front door opened and Esther walked in.

"Where's Becky?" she said. "Her mother's asking for her."

Becky answered the question by appearing in the doorway to Jake's apartment, Sam right behind her. But Becky didn't see Esther. Her eyes sought her son, and she came to me and took the sleeping Trevor. She bent and kissed his brow, his cheek. Then she turned to Sam.

"This is your son," she said proudly, laying the baby in Sam's arms.

Sam looked startled. "This is our Trevor? I thought he was Jake and Rose's baby."

I turned a fiery red and couldn't even look in Jake's direction. Becky looked at me and smiled. "They aren't married," she whispered to Sam. Then she blushed. "But then, neither are we."

Sam smiled at her, love all over his face. "It's just a matter of time, sweetheart. We'll see how fast it can happen in Pennsylvania. I'm not letting anyone take you away from me again, believe me."

Then he turned his attention to his son, kissing his

head, stroking his cheek.

"Becky, he's beautiful," he whispered in a choked voice. He looked at her. "You're beautiful."

She glowed and the little family drifted back into Jake's rooms.

Esther stared after them.

"That was Samuel?" she whispered. She looked unhappy, distressed.

I nodded. "He showed up this morning, looking for Becky. He followed her parents here."

"But he's meidung. He shouldn't be here," she said, agitated. She had lost all color and looked ready to weep.

I didn't know what to do. I understood Esther's concern, though I thought both the concern and the reason for it extreme, and I certainly didn't want to add to the emotional struggles she was already having. I also didn't want to offend Mary and John who had been nothing but kind to me. However, I wasn't about to tell Sam to leave.

I turned, as I found myself doing more and more these days, to Jake.

"Esther, look at me," Jake said, easily taking the problem on his broad shoulders.

She glanced at him warily. I could almost read her mind. Here was a man who would be meidung too if he had taken his vows. He had just been smart enough not to, knowing his own heart for the rebellious thing it was. His family had also been smart enough not to force him.

Jake's voice was soft, for he too understood her distress. Here was a situation the rules didn't cover, and she was truly on the horns of a dilemma. The simple life had suddenly become very complex.

"No one in your district even knows Sam," Jake said. "He's under the ban in Ohio where he lives, not here. Here he is an English man just like me. Here no one has to know he's meidung."

She stared at him, not certain she believed him. I doubted she knew the phrase situation ethics, but if she did, she'd be screaming it.

"Say you didn't know Sam was Becky's boyfriend and you didn't know he was shunned. If I brought him home to dinner with the family, would you be polite? Would you eat at the same table with him? Would you talk with him and give him a piece of that wonderful apple pie of yours?"

She nodded. "I would always show hospitality. If I didn't know."

"Then think of him that way, okay? Think of him as my friend, an Englisher named Sam Hershberger. Because I'm inviting him to dinner."

I looked at Jake. He was inviting Sam to dinner? Why? To rebel against the Amish strictures just a bit more? To force Esther to bend a bit? Or to be kind to Sam? Or all of the above?

"I'm even going to ask him to spend the night if he wants to sleep on my sofa. In fact, he can spend every night here until he and Becky marry, if he wants to."

I looked at Esther and saw she was ready to cry. Too many difficult things were hitting her all at once. I went to her and hugged her.

"He loves God, Esther," I said. "He was just telling us how God took away the hatred in his heart and taught him to forgive. Isn't a man's heart what counts?"

"Yes, I guess. No. There's the Ordnung." She looked at me in despair. "I don't know," she said in a tiny voice. She covered her face with her hands.

Elam walked in at that moment.

"Esther!" He hurried to her. "What's wrong?"

She stiffened at his approach, and since I still had a hand on her shoulder, I felt a shiver of emotion pass over her. She turned away from him. "Nothing's wrong." She swiped at her eyes. "I'm fine."

He stood awkwardly, not believing her but not certain what to do about it. He looked at me, questions in his eyes. I merely smiled. I wasn't going to make things any easier for him as he struggled with his feelings for this wonderful woman.

After studying the toes of his boots for a few minutes, he seemed to remember why he came. "Rachel is worried about Becky and Trevor," he announced to the room at large. Then he looked at Esther who still wouldn't look at him. His voice grew soft. "And Mom is worried about you, so I came to get you." He stared at her bowed head and the curve of her neck beneath its black bonnet. Then he blinked. "Both of you, I mean."

She nodded and walked to the sink. She turned on the cold water and wet a cloth that sat there. "In a minute." She held the cloth to her face. "In a minute."

"I'll get Becky," I said and hurried into Jake's apartment.

Becky, Sam, and Trevor sat on the sofa, a little family clustered together for the first time. Sam was playing with his son's hands, reveling in the tiny fingers wrapping around his large, calloused ones.

"Stay there," I ordered, though they showed no signs of moving. I raced upstairs and got my camera. As soon as I got back to Jake's living room, I began snapping. I took pictures until all the film was spent.

"Becky," I said as the camera, now useless, dangled from my hand. "You've got to go back to the farm. They're expecting you. They sent Esther and Elam for you. If you don't return, Annie will be terribly hurt. Or they'll send someone else to look for you."

"No!" Sam turned to Becky. "You can't go back. I'm not letting you out of my sight." He put his arm around her, holding her tight against his side.

She smiled at him, eyes aglow with love. "It's okay, Samuel. I'll only be there until we make arrangements to marry. And Rose is right about Grandmother Annie. She has been so kind. Trevor and I will be back here tomorrow morning for you to see us."

"I'll baby-sit the little guy while you two go get your blood tests and do the paperwork for a marriage license," I said.

"I'll come with you now," Sam said to Becky like he hadn't even heard me. "I don't care what they think."

"You can't, Samuel." Becky rested her hand on his jaw.

"Mama and Papa would be so upset! Today isn't the day to face them, not just after Grandfather Nate's funeral."

Sam sighed. "It's hard to care about upsetting them after what they've put you and me through these past months."

Becky's arms slid around his waist. "I know, you poor guy. But you know I'm right. Today has been very hard for my mother."

He nodded. "Okay. I agree. You have to go. I want to do things in a way that honors God and starts to build good feelings, not momentarily satisfies vengeful desires." He took Becky's hand and looked her in the eye. "We're going to do things God's way from now on, Becky."

She stood on tiptoe and kissed his cheek. "You couldn't have said anything that would make me happier," she said. "I love you, Samuel."

She took Trevor from Sam and started for the door. Sam made to follow her, but I shook my head.

"Jake's brother is out there. Let him meet you as a friend of Jake's, not as Becky's boyfriend. There's no sense putting him in the same theological quandary over your shunning as we did Esther."

Sam paused, thought, then nodded. He turned Becky toward him, kissed her hard, then leaned over Trevor and kissed his head. "Sleep well, little guy. I love you." He gave Becky a final hug. "And I love you, Beck."

When she and I walked into the main house living room, Elam stood looking at Esther who stood looking

213

at the floor. Elam glanced at us, then took a second look at Becky. She glowed, as incandescent as a brilliant chandelier. He frowned and looked at me. I smiled innocently back.

The three of them left, Elam in the middle with Becky floating on one side and Esther studying the ground on the other. Elam himself looked straight ahead.

Sam strode into the room and watched out a window. As the three turned into the lane, Becky glanced back over her shoulder and smiled with enough wattage to power an Amishman's household for a year. She held Trevor on her shoulder and waved his little fist. Sam grinned and waved back.

It was hours later up in my bedroom when I finally had time to consider the conversation about forgiving myself that I'd had with Jake and Sam that afternoon. Was I making myself equal with or more important than God when I insisted I forgive myself? I certainly had no conscious desire to rival God's authority and person. Unlike Lucifer, I did not want to be like the Most High.

I thought long and hard about what the Bible said about forgiveness. There were lots of verses about God forgiving us and lots more verses that commanded us to forgive each other. What verses told us to forgive ourselves? I wracked my memories from a lifetime of Sunday school and church. Surely I'd heard someone somewhere preach on such an important topic. When nothing came to mind, I looked in my study Bible and in my concordance. I reached a surprising and unsettling conclusion.

There was nothing in the Bible about forgiving one's self.

When that thought crystallized in my mind, I wondered why not. Why didn't God tell us to forgive ourselves? Didn't He realize we would feel guilty over the heinous things we did, the sins of commission and omission that haunted us? That we would need absolution before our souls could find rest?

The only possible reason He didn't tell us to forgive ourselves was that His forgiveness bought for us by Christ on Calvary was all that we needed. In His economy, we needed not to forgive ourselves but to truly accept His forgiveness. Part of that forgiveness was remembering that Jesus is the Great Burden Bearer. *"For my yoke fits perfectly, and the burden I give you is light."* My burden had been heavy and hard for years.

But, Lord, what I did had such terrible consequences! How can You just let it go? How can You just remove my feelings of guilt? Don't I need to suffer?

A Spirit-whisper softly seemed to say, "Sin is sin, Rose. And offense is offense. A lie needs just as much forgiveness from a Holy God as a murder. An angry comment is as offensive to Him as adultery. What you did or didn't do is no better or worse than what thousands upon thousands of others have done. The ground is level at the foot of the Cross."

But, God, it's too easy, and I'm too undeserving!

It hit me that I sounded just like Jake. He couldn't accept the forgiveness that brings salvation; I couldn't accept the forgiveness that was already mine as a believer. I had been able to accept the idea that I was forgiven eternally, but I hadn't been able to believe that I was guilt-free on a daily basis, probably because I had the consequences of my actions ever before me.

I felt my heart swell as I finally understood the aspect of God's forgiveness that had eluded me for so long. God forgave me in Christ both today and forever. I was totally clean and clear both now and then. All my burdens had been borne by Christ, even the burden of being careless to the point that I caused my father's and sister's deaths. While I might have to live with the consequences, I didn't have to live with the guilt.

"Everyone who believes in him is freed from all guilt and declared right with God."

I lay back on my bed, my eyes brimming with tears. Release! Relief! Freedom! I fell asleep still thanking my Burden Bearer.

My cell phone woke me from deep slumber at 1:35 A.M. I squinted at the clock as I climbed out of bed and clicked open the phone.

"Rose," a sobbing voice said.

"Becky." I went weak in the legs and cold all over. I sank to the bed.

She didn't say anything more, just sobbed.

"I'll be right there." I hung up and called Dr. Braeborn.

"This is Rose Martin."

"Rose?" I heard the disbelief in his voice. "I thought you were—I mean, I heard on the news—" He couldn't make himself say it.

"It's a long story, but I'm fine. I'm calling about Trevor Stoltzfus."

"Bring him in no matter what," Dr. Braeborn said. "I'll meet you at Lancaster General."

I grabbed a pair of jeans and a sweatshirt. I threw on some sneakers, grabbed my coat, and ran for the car. I drove down the road and raced up the Stoltzfus's front walk, my emergency medical bag in hand.

The Stoltzfus house was dark except for a coal oil lamp in the living room. I let myself in and saw Annie seated in her rocker, Trevor in her arms, and Becky in her nightgown on her knees beside her, her head in Annie's lap. One of Annie's hands stroked the weeping girl's head.

Annie looked at me with such sorrow in her eyes that the breath went out of me. I felt a spiral of pain whirl through my chest, settling in my breastbone.

I walked to the chair and held out my hand to the baby. He was already cold to the touch.

"Let me look at him," I said to Annie.

She nodded and wordlessly handed me the infant. I took him to the kitchen table and removed his blankets, then his clothes, then his diaper. His little body looked so fragile, so perfect except for the great weal of a scar on his chest. I turned him over and studied him. I could see no external cause of death. I put his clothes back on and took him to Becky.

"Dr. Braeborn says we're to bring him, no matter what," I said softly.

Annie rose and took her great-grandson from Becky. "Go get dressed, child."

She held Trevor while Becky hurried to the beautiful blue and yellow bedroom.

"Thank Herr Gott that I got to love mein bubbli," she said in a trembling voice. She sank to her rocker.

"Do you want me to get Rachel?" I asked. "So you won't be alone when we leave?"

She shook her head. "We decided not to waken Rachel and the others," she said. "They wouldn't understand." She laid her warm, wrinkled cheek on Trevor's cold one. "Becky knows I loved him. She doesn't know I would go up and hold him when Nate was in the fields and she was busy. I didn't mean to sin, but he was mein bubbli. No matter how much I held him, it was never enough."

She sighed from a place of pain deep in her heart. "Now it has to be enough." Tears trailed down her cheeks, following the furrows of the years, dripping onto the still body in her arms.

Becky appeared and took Trevor. Her hand curled around his head.

"*Schloff, bubbli, schloff,*" she whispered, her voice breaking. "May your dreams be forever fine."

Annie stood in the door and watched us as we

walked to my car. I held Trevor while Becky got in and buckled her seatbelt. Then I placed the child in her arms. I got in and turned the key.

We had barely left the farm lane when Becky said, "Call Samuel."

I nodded and got out my cell phone. I dialed Jake.

"Hello? Is that you, Rose?" said a very alert voice.

I started. "How did you know?"

"I heard you leave. What's wrong?"

"Oh, Jake." I started to cry so hard I could barely talk, let alone drive.

"Rose? Is it—?"

"It's T-Trevor." I couldn't go on.

After a brief pause Jake asked, "Dead?"

I sniffed. "Yeah." That huge stone pressing on my breastbone was getting heavier by the moment. I couldn't even imagine Becky's pain. "Becky and I are on our way to LGH. She wants Sam to come."

"Sure she does. We'll be there as soon as we can."

I hung up and turned onto 340. I barely noticed an Amishman racing down the road on his scooter. It wasn't until we went under the railroad underpass and I saw another man on his scooter as well as three cars with lights flashing that I realized there was a calamity somewhere else tonight, too. The volunteer firemen were responding to a call.

"Are you all right, Beck?" I asked when I was certain there were no more volunteer firemen lurking for me to accidentally run over.

She didn't answer and I didn't blame her. Dumb question.

"It's so hard to think he's gone," she said as we passed the light in Smoketown. She held Trevor cradled in her arms like he was nursing, and I thought that soon she'd also have physical pain to endure when her milk came in.

"Talk to me about him, Becky. Tell me some good Trevor stories."

She was quiet so long, I wasn't certain she heard me. Then: "When I first realized I was pregnant, I couldn't believe it. I was so upset! But as time went on, I grew to love the child inside. He was my baby. Mine and Samuel's. It didn't matter when or how he was conceived. He was mine, ours. I talked to him and prayed for him. I gave him to Herr Gott."

Her voice thickened, and it was a few minutes before she could continue. "Then he was born so sick, and he had that terrible operation. I pleaded with Herr Gott to let him live. He lived, but I knew he would die. I decided I would love him with everything that was in me every day that Herr Gott let me have him."

"Most people would be furious at God for letting their baby be so sick," I said.

"Oh no," she said, cuddling Trevor close. "I was too busy being thankful that Herr Gott gave me Trevor. If it weren't for Trevor, I never would have gone to Mrs. Trowbridge like I did. I never would have learned about grace. I never would have believed in Jesus. Trevor was a gift, a wonderful gift."

I was moved by her sincerity and couldn't help but wonder if I'd feel the same way if he were my baby.

"A lot of people have told me that Trevor's illness is Herr Gott's punishment for what Samuel and I did. But I know iss not so."

"How do you know this?" I glanced at this child-woman of uncommon grace.

"Because fine people have sick babies too, don't they? And terrible people, people much worse than Samuel and me, have fine babies, all beautiful and healthy."

"So you think anyone can have a sick baby?"

"I do. Or a healthy one. And if I ever start to get mad at Herr Gott for letting Trevor die, I will remember that God let his Son die, too."

We drove through the silent clusters of houses, past Anderson Pretzels and into Lancaster City. We went past the prison that looks like a castle with crenellated towers and along the narrow city streets until we reached the hospital. I drove up to the Emergency entrance.

"You get out here, Becky. I'll go park and be right back."

She nodded and got out. When I came back to the entrance, she was huddled under the portico, Trevor held against her heart. We went inside and were shown into a cubicle immediately by Nancy, an ER nurse I frequently ran into on late nights as we passed our victims off to the hospital staff.

"Rose?" she said. "It is Rose?"

I looked at her strangely. Of course it was me. Then I drew the curtains around the cubicle and stood beside Becky as she sat on the lone chair holding her baby. She talked to him, crooned to him, sang to him. She kissed his forehead, his nose, his hands, all the time letting her tears wet his blankets.

Dr. Braeborn, a small man who took illness as a personal affront and who fought for the lives of his small patients with unfailing energy, arrived minutes after we did. He walked up to Becky and laid his hand on her head.

"I'm so sorry, my dear." He stopped and cleared his throat. "I failed."

Becky looked at him and shook her head. "No," she said softly. "I gave him to Herr Gott, Dr. Braeborn. It was His choice. Not yours."

The doctor blinked at her words, then took Trevor and laid him on the gurney. He started to unwrap Trevor's blanket when he stopped. "Would you undress him for me, Becky?"

I watched the grateful look that spread over her face. She rose and slowly, for the last time, removed her son's clothes. The doctor examined him as Becky and I stood watching, wrapped in each other's arms. He, as I, found no overt cause of death.

"I know this is a hard question for you, Becky, but may I perform an autopsy on Trevor?"

Becky opened her mouth to answer when a frantic

voice yelled, "Becky! Becky! Where are you?"

I came out of the curtained cubicle where Trevor lay just as a nurse came up to Sam and tried to shush him.

I hurried forward. "It's okay, Nancy. I'll take him." I looked into Sam's wild eyes.

"Rose?" Nancy said again. "Rose?"

But I ignored her.

"They're over here, Sam." I said and led him to his family.

He fell to his knees beside the gurney and sobbed as he looked at the little body. Becky came up behind him and wound her arms around his neck. She laid her cheek on the top of his head and her tears wet his hair.

"Thank God I held him," Sam said over and over. "Thank God I held him."

I looked at Dr. Braeborn who nodded. I wrapped Trevor in his blanket and held him out to Sam. Tears streamed down his face as he looked at the little boy.

"Take him, Sam," I said. "Say good-bye to your boy."

Dr. Braeborn and I backed out of the cubicle and left the three of them together. Both he and I were sniffing and blotting tears with our sleeves.

A familiar voice said, "Rosie?" and I came undone.

Jake opened his arms, and I fell into them. For the second time in less than a week, I sat on his lap, my face pressed to his chest, and sobbed.

Eleven

WHEN I FINALLY CALMED DOWN, I SAT UP UNDER MY OWN steam and climbed off Jake's lap. I felt Jake's hand remain on my waist and was grateful for his support. Poor man. He'd catch his death of cold if he went outside in his tear-saturated shirt.

Sniffling, I began searching through my pockets for a tissue and could find none. I began to feel desperate. "You don't have a handkerchief, do you?"

"I didn't exactly have lots of time to dress," he said, running his hand through his sleep-tousled hair.

I glanced at his jeans and T-shirt, then at my clothes and knew what he meant. I didn't even want to think about my hair.

Nancy came up just then and shoved a box under my nose.

"Thanks," I muttered through a clogged nose as I pulled a tissue free.

"No problem."

I grinned at her, then buried my face and blew. Relief! When I finished, I looked up to find her standing in exactly the same spot, staring at me. I grabbed another tissue, certain my nose was dirty.

"Oh, Rose," Nancy said, her eyes suddenly tearing, her voice thick. "Oh, Rose!" And she threw her arms around my neck. "I thought—I thought—" And she began to cry in earnest.

I automatically hugged her back. Then it hit me. I looked at Jake in consternation as I patted Nancy on the back. "I forgot I'm supposed to be dead."

"But you're not!" Nancy said, pulling back. "How did the news get it so wrong?"

I smiled wanly. I didn't know what to say.

"There was nothing you could have done differently, Tiger," Jake said. "Becky needed you."

I nodded. He was right. Still, the fact remained that I'd blown my story.

"Look, Nancy," I said. Maybe I could convince her to forget she'd seen me, talked to me. Maybe when the larger emergency care family commiserated about my death, she'd be able to bite her tongue.

I sighed. That was a lot of maybes and called for an inhuman amount of discipline. If the situation were reversed, I'm not certain I'd have the strength to keep quiet. Things would just slip out.

And then there was Dr. Braeborn. And the nurse staring at me from across the room, looking like she was seeing a ghost. And the receptionist who waved three fingers at me from her desk.

Just then the door flew open and an ambulance crew surged in with an accident victim strapped to a gurney. Everyone in the emergency room was galvanized into action, even Nancy who wiped at her eyes, thrust the tissue box at me, and grabbed the victim's flailing wrist.

"Auto accident with fire, victim trapped against steering wheel," the EMT shouted. "BP 90 over—" And he froze midstep, staring at me.

"Hi, Harry," I said softly.

"Rose." He breathed my name as the gurney bumped into him hard.

"Harry!" yelled Alice Moyer, his partner for the run. "Move it!"

He blinked and turned back to his work. "BP 90 over 50 and falling," he shouted as they wheeled the victim into a cubicle across the room from Becky and Sam.

"Fat's in the fire," Jake said.

I nodded. "Wait until Lem hears."

Harry peered out of the cubicle for just an instant, like he was checking to see if he'd seen what he thought. I sent him a small wave. He shook his head like a dog that's been out in the rain and moved back behind the curtain.

Poor Harry.

Jake touched my arm and I turned to him.

"Why don't you give me your car keys? I'll give them to Sam so he and Becky can leave whenever they want," he said.

I nodded and fished them from my pocket. "The doctor should be finished with them anytime now."

He took the keys and started to roll across the floor. He paused and turned. "I'll wait and take you home when you can finally get free from Harry and the others."

I smiled. "I know."

He wheeled off to do his errand just as Harry and Alice stepped out of the cubicle where the accident victim lay. Harry stared at me as he walked across the room.

I rushed to him and wrapped my arms around his neck. "I'm sorry, Harry. I'm sorry. I didn't want to do it. They made me."

He hugged me back, his arms like bands of iron. "My heart's going a million miles an hour, kid. My BP is probably through the roof."

He pulled back and stared at me, then laughed. "Oh, God, thank You, thank You," he shouted to the ceiling. And he hugged me again. Alice patted me on the back.

"You have no idea the hell you've put me through, girl," he said. "I've been so upset, so angry." Suddenly that anger licked across his face. Harry, my gentle Mennonite, looked ready to explode.

"I'm sorry, Harry. I'm sorry."

"A lot of good that does," he groused in a tone of

voice that was, for him, positively incendiary. "I lost twenty years off my life, and I can't afford that at my age. And I'm still two night's short on sleep."

"The police asked her to do it, Harry." Jake had come up beside me and rested his hand on my waist again. "She had no choice."

"Who's he?" Harry asked me, looking at Jake.

"I'm Jake Zook." He offered his hand. "I'm a friend of Rose's. She's been staying at our family farm."

Harry looked at him suspiciously, like this whole misunderstanding was somehow Jake's fault.

"The police have been trying to keep her alive by letting the bomber think he killed her," Jake said. "I've been more than willing to help."

Harry grunted.

"So who did he kill if it wasn't you?" Alice asked. I could see the collar of a pair of pink pajamas peeking out from under the collar of her uniform. I bet there was a pair of pink pj bottoms under the navy pants she had on. "Or wasn't it anyone at all? It was all a line the police fed us to keep you safe."

"There was definitely a body," I said, "but they don't know for sure whose yet. Or maybe I should say, at least they haven't told me. It was probably my landlord."

"Whose idea was it to let everyone think it was you?" Harry asked, his anger draining away.

"Lem Huber of the Lancaster City police."

Harry nodded. He knew Lem.

Nancy approached us. "Would you mind moving to

the waiting room?" she asked. "There's another victim of the car fire arriving."

We just started in that direction when the door flew open again and the other accident victim was wheeled in. Another flurry of "Rose! You're dead!" echoed through the emergency room, blending with the groans of the survivors. None of us even noticed the TV crew until a microphone was shoved in my face and WGAI's Patty Carlson asked, "Rose Martin, what's it like to return from the dead?"

I took a deep breath and told myself not to panic. My secret was already blown. What did it matter if all of Lancaster County would be privy to my resurrection, not just my friends and coworkers?

It mattered. I didn't dare hope that Ernie wouldn't see TV or read the paper for the next few days.

I turned to smile sweetly at Patty. "Do you realize that my death was announced to keep me alive? If you put this report on the air, I could once again become the bomber's target. Do you want that on your conscience?"

She yelled, "Cut!" The TV crew put their camera down and she grinned at me. "What a great interview," she said. "Right to the point. Thanks! We'll just cut the conscience crack." And they disappeared.

I stifled a groan and turned to find the whole Bird-in-Hand ambulance crew waiting for me plus a couple of our firemen who'd come in to get minor burns treated. They hugged me and patted me on the back and yee-hawed loudly enough to cause Nancy to send us packing again. Out in the parking lot they crowded around me once more.

Suddenly Alice said, "Denny's, everybody. We can't stand here forever. Besides, I'm hungry."

"Right," Harry said. "We need a celebratory cup of coffee to toast our Rose."

"Only coffee?" someone yelled. I think it was one of the Amish firemen.

"Coffee," Alice said. "This is our sweet Rose we're celebrating, not a deadbeat like you, Amos."

And everybody laughed.

We sat around several tables pushed together at Denny's. Half the crowd had breakfast, the other half had hamburgers. I had a Grand Slam with my eggs over easy and lots of hot tea. I held Jake's hand under the table.

"Did you know we were planning a memorial service for you?" Harry asked as he poured syrup over his pancakes until even his eggs were floating in the sweet liquid. He sat directly across from me and seemed to have trouble taking his eyes off me.

"He was in charge." Ben Zuckerman pointed to Harry. "He was pulling out all the stops, let me tell you. And Alice was going to sing."

"I was already practicing," she said. She gave a few la-la-la's and was booed by the rest of the crew.

"Harry even asked the mayor to come and give the eulogy," Ben said.

"The mayor!" I protested. "He doesn't have the faintest idea who I am."

"I know." Harry grinned. "But you deserved all the stops pulled out and he loves photo ops."

"You guys are wonderful," I said, loving them all. "I'm sorry for what I put you through, especially you, Harry. And I can't thank you enough for caring so much."

"Hey," shouted Alice, checking her watch. "I've got to get going. I need to have time to get beautiful for my students." She sighed. "This won't be one of my better days as a teacher, I don't think."

"Count it a success if you stay awake," Harry said. "Now, me. I'm going home to sleep, at least as long as the wife lets me. It's the chief perk of retirement."

I felt like the guest of honor at a shower as everyone came by my chair and gave me a kiss. Several of the men looked hard at Jake. He glared right back.

"In case you haven't noticed," Harry spoke along with his stare, "she's special."

"You'll get no argument from me," Jake said as he smiled at me.

Harry looked from one of us to the other and grunted. He lumbered off calling after Alice, "Don't worry about the reports! I'll do them. Go home and get a good hot shower. At least it'll help you stay awake through first period."

Finally we headed for the farm, and adrenaline shutdown struck. I was so wiped out I could hardly sit up straight.

"Sleep, Tiger. Even the few minutes from here to home will help."

I leaned my head back and closed my eyes, but I couldn't sleep. I felt emotionally torn apart. On one hand, my mind kept pulling up images of the first part of the night: Becky weeping with her head in Annie's lap. Annie rocking Trevor. Trevor lying on the gurney. Dr. Braeborn's anger. Sam's tears.

Then I'd see a beaming Harry and a singing Alice and a tissue-toting Nancy. I'd see a table full of people rejoicing that the report of my demise was premature.

"Oh, Jake." My voice shook more than I meant it to.

"Hang on, Tiger. We're almost home. You can make it."

"I don't know what Lem's going to say when he hears the news tomorrow morning," I mumbled.

"That doesn't worry me near as much as what the bomber's going to do."

I shivered. "He still doesn't know where I am."

"And it better stay that way."

When we got back to the farm, it was almost 5 A.M. Soon the men would be up and heading for the barn. Soon Esther's new employer would be coming to collect her. Soon I would collapse in my bed and sleep.

I stumbled from the passenger seat and waited for Jake to round the van from his side.

"Rose?"

"Jake?" I started around the van. "Are you okay?"

"Come here."

I hurried to him and found him sitting in the shadows. He reached for my hand and pulled me onto his lap.

"Are you going to be all right?" He searched my face as he pushed my tousled hair out of my face. "You've been from the depths of sorrow to the heights of reunions. That's a lot to deal with."

I was moved by his concern, this man who refused to love me. Tears pricked my eyes.

"I'll be okay," I said as I fingered the dark lock that always fell across his forehead. "I'm liable to burst into tears at random moments for the next few days, but I'll be fine."

He wrapped his arms around me and hugged me, the first time he'd initiated such a move. I lowered my head and rested it on his shoulder, my arms about his neck. We sat there quietly for several minutes. I let out a deep sigh, grateful beyond words for his comfort and presence.

"You're wonderful, Jake." I sat up and looked at him. "I can't thank you enough for being my tower of strength these last few days. I don't know how I would have survived without you."

He looked acutely embarrassed but pleased. I leaned over to give him a gentle thank-you peck on the cheek, but he turned his head and suddenly we were kissing and my heart was pounding. I clutched at him, holding tight as my head spun like a mad top and my insides melted as under a summer's desert sun.

Jake pulled back to gasp for air. "There's this woman," he mumbled against my lips.

"I know." I ran my finger down his jaw. "You won't love her."

"I won't." And he kissed me again.

But she'll love you, I thought. Always and forever.

And I knew that no matter what Jake said or did, I wasn't being merely poetic or romantic. I *would* love him always and forever.

The headlights from my car spotlighted us as Sam turned into the drive. We pulled apart reluctantly. Jake held me in the chair as Sam walked over to us. The first light of dawn showed a face full of fatigue and grief beyond words.

"Thanks, you guys." He smiled wanly at us. "You were so great."

"Is Becky at home?" I asked.

Sam nodded. "She made me leave her there. She wouldn't let me go in. She said she needed to talk to people about me before I came to the house."

I took his hand. "She's right, Sam. Hard as it is for both of you, she's right."

He put his other hand on top of mine and patted it. "I know. But that doesn't make it any easier. I want to be there with her, holding her, comforting her." He sighed. "But we did things out of order, and we have to pay the price."

We watched him walk disconsolately to the house.

"I guess we'd better go in, too," I said.

Jake nodded. "Are you mad at God about Trevor? Do you think He took him to punish Becky and Sam?"

I shook my head. "Becky said she gave Trevor to God. She promised God she'd love Trevor as long as she had him, but how long was up to God."

I pictured her sitting there, her dead child in her arms as she talked about how gracious God was. "She said that if it weren't for Trevor, she and Sam wouldn't have come to Christ." I shook my head. "She has the most wonderful faith."

"Yours isn't too shabby either, sweetheart." And he shifted to let me know it was time for me to stand up.

As I stood, one side of Jake's jacket fell open and hit the side of his chair with a heavy clunk.

"What have you got in your pocket?" I asked absently.

He looked at me and smiled but said nothing.

The hairs on the back of my neck stood up. "Jake!" I reached for the pocket.

He caught my wrist and said, "Don't touch."

"It's a gun," I whispered, appalled.

"It's a gun." He reached into his pocket and pulled out the weapon. It sat heavily in his hand.

I shivered. "I hate guns. I absolutely hate them. One night we picked up a little boy suffering from a gunshot wound his nine-year-old brother had given him. The father had the gun in his night table in case of intruders. The boys found it. The seven-year-old died."

I stared at the gun and thought about causing death. "I know how the nine-year-old feels."

"And the father," Jake said.

I shook my head. "Somehow I don't seem to have much pity for him. He was old enough to know better."

Jake released the clip from the gun and put both

parts back in his pocket. He took my hand.

"It's okay, Rose."

I didn't ask what *it* was and he didn't say. Guns? Bombs? Life? Probably neither of us knew, but there was a strange comfort in the saying.

We approached the front steps, then paused.

"See you for a late breakfast," Jake said, taking my hand. "About noon."

"Sounds wonderful." I placed my other hand on his shoulder.

He reached up and pulled my head down so that our lips met. The sweet, gentle kiss moved me deeply.

"Good night, Tiger." He smiled with his heart and wheeled away.

I stood for a minute, bemused. Then I floated up the stairs and inside.

"Esther!" I was startled to see her in her robe and gown, her hair in a braid hanging down her back. "What are you doing up so early?"

"I heard you leave." She looked at her hands. "I was having trouble sleeping, and so I heard you. I stayed in bed as long as I could stand it. I finally got up to have some tea ready for you when you got home."

"Oh, my dear," I said, moved by her kindness. "How long have you been waiting?"

She shrugged as if it didn't matter. To her it probably didn't. She wouldn't have slept anyway.

I sank into a chair at the table. "Join me. It might be our last chance to drink together."

"I saw you and Jake come back."

I was suddenly glad he had kissed me on the far side of the van. Then I thought of the kiss by the front porch and blushed.

"Things are better between you," she said.

I nodded. "I think."

"You love each other."

"He'll never agree," I said, sighing.

She looked at me and gave me a shadow of her former smile. "But you will."

"I will."

"Men," she said with more than a touch of anger.

I nodded. "Men."

She put a pot of tea on the table and a plate of freshly baked cinnamon rolls. I looked at them and thought ruefully of my Grand Slam. But a gift is a gift, no matter how full the stomach. I slipped a roll onto my plate and began working my way through it. After the first bite, it was no great effort.

"These are wonderful," I said. "You are definitely a gifted cook. If you ever want to go into business either with a restaurant or a bakery, let me know. I want to invest."

She smiled wanly. "All I want to do is cook for my husband and children." Her slumped shoulders said she had no hope of that in the near future or maybe ever.

Mentally I shook my head as I thought of Elam. The guy was throwing away the greatest potential blessing of his life, not to mention a marvelous cook! And over what? A misbegotten and unrequited love.

Esther took a fortifying sip of tea. "All right," she said as she set the mug on the table. She squared her shoulders. "Tell me."

I sighed. I recognized that we had been stalling, and I cast about for some other topic to hold the real subject of our morning at bay. I could think of nothing.

Esther was more forthright than I. "Was it Trevor?"

I nodded. "Becky called. I went down right away."

"Were you in time? Is he okay?" Her eyes pleaded for affirmative answers.

I shook my head. "No."

She shot to her feet and walked to the sink. She grabbed the edge as if to hold herself up. Tears streamed down her face.

"I knew it," she said. "I didn't want to admit it, but I knew. As soon as I heard you leave, I knew." She grabbed a paper towel and wiped futilely at her tears. She turned to me. "What happened?"

"I don't know." I stared past her out the window at the soft new day being born as we spoke of death. "The doctor's going to do an autopsy. My bet is that his little heart just stopped."

She wrapped her arms around her body as if to hold herself together through the pain. "Do you think he suffered?"

I shrugged. "I don't know that either."

"Did he look—" she faltered.

I knew what she wanted and was thankful I could

239

give it to her. "He looked fine. No marks, no signs of struggle, no evidence of pain."

"Denki, Herr Gott," she whispered. Then she lowered her face into her hands and was overwhelmed by deep, gut-wrenching sobs.

"Oh, Esther!" I got up from my chair and started toward her, but Elam got there first. I hadn't even heard him come downstairs, clad as he was in his stockinged feet.

"Esther!" He pulled her into his arms and began making small soothing noises.

I started toward the stairs, glad he was there to comfort her. I didn't think I had the emotional resources left to do a decent job. I wasn't even sure I had the strength to get myself to my bed.

"Trevor's dead," Esther told him when she got her breath back, her voice quivering. "That beautiful little boy. Oh, but it breaks my heart!"

As I put my foot on the first step, I glanced back to make certain she was all right. Bemused by what I saw, I continued to stare. Neither Elam nor Esther was even aware that I was still around.

"Shh, iss all right," Elam said as he stroked her hair. "Iss all right."

"No, it's not!" she shouted and punched him. His eyes opened wide in surprise. Docile, sweet Esther had become a Marah, weeping in anger for her children.

"Don't you ever say it's all right!" She punched him again and again, sobbing the whole time. "Never, never, never!"

He held her and let her strike him. I looked at his sorrow-filled face and understood that the sorrow was for her and her pain. The fear beneath the sadness was for himself.

When she once again let her hands lie still, he said softly, "Esther, look at me."

She kept her head down and shook it. "I can't," she whispered.

"Why not?"

"I'm too embarrassed."

"Because you cried?"

"Because I hit you."

He grinned gently at her bowed head. "It's all right. I understand."

"It's not all right! It's terrible."

"Esther, I said it's all right. Now look at me."

She kept her head down, but she didn't shake it, nor did she say anything.

"Esther." There was a command in his voice.

She sighed deeply. Slowly, reluctantly, she raised her face to his. I could see such self-exposure there that my heart clutched. No wonder she hadn't been willing to look at him all this time. She knew he'd see her heart and her hurt written there clearly. She may consider pride a terrible sin, but it had been all she had left. Now she hadn't even that.

Apparently my heart wasn't the only one moved by her beauty and vulnerability.

"Esther," he breathed. "Oh, Esther." He bent and

kissed her cheek, then her eyebrow, her forehead, her cheek again.

"Don't," she pleaded, her eyes closed. "Please don't. I can't bear it."

In answer he pulled her against him, burying his face in her hair. He made a deep-in-the-throat noise much like his brother did, only Elam's was one of agony not warning.

"Don't go, Esther. Don't leave me. Please."

"Elam?" She leaned back and studied his face, resting a hand along his jaw. Whatever she saw shocked her. Their eyes locked for a long moment. Then she whispered in a voice full of joy, "Elam." She wrapped her arms about his waist and buried her face in his neck. "Oh, Elam."

"*Ich lieb dich*, Esther," he breathed. "How I could have been so foolish, I'll never understand. But *ich lieb dich. Ich lieb dich.*"

I made myself turn away from the deeply private moment and continue up the stairs to my room. At least the night had ended well, I thought as I fell into bed without brushing my teeth or washing my face. Now Esther wouldn't have to leave.

And all Jake had to do was get his act together as his brother had finally done. Surely he could do that.

Couldn't he?

Twelve

I HAD BARELY FALLEN ASLEEP WHEN THE PHONE RANG. AND rang and rang. Muttering under my breath about sleep deprivation and its effect on the human psyche, I fumbled through the pile of clothes I'd dropped on the floor when I fell into bed. Then I remembered that the cell phone was in my jacket pocket. By the time I located it, my mood was foul.

"Hello," I muttered with all the graciousness of a bouncer in a third-rate bar.

"And good morning to you too, Merry Sunshine," said Lem Huber. I could hear laughter in his voice, and it made me grind my teeth.

I groaned as I flopped back onto the bed. I pulled the calico quilt up under my chin and slid one hand behind my head. "I knew you'd call, but I thought you'd have the decency to wait until the afternoon."

"Why?"

"Because I was up all night!"

"Ah yes. Giving TV interviews, I presume." There was now an edge to his voice that even I couldn't miss.

"Give me a break." I hoped I didn't sound as defensive or guilty as I felt. "I'm not that dumb."

He made a noncommittal noise.

"I had to make a hospital run," I explained. "Carlson was there looking for a story, and that was that."

"You aren't supposed to be riding with the ambulance crew now," Lem said carefully and clearly. "You're supposed to be dead."

"I wasn't riding with the ambulance. It was the girl down the street. Her baby died."

"Oh." Lem took a deep breath. "I'm sorry. That must have been rough."

Tears pooled in my eyes and I blinked. I brushed at the side of my face, trying to get the wetness that overflowed. "Yeah. It was." My voice broke.

After giving me a minute to get control, he asked, "Does anyone know you're living at the Zooks?"

"Just the ambulance crew."

Lem made an unhappy noise. "Too many. That makes me uncomfortable."

"That makes *you* uncomfortable? Think about me!"

"Look, Rose, I wish I could put a guard on you, someone to be with you all day every day, but we just don't have the manpower."

"I don't think I want a bodyguard anyway," I said.

"And Jake's here, don't forget." I watched dust motes dance by in a sunbeam and listened to Lem's silence.

Finally he said, "Well, don't open any packages in the near future, okay?"

"Is that what blew up my apartment? A package?"

"We found a couple of pieces of brown wrapping paper on the grass under the living room window. Apparently when the bomb exploded, the scraps were blown out the shattered windows and fell to the ground with the glass. The fire didn't touch them, though the water damage was considerable. One scrap had nothing written on it, but the other had M S period R O. It's a good thing it was written in ink not a felt pen, or we wouldn't have even this much."

I tried to picture the letters in my mind. MS. RO "The beginnings of Ms. Rose Martin?"

"We think so."

I shivered. Suddenly being the abstract target of a bomber had become much more personal. "And Mr. Metz, being really mad at me and a nasty man besides, was going to open the package just for spite?"

"That's the best we can come up with."

I sighed. "How sad."

"You'd rather you'd opened it?" Lem asked.

"I'd rather no one opened it. Or no one sent it."

"But there's a great lesson for you here, Rose. No packages. And can you park your car somewhere safe? I don't want him getting to your vehicle like he did the Hostetters'."

"I'll keep it out of sight and try not to drive it until this thing's over."

"Yeah," he said. "Don't drive it. That's the best."

"What about Peter Hostetter?" I asked. "I've thought about him so much. Are you taking good care of him?"

"That we are," Lem said. "That we are."

"And Ernie? Have you got enough evidence against him yet? No," I said, answering my own question. "You wouldn't still be worried about me if you had."

"If we had the evidence we needed, you'd be home free," Lem agreed.

"By the way, I was wondering who inherits all that Hostetter money and who gets Pockets. Is it Ernie? That wealth has got to be a great motive for murder."

"Right now Peter gets it all, but if something happens to him—well, he's got to make a will stipulating his desires."

"Don't let him name Uncle Ernie as his heir!"

"Rose, he can name whoever he wants." Lem sounded tired. "Look. I've got to go. Just stay safe!"

When Lem and I hung up, I buried my head in my pillow and fell asleep again.

A shrill whistle woke me at one o'clock.

"Hey, Tiger, get down here. Lunch is ready."

I ran a hand over my bleary eyes. "In a minute," I yelled.

It was closer to a half hour before I made it downstairs, freshly showered and brushed, both hair and teeth. Jake was nowhere in sight, but a ham and Swiss sandwich garnished with several of Mary's bread and butter pickles and homemade potato chips sat in the middle of the table.

The house was very quiet.

"Jake?" I called. "Where are you? Have you already eaten? How come you didn't wait for me?" I wandered over to the door of his apartment with my sandwich in my hand. "Jake?"

My answer was a groan.

Goose bumps covered my arms. "Jake?" I pushed open the door of his place. "Jake?"

Another groan, this one coming from his bedroom where the door was partly ajar.

"Jake?"

There was no answer for a full minute. I had just decided I had misheard and that nothing was wrong when he spoke. "Go away." His voice was hoarse and full of pain.

The nurse in me jumped to attention. "What's wrong? Tell me."

"Rose, just go away."

I stood paralyzed, undecided. The health professional wanted to run in and help him. The woman who loved him knew of his fierce pride and wanted to respect him.

"Rose," Jake choked out, "just leave me alone. If you come in here, I'll never forgive you."

"If I don't come in, I'll never forgive myself."

"No!" If ever I'd heard an anguished cry, that was it.

I reached for the doorknob, my hand shaking. "I'm coming in."

I threw open the door and rushed in. Pride was a highly questionable virtue anyway.

Jake sat in his chair with a wastebasket in his lap. He sat still, his forehead resting on one palm. He didn't lift his head.

"Go away, Rose. Please. Let me have some pride."

"No one's home but me, Jake. Someone's got to help you." I spoke in my efficient nurse voice. I walked past him into his bathroom with its shower stall large enough to hold him in his chair. I took a washcloth and wet it and grabbed a large towel.

"Look here," I ordered as I stood beside him. I reached out to wipe his face.

He grasped my wrist and squeezed. "Go away!"

Then violent spasms seized him and his whole body shook. I felt his forehead. He was burning with fever.

I took the wastebasket and emptied and rinsed it. I put it on the floor beside him and this time I washed his face whether he liked it or not. He swatted weakly at my hand, but I ignored him. I began unbuttoning his shirt.

"What are you doing?" he rasped, batting at my hands again.

"Getting you out of these dirty clothes."

"Rose, you're killing me here," he said, staring at his knees. His shoulders were hunched and his arms wrapped around his body.

My heart broke for him. "I know," I said softly. I bent

and kissed the top of his head. "I'm sorry."

He sighed in resignation and said, "Basket. Fast."

I shoved the container into his hands and went back to the bathroom where I had seen neat piles of clothes arranged on a wheelchair-height shelf. I selected a clean long-sleeved T-shirt. I'd never thought about it before, but drawers would be a hardship for a person like Jake, opening into his knees, requiring all sorts of maneuvering.

I took another wet cloth with me and wiped his face again. He was clearly weak and sitting was becoming harder by the minute. He didn't complain as I took off his shirt.

I filled the bathroom sink with cool water, wheeled him close, and washed his back and chest. His face told me how much he hated it, but when I was finished, he was a little less fevered.

"Pants off," I said as casually as I could. "Then into bed."

I knelt and undid his shoes and took them and his socks off. I glanced up and saw the anguish in his eyes as he watched me. He lifted himself on the third try and I slid his trousers down. I pushed the chair to the bed where I turned the quilt and sheets back far enough to get his legs under with ease.

"Hand me that board," Jake said, pointing to a highly polished piece of wood about three feet long and a foot wide.

I did so, and he placed the board so that one end

rested on the bed and the other on his chair. Using his arms, he slid onto the board. When he stopped to regain his strength, I moved behind him. He was so weak that I was afraid he'd fall. A fit of chills hit him. I grabbed him, holding him about the chest, keeping him steady. For a minute he allowed himself to lean back on me. Then with great effort he moved himself onto the bed where he fell back, exhausted.

"Come on," I said heartlessly. "You can't lie there like that. You need to move higher on the bed so your legs can straighten out. Let me help you." And I moved toward him.

His eyes snapped open and he glared. "You're not touching me again. I can manage on my own. I've been demeaned enough for one day."

"You haven't got the strength to stop me," I said.

Recognizing a challenge when he heard one, Jake pushed himself up, but his arms were shaking from the effort.

"I'm going to put my arms around your chest whether you like it or not," I said. "When you give the word, we're both going to move you."

I put my arms around him as I'd said, resisting the urge to rest my head on his shoulder. "Ready when you are."

Eventually he was lying comfortably, covered by a sheet and a blanket I found in his bathroom. A wide-mouthed pan I'd snitched from Mary's kitchen sat within easy arm's reach.

"I felt fine when I called you for lunch," he muttered. "In fact, you took so long to come down, I ate my own sandwich. Then all of a sudden I was in trouble." He swallowed a couple of times and we both reached for the pan. In a minute he relaxed. "Not this time. Sheesh, I hope this is only the twenty-four-hour kind."

"Shush," I said. "Just sleep if you can."

"Mmm." He closed his eyes.

I bent down to kiss his forehead as much to check for fever as for affection.

Without opening his eyes, he mumbled, "I won't love her."

"I know." I brushed his hair back. "I know."

He was so weary from the virus and the efforts to get into bed that he soon fell asleep. In repose, his often forbidding expression was soft and vulnerable. His chest rose and fell as he breathed, and he rested one arm along his side and had the other flung up beside his head.

We spent the rest of the afternoon in a pattern of illness, cleanup, sleep. Whenever he had the energy to be angry, Jake was grumpy and out of sorts with me.

"Is your bedside manner always so heavy-handed?"

"If I'd realized I was renting to Florence Nightingale, I'd never have done it."

"You think because you smile at me, I'm going to be happy you're here? Hah!"

But once when he slept and I leaned over to check on him, I laid my hand on his cheek. Without consciously knowing, he turned his face into my palm and kissed my wrist.

Oh, Jake, what are we going to do? *Oh, Lord, help us find Your way!*

It was almost dark when I heard the front door of the main house open. Jake was sleeping and I had been sitting in his living room reading. I put down my book and went to see who had come home.

Mary and John looked at me in surprise as I walked from Jake's apartment.

"Jake's sick," I said. "The stomach virus."

Mary gasped and started toward his door.

"Stop," John said in firm, soft command.

Mary stopped.

"You're caring for Jake?" John asked me.

I nodded.

"Does he mind?"

I grinned. "He hates it."

Mary started for the door again.

"Stop, I said." John looked at his wife. When she had stilled again, he turned to me. "Will you keep caring for him?"

I nodded.

John looked at his wife. "You will fix supper. It has been a long day with Annie and Rachel. You don't need nothing else to do. Rose will care for Chake."

Mary looked at the floor, obviously not happy with John's decisions. After a minute, she took a deep breath, squared her shoulders, and walked to the kitchen.

I followed her. "I borrowed one of your pans for Jake. I hope you don't mind."

She shook her head as she all but threw a large cast-iron frying pan on the cookstove. The clatter of iron against iron was deafening.

"Wife!"

Mary spun and looked at John. Neither spoke, but communication flashed through the air faster than the speed of sound. Finally Mary sighed, nodded, and turned to her pan. She picked it up and set it gently back on the stove.

John made a satisfied grunt.

Soon canned beets and lima beans were warming while pork chops sizzled. After I set the table, I found sweetened iced tea in the refrigerator and placed the pitcher on the table. Mary had just put the pork chops on a plate when Elam and Esther walked in, cheeks rosy, smiles broad.

"The cow is all milked and cared for," he said.

Esther grinned shyly at Elam and nodded. "Everything is fine for the night."

John grunted and Mary didn't respond at all. No one seemed to even notice the fact that Elam and Esther had done the work together, something they had never done before.

We sat down to eat.

"Only five?" Elam asked.

"Jake's sick," I said. "Stomach virus."

When Esther served us her pound cake for dessert, I said, "I'll take my cake and go check on Jake."

"No, you don't have to," Mary said. "I'll go."

As she started to rise, her eyes caught John's. Immediately she sat again.

I took some ginger ale with me, thinking that maybe Jake would enjoy it. I didn't want dehydration to become a problem. When I walked into his bedroom with the soda in one hand and my pound cake in the other, he was awake.

"Do you always desert your patients in their hour of great need?" he demanded, hostile and antagonistic.

"Do you always speak so nicely to those who help you?" I countered.

For an answer, he sneered. I gave him my most seraphic smile, and I think I saw steam come out of his ears.

As I handed him a glass of ginger ale, I said, "Time to take those heavy stockings off."

I had to pull the covers out of his hands as he was overcome with a sudden attack of modesty. I carefully rolled down the TED stockings he wore to keep his legs from swelling. I could feel his eyes on me, watching for my reaction as I saw his legs for the first time. They were painfully thin, the muscles atrophied. I couldn't help but think how strong they must have been before and what he had lost.

I was very careful not to let any of the sorrow I felt show on my face. I acted the consummate professional, not like a woman in love. When I did look up at him again, at his fierce eyes and strong brows, at the stubborn set of his jaw, I was struck by the sheer strength of his personality. Legs were only legs. Force of character and will made the man, and Jake had both in abundance. Certainly he had more than enough for me.

Jake's front door opened and I heard Sam and Becky's voices.

"I'll go see what's up," I said as I pulled the covers up over him. "Will you be okay?"

He glared at me and I could see him trying to think up a smart-mouthed retort.

"Don't waste the energy," I said, bending to brush a kiss on his forehead. "You need it to get better."

"I won't love you," he whispered.

"I know." I kissed him again. "I know."

I went into the living room and greeted Becky and Sam.

"Where's Jake?" Sam asked.

"In there sick as a dog," I said, pointing to the bedroom. "Stomach virus."

Sam walked to the door and peeked in. "Hey, guy, when I get sick, can I borrow your nurse?"

I heard a low rumble from Jake but couldn't make out the words. It was just as well. He was probably offering me to Sam on a silver platter. I walked over to Becky.

"How are you doing?" I gave her a hug.

"It depends on the minute," she said. "One minute I'm in tears over Trevor, the next I can hardly breathe, I'm so happy Samuel's here. My head aches, my breasts ache, and I wonder if my heart will ever stop hurting." She looked at me through tears. "In other words, I'm a mess."

"That's not surprising. In fact, it'd be surprising if it were different."

She stared down at her hands. "I find a lot of comfort in the fact that God knows how it hurts because He let Jesus die." She drew a long, shaky breath.

Sam came up behind her, put his arms around her, and gave her a kiss on the top of her head. She turned, wrapped her arms around his middle, and held on for dear life.

"It'll be okay, sweetheart," Sam said softly. "It'll be okay."

Becky nodded, but I imagined she wasn't any more convinced than he was.

Sam looked at me over Becky's head. He seemed to want to change the subject. "He's a pretty grouchy patient, isn't he?"

I glanced at the bedroom door. "I think it's having me as his nurse."

"The man doesn't know how lucky he is."

I smiled at Sam. "Becky, you've picked a man of taste and insight here."

She pulled away from Sam and smiled at him through her tears. "I know."

Sam wiped the tears from her cheeks and said, "Do you mind if we sit in here and talk? We're having a hard time finding somewhere to be alone."

"I'll bet you are," I said.

"We'll be good," Becky said quickly. "You don't have to worry. We've already talked about that, and we know we can't sleep together until we're married."

"We made so many mistakes before," Sam said. "But now that we both love Jesus, we want to obey Him. We will be pure."

I smiled at them. "I think that's wonderful. And just the way it should be. You sit and talk. I'll go back to my patient."

"We applied for a marriage license today," Becky said shyly just before I left the room. "Of course, we can't marry until after Trevor's buried. And we need to decide whether to live here or go back to Ohio." She looked at Sam, pain etched on her face. "I don't know if I can leave here if Trevor's buried here."

When I entered the bedroom, Jake glowered at me, his arms folded across his chest. He continued to grump and complain as I took his temperature and wiped down his back and chest again.

"Oh, shut up," I finally hissed.

Surprisingly, he did. He catnapped through the evening while I read. Every time he woke up, I forced some more ginger ale on him. He scowled ferociously but said nothing. The peace and quiet were refreshing.

Becky went home around ten, Sam settled on the sofa about eleven, and I sat watch through the night. Once I had Jake roll over and I rubbed his back for him. He forgot himself and almost purred with contentment.

At about midnight he fell into a deep sleep. Enviously I stared at him, exhausted. With last night's lack of sleep and this morning's interrupted sleep, I was running on empty. I thought longingly of the sofa in the living room, close enough that I could hear Jake if he needed me. But Sam's tall form already filled it.

I looked at Jake's floor. Too hard. I looked at the rocker I'd dragged into the room. Too cramped. I looked at his bed and grinned.

I grabbed the quilt I'd taken off the bed earlier and wrapped it around myself. Then I lay down on the edge of the bed and fell immediately asleep. Nothing woke me until morning when the sounds of Jake moaning pulled me from a warm and cozy dream that I couldn't remember when I awoke.

I sat up so quickly that I rolled off the bed and landed in a heap of quilt on the floor. The very hard floor.

If I'd hoped for sympathy from Jake, I could hope again. He was feeling so vile that he barely noticed me as I picked myself up. I unwound myself from the quilt and we began yesterday's pattern of illness, cleanup, and sleep all over again. Mary spelled me while I ate breakfast and lunch, but otherwise Jake's care was my responsibility. My privilege. His worst nightmare.

I was dozing in the rocker shortly after lunch when a peeved voice said, "Don't you think you'd do better sleeping in your own bed? Then I could get some clothes on."

I sat up straight and faced Jake, also sitting up straight and radiating health and energy. He looked terrible, his heavy beard shadowing his jaw, his hair hanging in his eyes, his T-shirt a mass of wrinkles, but his eyes were alert and staring at me.

I knew I must look every bit as terrible as he did. I hadn't brushed my hair or washed my face in twenty-four hours. I, too, had slept in my clothes. The only thing I was missing was the beard.

Suddenly my stomach clenched, my mouth filled with saliva, and I raced for the bathroom. I fell to my knees just in time to heave my lunch.

His twenty-four hours may be over, but apparently mine were just beginning.

Thirteen

I WAS HUDDLED IN MY BED, ABOUT TWENTY HOURS INTO MY twenty-four-hour virus when I heard Jake in my living room.

I told myself it was my spinning head; I was hearing things. When his voice continued, I told myself I was hallucinating. When he appeared in my doorway, I told myself I was having a full-blown psychotic episode. Anything was better than the truth.

He wheeled into my room looking beautiful, all cleanly shaven, freshly pressed, and in appallingly good humor. At least that's how he looked to me without the aid of my glasses. They were somewhere on my night table, but I hadn't the strength or will to find them.

I, on the other hand, was a mess. My mouth tasted like a swamp, my flannel nightgown was wrapped about me like a mummy's grave clothes, and my eyes were bleary with pain.

"Hey, Tiger," he said as he smiled at me. "How are you doing?"

His aftershave made me gag, and I grabbed for Mary's pan, now my constant and faithful companion. As I made ghastly wretching sounds, so ladylike and endearing, I understood clearly his resentment of me in his room yesterday.

"How did you get up here?" I muttered with great ill-humor when it became obvious I wasn't going to throw up after all.

"Elam helped me. First he carried the chair. Then he lugged me."

I made a mental note to do something terrible to Elam in revenge, but I was too weak to come up with a decent plan at the moment.

"I'm a mess," I said in massive understatement.

He shrugged. "Probably no worse than I was yesterday."

"Somehow that doesn't make me feel any better. I know what you were like yesterday."

I thought about pushing myself into a sitting position, but all that would accomplish was a wave of dizziness and another bout of nausea. I lay there ignominiously on my back, hair plastered to my forehead, face a ghastly avocado green, teeth so fuzzy they could have been harvested for chenille.

I closed my eyes and wondered if I could feign narcolepsy. Recognizing that as a foolish idea the instant it crossed my mind, I glared at him and asked with a deplorable lack of civility, "Why are you here?"

"Well, I could say I'm your landlord checking to see if you're taking good care of my property."

"Like you need to do that while I lie here feeling like roadkill."

"Or I could tell you I came to apologize for being such an ingrate yesterday." His voice had become soft and gentle, almost pleading.

I turned my head and looked at him in surprise.

"Can you ever forgive me?" he asked, his black eyes earnest. "You were so kind and I was such a jerk."

"Sure," I said. "You're forgiven. And thanks for the apology." It was really more than I had expected. After all, I'd been dealing with sick people for years.

He frowned at me.

"What?" I said, irritated. "I forgive you."

"You make it too easy." He scowled. "I made your life miserable for twenty-four hours and all you say is okay?"

"I didn't say okay. I said I forgive you. You weren't okay. You were rude. You were nasty. I agree. But I forgive you."

He opened his mouth to protest, but I threw back the covers and rushed past him. I slammed the bathroom door and did what my ex-fiancé Ben used to call worshiping the porcelain goddess.

When I finally pulled myself to my feet, I looked in

the bathroom mirror. It was enough to set the gag reflex to work all over again. And I couldn't even see myself clearly without my glasses.

I managed to brush my teeth and hair. I thought about washing my face, but I was out of energy. I opened the door and made for the bed, hoping to reach it before collapsing. I had just found a comfortable position in which to die when Jake reached out to me with a warm cloth and washed my face for me. He was very awkward about it, and he poked me in the eye once, but I was moved to tears by his action.

Dear Father, what do I do about this man?

"Now, Tiger," he said earnestly when I was finally settled, "I've got to know. How can you forgive me so easily?"

"Because I choose to," I said wearily.

"But I don't deserve it," he countered. "I was a jerk."

"I already agreed you were a jerk. And who said forgiveness is given because it's deserved?"

He stared at me, and I suddenly realized that a lot more was at stake than my forgiving him for yesterday.

"Listen closely, Jake, because I only have strength to say this once. Forgiveness is a gift. You can't earn it. You never deserve it. It is a gift, whether it's mine to you or God's to you. Remember those verses Sam quoted? 'God saved you by his special favor when you believed. And you can't take credit for this; it is a gift from God. Salvation is not a reward for the good things we have done, so none of us can boast about it.'"

I looked into his eyes and willed all the strength I had to say, "None of us deserve salvation or forgiveness. It pleases God to grant it through Jesus. It's a gift."

"I can't buy that," he said. "It's too easy."

"You don't get to set the rules here, Jake. God does." I forced my scattered wits to focus. "It all starts with His decision to love us and forgive us. Are you going to tell Him that He can't offer you forgiveness and grace? Why do you think Jesus died? So we could have another holiday?"

"You're getting sarcastic," he said.

I nodded. "I am. I'm sorry."

I paused, feeling as weak as the proverbial newborn. I lay with my eyes closed, trying to gather the strength to finish stating my position. I was surprised to feel a strong hand press against the side of my face.

"It's okay, sweetheart," Jake said as he stroked my cheek. "We can talk about it later."

I turned my head into his hand and kissed him. How comforting he was.

"I love you," I whispered.

"I can't love you," he whispered back.

"I know." I smiled sadly. "I know."

We were silent for a few minutes.

Lord, so much is at stake here! And I am so weak. Help!

I reached for his hand. "Jake, it's okay to let God call the shots, you know. He is, after all, God."

His answer was a grunt.

Suddenly I was so weak I could no longer grip his

hand, let alone debate theology. He felt my hand go slack and held it between his.

"You'll be well soon, Tiger. We're celebrating Thanksgiving today, you know, and Mom's making a huge turkey. The whole family's coming."

The thought of a turkey, usually one of my favorite dinners, made me bilious. Then the rest of his comment hit me.

"It's Thanksgiving?" I'd lost track through my gray haze. "Oh no! My mother's expecting me."

Jake shook his head. "Not today. Definitely not today. You're not going anywhere. Besides, today's not Thanksgiving. Yesterday was."

Yesterday! Mom had been expecting me!

Jake continued, "We're just celebrating today. Tomorrow's Father's birthday, so Mom selected the day in between to get everyone together."

I looked at my cell phone resting by my glasses on the night table. The very thought of putting on the glasses so I could see and dial the numbers, then explain to Mom why I hadn't called her exhausted me. I looked helplessly at Jake. "Could you call her for me?"

And why hadn't she called me? Surely she wondered what had happened to me.

He picked up the cell phone and hit the power button. He shook his head. "Dead."

Now I knew why she hadn't called. She was probably beside herself, especially with the bomber still on the loose.

"Don't worry," he said. "I'll use my phone."

Don't worry. Hah! I gave him Mom's number, and soon he was talking with her like they were old friends. "Don't worry, Mrs. Martin. We're taking good care of her."

He grinned at me and squeezed my hand.

"Yes, she's very sick. Throwing up all over the place. I feel badly because I think she caught it from me."

Pause.

"She took care of me yesterday. That's why she didn't make it for dinner. You know how involved she gets in her work."

That was a true statement, though in this case, it hadn't been the work but the patient.

"I'm sure you tried to call. Unfortunately her phone was dead. Cell phones may be marvels of technology, but they do have this one serious drawback, don't they?"

I would have been so defensive with Mom, and he was just the opposite. You do catch more flies with honey.

"Your loss was my gain, though I'm sorry you were so worried. But let me tell you, she was wonderful, so kind and gentle. I almost want to get sick again so she can nurse me."

Now there was a line if I ever heard one.

"You're absolutely right. She's a marvel, a beautiful marvel."

I looked at Jake skeptically. My mother never in my whole life said I was a marvel, let alone a beautiful one.

"How about if I drive her down tomorrow if she's up to it? That way she won't tire herself prematurely."

What a sneaky way to get to check out my family.

"It'd be fun to put up the Christmas tree. I'd love to help. I can do the bottom."

Pause.

"I may sound tall, but I'm not. In fact, I'm pretty short these days."

I rolled my eyes. Talk about black humor.

"Don't give it a thought. We'll stop at the hardware store and get a new tree stand on our way."

Pause.

"It's no trouble at all. In fact, we're glad to do it. And dinner sounds like a great treat. Yes, I love leftover turkey."

I listened to him in a state of semisleep, marveling at his ease with Mom. I fell asleep thinking about how wonderful he was. I woke to a knocking at my door.

I looked up and saw Elam standing there.

"Jake, Mom sent me up because Andy and Sally are here. Also, she thinks you need something to eat."

"What time is it?" I asked. Neither answered. I turned my head to look at the clock radio and was delighted that I didn't feel any vertigo. It was 1:10.

Jake nodded. "I'll be ready to come down soon."

"You can go now," I said, pushing myself to a half-sitting position. "I feel much better."

"Your twenty-four hours are almost up," Elam said. "If you've got what Jake had, you should feel miraculously healed anytime now."

I watched the brothers leave the room and wondered how long it would be before Esther and Elam were married. This was marrying season, after all.

I napped a bit more and awoke feeling fine. I showered and washed my hair, then sprayed myself with enough perfume and gargled with enough mouthwash to make the sourness of illness but a memory. I even did my nails. I had just finished changing my bed when I heard a knock on my door. By then it was late in the afternoon.

I looked up, and there stood Esther.

I smiled at this young woman so immersed in a culture vastly different from mine, and I realized our hearts belonged to a pair of incredibly dissimilar brothers. Who would have thought, even as little as a week ago?

"Jake and Mary sent me to get you," Esther said. "They say you must come down before Elam has to bring Jake up again." She put her hand to her mouth to prevent a giggle from escaping. "I don't think Elam's back can stand another trip like that."

I was nervous as I came downstairs, but the Zooks quickly made me feel part of the party. I met the two Plain married daughters. Sarah, the oldest child, was married to a farmer named Abner, and they had four children. Ruth was the youngest child and was married to Isaiah, a farmer with a penchant for practical jokes. They had one child, a brand-new baby boy named John after his grandfather.

I met the two fancy brothers. Zeke was married to

Patsy, the woman he left the community for. He was an electrician and they had three kids. Andy was the brother who left the community over the issue of grace versus works. He and his wife Sally had two kids and went to my church, though I'd never met them before.

It fascinated me how the family was split right down the middle on the Plain/fancy issue but seemed to love each other anyway.

"It's Mom," Patsy confided when I mentioned my observation to her. "I know it was very difficult for her when Zeke left for me, but she's absolutely determined that there not be division in this generation of the family like there was in the last."

"What happened in the last generation?" Here was a story I'd never heard.

"Father's brother Jake broke with the church when he was twenty-two over the issue of works and grace. The senior Zooks never saw Jake again, and Father's seen him only rarely since then, and only when Uncle Jake has come to the farm."

"John has never initiated the visits?"

Patsy shook her head. "He doesn't believe he can. And I think it's hurt both of them deeply."

"Is Jake named after this brother?"

"Father and Mom never say so, but we kids all think yes. Uncle Jake used to be Father's favorite brother."

"I guess shunning keeps the community pure, but at such a cost!"

Patsy nodded and adjusted the dress of the beautiful child she held in her arms. The little one grabbed Patsy's gold necklace and tried to eat it.

"Whose little girl is this?" I said.

"This little girl is Young Abner," Patsy said with a smile. "He's Sarah's youngest. He goes into pants in about three months."

Just then two of the grandchildren began squabbling over the same toy.

"Oh, dear," Patsy said. "That's my Aaron and Sarah's Jonathan." She hiked the baby onto her hip more firmly and took a step toward the children. Sarah reached them first and leaned over to talk to her son. In no time, Jonathan held out the coveted toy, which looked like a blue Pockets car to me, and Aaron took it gladly.

Patsy came back to me. "Sometimes I applaud the Plain custom of others first always. Other times I think it makes little monsters of the ones that always get their way."

"I've got a whole collection of Pockets upstairs," I said. "About sixty cars. Maybe the kids would like to play with them?"

I glanced at Patsy and saw her questioning look.

"Sixty cars?"

"The Sophie Hostetter of Pockets fame used to be one of my patients. She gave me the whole set plus all the accessories."

"Isn't she the woman who was killed last week?"

I nodded. "Yes. It makes me so sad. She was a sweetheart."

Suddenly Patsy squinted at me. I saw the recognition leap to her eyes.

"Mary and John don't know anything about the bombs or my temporary death," I said quickly. "I don't think Elam and Esther do, either."

"But Jake does?"

I nodded. "He's become my bodyguard."

Patsy grinned. "Then you're in good hands. I always liked Jake, even when he was at his worst. He had a roguish charm that reminded me of Zeke when I first met him. A good boy gone bad and determined to do it well." She laughed.

I wasn't sure I wanted to hear about Jake as a bad boy, even though I knew that was the Jake of then, not now. His accident had forced all kinds of changes on him, the least of which were the physical limitations. There were also the life reevaluation, the choice to seek higher education, and the empathy and gentleness learned in the crucible. But it was the spiritual changes that I prayed for most. More than anything I wanted to hear that he'd accepted God's forgiveness and become a believer.

Dear God, please!

As if he heard my plea on his behalf, Jake turned and our eyes met. He smiled that sweet, charming smile that melted my heart and dropped one lid in an exaggerated wink. I shook my head in wonder as I grinned back.

Patsy saw the wink and smiled knowingly. She

looked across the room at her husband who was laughing at something Isaiah the joker had just done. "They wear well, these Zook men." She glanced at me with mischief in her eyes. "I just thought you'd like to know."

I smiled and said, "I think I'll ask Sarah how she feels about Jonathan and her other kids playing with the Pockets."

It was a very late night by Zook standards, and I went up to my rooms at ten with a warm glow. I had enjoyed the unique experience of being part of a large family gathering. No, to be perfectly honest, I had enjoyed being part of the Zook family gathering.

Oh, Lord, thank You for letting me have today. It was wonderful, even when I sat on Isaiah's whoopie cushion. Knowing these people and loving Jake have made my life so rich. I love Mom, but it's been just the two of us for years. Being part of this loving group is so exciting, so marvelous. Now how do I stand the agony of losing it all? Jake won't love You, and he won't love me. What do we do?

Fourteen

Saturday morning was a crystal clear day with temperatures much more in keeping with late November than those of earlier in the week. When I climbed out of the van at the cemetery, my breath vaporized into a small cloud. I walked around the vehicle to wait for Jake to emerge, pushing my hands into my gloves and pulling my collar up against the sneaky breeze that wrapped itself about my neck.

I was nervous about what to expect in the next hour. I'd never been to a baby's burial before.

My pastor, Adam Trempler, climbed out of his car ahead of us. Becky had said that she didn't know what to do about a service. She and Sam were believers, but they didn't have a church. I talked to Pastor Adam, and he was more than willing to be Becky and Sam's pastor. He met with them and prayed with them and cried with them. I knew that next week he would marry them.

A white rental car pulled behind us on the narrow road that wound through the cemetery, and Davy and Lauren Stoltzfus got out. Davy was a lean, powerful man with snapping brown eyes and a Stetson. Lauren was about my height and had a charming smile, which she poured on us as she introduced herself. I immediately liked her.

"I feel like I already know you," she said to Jake. "I've heard so many stories about you from Davy."

"And they're all true," Davy said as he opened the back door of the car and helped Annie out.

Another van slowed and parked behind Davy. The back door slid open and John climbed out. He turned and helped Mary down. Esther and Elam followed. Esther's eyes were already red from tears.

We walked in a cluster toward the grave site, a pile of raw dirt covered with a green tarp showing us the way.

"How was Becky this morning?" I asked Annie as we walked. I really wanted to ask where the rest of Becky's family was, but I didn't. Though I found it hard to believe that Rachel and Emmett wouldn't come to help bury their grandson, even if the baby's father was mei-dung, I knew it was none of my business what their choices were.

"Becky seemed fine," Annie said. "It was Rachel who was upset."

"Was she?" I felt relieved. The woman had normal emotional responses after all.

"She was so torn. She wanted to be here for Becky's sake, she wanted to honor Samuel's shunning for the church's sake, and she wanted to go home and forget it all. She's not sure what to do because she feels caught in the middle. She doesn't want to loose her daughter, but her whole life is her community." Annie smiled wanly. "Believe me, iss not a goot place to be."

I nodded and glanced at Davy. Annie knew what she was talking about.

Annie shook her head. "Emmett decided they would go home. They had bought return tickets for today when they came for Nate. He said it would be simpler if they just followed their original plan."

"I don't want to upset you," I said honestly, "but I don't understand. Aren't some things more important than others? Aren't daughters and grandsons more important that rules?"

"Don't feel bad," Annie said. "Becky understands. So does Samuel. And Emmett made the best choice for Rachel. She will cry, but she won't feel torn."

I nodded, but I still couldn't think in patterns so foreign to me. It should be people first, regulations second when a choice had to be made. I glanced at Jake and realized with a start that others would find my pattern equally hard-nosed if I held to my decision not to become any more involved with him due to his unbelief. I sighed as I understood that it was always the other person's patterns that were so foolish.

Lord, why does life have to be so difficult?

A dark green sedan pulled through the gate into the cemetery. It drove slowly along the narrow road and came to a stop behind the white van. We all turned to watch.

A man I had never seen before climbed out of the front. He walked to the back and opened the door. He reached in and helped Becky out, then Sam.

I walked over to Jake, needing to be near him. My eyes filled with tears as I watched the young couple struggling with such sorrow.

The man walked to the trunk of the car and Becky and Sam followed. They stood quietly while he raised the lid. He reached inside and emerged with a small coffin in his arms. He began walking toward us, bearing his little burden. Becky and Sam, hands linked, followed.

When I saw the man lift the little coffin from the trunk, my heart stopped midbeat. I gasped at the unexpected sight, my breath catching in my throat and becoming a sob. So small. So very small! The man could carry the coffin by himself!

Jake clasped my hand, and I hung on as the burial party approached. I could hear Esther's sobs and saw Elam standing shoulder to shoulder with her, offering his comfort.

Becky and Sam took the two folding chairs set beside the grave. The man bent and laid Trevor on the straps suspended over what I now saw was a very small opening. The man backed away and stood quietly to the side.

Everything was quiet for a few minutes. I gazed at Trevor and his parents through a haze of tears. I kept hearing Becky's words: "He was my baby, mine and Samuel's. It didn't matter when or how he was conceived. He was mine, ours. I talked to him and prayed for him. I gave him to Herr Gott... And if I ever start to get mad at Herr Gott for letting Trevor die, I will remember that He let His Son die, too."

Sam stood, his hand still linked to Becky's, and turned to face all of us.

"It was difficult for us to know how to plan a service for Trevor," he said, strain and sorrow evident on his face. "Pastor Adam has helped us, and he will say some words and pray, but I've got to say something too."

He swallowed convulsively and looked at Becky. She turned her tear-stained face to him and I could hear her say softly, encouragingly, "Go on, Samuel. You can do it."

He took a deep breath and looked back at all of us.

"We are so thankful to God for our son. Becky got to enjoy him for two wonderful months. I only knew him one day." His voice wobbled on the last two words. He stopped and took a deep breath before he could continue. "How I thank God I met him and held him and loved him."

I put my hand to my trembling lips in an unconscious gesture. Maybe to contain my sobs?

"Becky and I know we were wrong to sleep together before we were married. We confess that to you as we've confessed it to God. But like Pastor Adam told us, our God is a redeeming God. He took that bad situation and used it to bring Becky and me to Him. We've committed our lives to God. We love Him and we're going to honor Him. That's Trevor's legacy. He made his mother and father realize that rebelling isn't the answer. Believing in Jesus is."

With a sound halfway between a sigh of relief and a sob, Sam took his seat and slumped forward, his head in his hands. Becky immediately slid her arm around his shoulders and leaned in to speak to him. Her words were soft, private, unheard by the rest of us. He listened, nodded his head, and sat up straight. She lowered her arm and wound it around his. Their fingers threaded.

Pastor Adam stepped forward. "What more can anyone ask of his life than that he turn hearts toward God?" he asked quietly. "Trevor did exactly that. We must thank God for this little boy, this redeeming child."

Soft sobs and sniffles mingled with the gentle rustling of clothes as people searched for tissues to mop cheeks and blow noses. Pastor Adam led in singing "Jesus Loves Me," and I was only able to sing half the words because my throat kept closing.

Suddenly John began praying in High German, his voice sonorous and urgent. I had no idea what he was saying, but I was blessed by the fact that he had chosen to participate in this unique service with its unusual band of mourners.

When he finished, there was a time of silence. Then Pastor Adam said, "And all God's children said—"

And we supplied, "Amen."

Becky and Sam were the last to leave the grave.

Davy and Lauren Stoltzfus came to visit Jake after they took Annie home from the funeral. At Becky's request there had been no funeral meal. "Too awkward," she said.

We sat in Jake's living room, Davy and Lauren on the sofa, me in the glider/rocker, and Jake in his chair. It took a while for the melancholy of the funeral to dissipate, but soon Lauren and I were listening to old war stories as the men recounted tales of growing up Amish. We rolled our eyes as they relived tomato wars, the beheading of chickens and the fun of watching them run around headless, the bounty of the groaning tables at church socials, the raising of a new barn for Big Joe Lapp when lightning burned his to the ground. We even listened tolerantly to their tales of courting in buggies.

"Then I discovered cars and you discovered motorcycles," Davy said. "And the troubles began."

"How old were you?" I asked.

"Seventeen or eighteen." Davy said. "Old enough to drive. Old enough to rent garages for our vehicles. My father didn't catch on for three years."

"I wonder what would have happened if we hadn't gone through our *rumschpriges* together," Jake said. "All we ever did was dare each other to try some new outrage. Would we have become such reprobates alone?"

"Hey," Davy said. "I'm not a reprobate. I'm a married

man." He grinned at Lauren.

"You may not be a reprobate now, but you certainly were when I met you," she said. "You had a chip on your shoulder big enough to weigh down the whole state of Texas." She grinned at her husband. "I still thought you were the cutest boy I'd ever seen."

"What happened to the chip?" I asked with interest. It was obvious that it had somehow disappeared, unlike the chip of someone else I could mention.

"Now there's a story," Lauren said.

"Well, tell us," I said.

Jake groaned.

Davy started. "I met Lauren when she was working her way through college as a waitress at a little restaurant I often went to. I kept asking her out, but she wouldn't go anywhere with me but church."

Jake laughed. "I bet you loved that! I know your tolerance level for anything religious was zero after the shunning fiasco."

Davy nodded. "But look at her."

Jake and I did, and we saw a cute woman about my height with brown curly hair and a wonderful smile.

"Isn't she worth going to church for?"

"Us Texas girls have standards," Lauren said. "Especially us Southern Baptist ones. And if you could have seen him, Rose, you'd have known he was one dangerous man to a virtuous little girl like me."

"So after six months—" Davy began, but Jake interrupted.

"Six months!" Jake looked incredulous. "She stood you off for six months? You, Mr. Ladies Man?"

I studied Davy's fair hair, strong jaw, and devastating smile. I could imagine a younger version killing the girls right and left, especially in his Stetson.

"Six months," Davy repeated, smiling wryly. "Finally I bit the bullet and went to church with her. Scared me to death!"

"We sang in English and at fast tempos and with guitars and even drums sometimes." Lauren grinned at Davy. "Talk about culture shock."

"And the pastor preached grace and forgiveness, not law and judgment. Let me tell you, Jake, it threw me for a loop. Here I was, this rebellious little Amish boy pining for this Texas lady who believed in a very personal God and a personal Jesus. I didn't know what to do."

He shook his head and reached for Lauren's hand. Their affection was real and mutual, and I ached for the same thing.

"Since church was the only place she'd go with me, I kept going. Next thing I knew, I was in Mexico on a missions trip with about seventy singles in their early twenties who all were as enthusiastic about Jesus as Lauren."

"He didn't know it at the time," Lauren said, "but everybody on the trip met regularly in small groups to pray for him. I'm sure the groups I wasn't in prayed for me too because it was obvious that I loved him, sinner that he was." She gave his hand an affectionate squeeze.

"Basically they loved me to Jesus," Davy said. "Life has never been the same."

"And you think God forgave you for all those secrets sins I know about?" Jake asked. "The ones you haven't told Lauren about?" There was an edge to his voice that indicated he was spoiling for a fight. The last thing he wanted to hear was that his fellow rebel was now a Jesus follower.

Davy nodded. "I do think that, and for two reasons. One, the Bible says He forgives us and does so freely when we believe. Secondly, I'm free. The bitterness is gone, Jake. So's the anger."

Jake's face wore a look of disgust. "I'm surrounded." He glowered at me like it was all my fault.

"He is," I said cheerfully. "There's me. There's his brother Andy. There's Sam and Becky. And now there's you."

"And you all think I'm going to believe it's all free?" He looked at the three of us with a fierce scowl. "You all think I'm going to fall on my knees and repent?"

Davy grinned at him. "I know just how you feel," he said. "But it's not us you have to wrestle with, guy. It's God. He's the one who made the decision that forgiveness and salvation are free."

"At least free to us," Lauren said. "Very costly to Jesus."

We were all silent for a minute. Then Jake said, "When do you two go home?"

"Now there's a subtle topic change if I ever heard one." Davy laughed.

"We're not sure. Sometime next week." Lauren shifted her position, tucking her legs under her and leaning her shoulder against Davy's. "We want to stay for Becky and Sam's wedding."

"We'll probably be the only immediate family there." Davy shook his head. "Poor kids. At least people came to the funeral."

"Mom'd come to the wedding if she could," Lauren said. "She loves Becky, and I think she likes Sam in spite of him being meidung."

Davy grinned. "She's a wonderful lady is my ma."

"She likes you in spite, too," Lauren said, patting Davy's knee.

"She *loves* me in spite," Davy corrected.

"I like Annie," I said. "She gave Becky a decent room."

The three of them looked at me to explain my non sequitur. I just held up my hand and shook my head. I couldn't explain without making Davy's father look like the hard man he had been.

Davy looked at the gun cabinet Jake had against the far wall. "Do you still do much shooting?"

"Not too much. I'd do more if I had more time. How about you?"

"Not nearly as much as I'd like." His eyes fogged with memories. "Do you remember how worldly and mature we felt the day we bought our first handguns? I don't know about you, but when I held that thing in my hand, I felt like I had finally found a way to get even with my father."

Lauren winced. "You sound like you planned to kill him."

Davy looked startled. "No. Never. It was more knowing that a personal weapon was something he'd never, ever approve of. It was worse by far than a car."

"The ultimate rebellion for a pair of ex-pacifists," Jake said. "We'd go to the target range in our Amish clothes, feeling so sophisticated that we were breaking out of the mold."

"That's because we always left our hats in the car. Bareheaded was sophisticated."

Lauren and I looked at each other in amazement.

"They seem so normal now," she said.

"We should be glad we didn't know them then," I said.

"We got to be pretty good with the pistols," Jake defended them. "And we soon got ourselves jeans with zippers and belt loops and leather patches at the waist. And boots. Black motorcycle boots. We weren't country bumpkins, you know."

"Just pistol-packin' papas," Lauren said.

"There's a gun club just down the street from my mother's," I said. "We hear the guys down there practicing all the time."

Jake's eyes grew speculative. "What are you doing this afternoon, Davy?"

He shook his head. "Nothing special."

Jake looked at me. "We're going down to Rose's Mom's this afternoon."

It didn't take many brains to figure out what Jake wanted. "Why don't you two come down, too," I said like the cooperative little girl I could be. "The guys can go target shooting, Lauren, while you and I visit with my mother and help decorate her Christmas tree." I had a new thought. "Or would you rather go target shooting? I don't know about Texas girls."

Lauren beamed. "I love decorating Christmas trees."

I thought it only fair to warn her. "Mom'll change everything you do the first time you leave the room."

Lauren shrugged. "I just won't leave the room until it's time to go back to Texas. Then I'll never know."

We made arrangements for Davy and Lauren to drive down to Mom's on their own, arriving about three. That would give the guys an hour or so to shoot before it started getting too dark.

Jake and I left for Mom's right after lunch. It was nice to be alone with him with both of us feeling well. It was also awkward. I kept remembering my confession of affection made as I lay in a weakened condition, unable to think straight, unable to exert my normal self-control. I would take back what I'd said if I could, though not because it wasn't true. It was. I'd take it back because it propelled us to a level I knew would force decisions I didn't want to make.

As I sat beside him and watched a pair of tethered sheep crop the grass along the road while a flock of chickens ran free in the middle of a field, all I could do was wonder what in the world was going to happen to us. He wouldn't love me, and I shouldn't love him, even though it was more than obvious that both of us were fully heart involved.

It wasn't so much that Jake wouldn't love me. What he actually meant was that he wouldn't marry me. It was a commitment issue, but not the normal kind. It was his legs, I was sure. For some reason he felt they precluded his marrying. I'm certain he saw himself as noble and self-sacrificing, but I saw him as foolish. Even if his injuries meant we could never have children, he could still love me. And we could adopt children.

And what I meant was that until he was a believer, I couldn't marry him no matter how much I loved him. And I had to admit that I loved him with all my heart.

The only answer to our quandary I could think of was for me to leave the farm as soon as I found another place to live. The very thought of saying good-bye caused intense pain to explode in my heart, emotional distress so strong that it produced a physical ache.

"Well, Tiger, what do you think?"

I jumped. "About what?" Certainly he wasn't reading my mind.

"About the best kind of tree stand. What else?"

What else indeed.

"I have no opinion on that subject," I said somewhat primly.

He glanced at me as we drove past the People's Place and the Kitchen Kettle in Intercourse. The usual couple was standing in front of the Intercourse sign having their picture taken, totally ignoring the true meaning of the town's name, social interaction and conversation. I sighed. What a difference two hundred-plus years makes in meanings of words. Now this wonderful little town was the butt of hundreds of unpleasant jokes.

Jake slowed for a buggy that wanted to turn left to tie at the hitching rail in front of Zimmerman's store.

"Somehow I don't think tree stands are on your mind," he said.

I looked out the window at the military museum across the street from Zimmerman's. A military museum in the middle of Amish/Mennonite country. I loved the dichotomy.

"They aren't," I agreed.

Jake was silent until we were through town and once again in farm country going east on 340.

"I hurt you yesterday," he said, taking care to look straight ahead.

I looked at him in surprise. "When you said you wouldn't love me? No, you didn't."

He risked a glance at me. "Are you sure?" It was as if he couldn't decide whether he was glad he hadn't offended me or upset that he hadn't.

I took care to frame my thoughts as clearly as I could. This wasn't the time for my usual tendency to blurt. "I understand what you're saying about refusing to love me. I think you're foolish to feel the way you do, but I understand what prompts you."

He made that deep-in-his-throat noise. "Believe me,

Rose, you haven't got a clue."

"Not about how you feel, the actual emotions," I agreed. "About why you feel that way."

He looked at me, a scowl darkening his face. "You are the most frustratingly empathetic person I've ever known! You drive me crazy!"

I scowled right back. "Like you have room to talk! You are the proudest, most obstinate man I've ever met! And you drive me equally crazy!"

We frowned at each other, pure venom leaping from our eyes, until suddenly the absurdity hit us and we began to laugh.

"I'm sorry I'm so empathetic," I said, grinning broadly. "I'll try to be nasty and spiteful from now on."

"See?" He pointed an accusing finger at me. "You're agreeing with me again."

I grabbed at his outstretched digit and missed, which was a good thing. He needed two hands on the controls.

"Don't worry about what you said yesterday," he said, eyes again straight ahead. "You were sick and weak and feeling grateful. I don't hold you to what you said."

"You mean when I said I loved you?"

A flash of feeling rippled across his face, but seeing only his profile, I couldn't identify what it was. Regret? Distress? Sorrow? "Yes. That's what I mean."

I took a deep breath and leaped off into the unknown. "Then I'll say it again now when I'm well and very aware." I turned in my seat and looked directly at him. "I love you, Jacob Zook."

Again that flash of something across his face.

"I'll always love you," I continued, "and I wish from the bottom of my heart that I could marry you. I wish you weren't so stubborn. I wish you would consider what I feel and think instead of unilaterally deciding against marriage. But in the end it doesn't matter what you decide because I can't marry you any more than you can marry me." I gave a quavery laugh. "We've come straight down a box canyon, and we're up against an impregnable, immovable wall of granite. We're trapped."

Silence laced with myriad emotions ricocheted around the van. I was literally shaking and thoroughly surprised that the agonizing pain I was feeling didn't fill the vehicle with shrieks and screams and banshee wails.

"Why?" Jake asked finally, quietly.

"Why what?"

"Why won't you marry me?"

I looked at him with a wry half smile. "It's okay if you won't marry me but not if I won't marry you?"

"Don't play verbal games, Rose." He glared at me. "Why won't you marry me?"

"You won't like my answer."

He snorted. "I know your answer. I don't believe. Right? Because I won't agree that God will forgive me freely, you won't marry me. And I thought the Amish were narrow!"

I squirmed under his disdain. "I'm sure it looks narrow to you, but that's the way it is. Again, God gets to set the rules, Jake. I have to accept them. The Bible says we shouldn't marry unbelievers. I may wish to overlook that because my heart is captive, but I can't."

"Can't or won't?"

"Can't and won't."

He clenched his jaw and stared straight ahead while I stared out the side window so he couldn't see my pain. We were going down the first of the twin hills south of Honey Brook. We drove through the intersection where Jake's accident had occurred. I saw my mother's house off to the right and the field where Ben had supposedly thrown my ring. Then we were climbing the second hill.

When we crested that hill and passed the sign for King's Wooden Furniture on the left and the greenhouses on the right, Jake looked at me, all traces of his anger gone. Instead he looked as forlorn as I felt. He reached quickly across the space between our seats and ran his finger down my cheek.

"I don't know what's going to become of us, Tiger."

I blinked back my tears. "I don't either," I whispered.

Kern's Hardware in Honey Brook had a large display of Christmas items, everything from lights to artificial tress, from wrapping paper to candles.

On one shelf near the artificial trees sat several types of tree stands. I studied them and tried to think like my mother. I picked up an old-fashioned tree stand with the green water container for the tree at its center and four spindly red metal legs jutting off it. Screws stood out like instruments of torture all around the stand. It was just like the one Mom now had but needed to replace since it had rusted through. I would go with this tried and true model. After all, it had lasted for years.

I looked at Jake. He was reading the label on another box. "This one tilts so you can straighten the tree without having to tighten all kinds of screws. You get the tree straight, lock the tilt, and there you are. Perfect tree. Let's get this one."

"But it costs a fortune. Mom'll never be happy forking over that kind of cash."

"So give it to her for a Christmas present."

"Can't. Presents are to be personal and only opened on Christmas morning."

"And she can't wait until Christmas morning for her Christmas tree?"

I grabbed another box. "Never. Today is already two days late." I held out the box and pointed to a picture of another green plastic stand. "How about this one? You have to tighten screws, but look how broad the base is. The tree will never fall over."

"Do your mother's trees often fall over?" Jake asked.

"Well, no."

"Then I still vote for the tilt one."

"Of course you do. Why should you care how much it costs?" I asked.

"Well, I'm certainly not getting down on the floor

293

and tightening screws."

"Of course you're not. I'm the one who will be on my stomach on the floor tightening, tightening while my mother yells, 'No, the other way, Rose. The other way!'"

"Then we should get the one that's best for you," Jake said. "The tilt one it is."

"But it's so expensive," I repeated.

Jake looked at me. "You're being a little bit obstructive here, woman."

"You just don't know my mother!"

He grinned. "Let me handle her. She thinks I'm nice."

I snorted. "She thinks you're tall, too."

He shrugged. "I am tall. I'm five eleven when I'm laid end to end. And that's tall for an Amishman."

"Really? No wonder I like you. I've always liked tall guys. My father was a tall guy."

"That's probably because you were a short girl."

"Now there's a new way to look at it."

As I said that, I noticed a man an aisle over looking at me. He wore a baseball cap reading Michigan pulled low over his brow and a pair of sunglasses, but even so I could tell he was staring. I smiled vaguely. When he saw me looking at him, he quickly turned away.

I was glad. I'm always uncomfortable when guys stare. I can never decide whether it's a compliment or an insult.

I turned my attention back to Jake and the tree stands.

Without realizing how it happened, I found myself in the checkout line with the tiltable tree stand in my hands. I turned and looked at Jake. "You're good. I don't even remember agreeing to buy this."

He grinned.

I handed him the tree stand and fished in my purse for some money. As I pulled out my cash, I saw the man with the Michigan hat at the other register. He was staring at me again.

I frowned as I turned back to my money. Somehow being watched that intently made me nervous. But maybe he'd seen me on TV and was interested in someone who had played dead. Whatever his reason for watching me, I was glad when he left the store.

Counting the money in my hand, I shuffled forward as the first person in line completed his transaction. As always happens to me, my line moved more slowly than the other, and it seemed like forever before I was at the register.

Maybe I ought to just put the stand on my credit card. Then I wouldn't clean myself out.

I put the tree stand on the counter and looked at the cashier, a kid whose name tag read Josh. He wasn't looking at me though. He was deep in conversation with the other cashier, a gray-haired gentleman whose tag read Tim. As they talked, Tim pushed a button under his counter.

My first thought was that there was a robbery in progress and he was pushing a silent alarm, like they do in banks. My second thought was that I watched too much TV. My third thought was that I hoped whatever the problem was, it didn't take too long. Mom was waiting for us, and I still had to go to the tree farm and pick out the tree.

The manager hurried up to the registers from wherever managers usually hide and said, "What's wrong, Tim? Why'd you ring?"

"I'm not sure," Tim said. "But I feel like I've got to tell you just so it doesn't weigh on my mind too much."

The manager looked unhappy as did all the people in the checkout lines. Lost register time was lost money and mangled schedules.

"There was just a guy in here," Tim said. "He bought a piece of pipe and two end caps."

The manager looked at Tim and shook his head. "I don't get your point."

"Well, if someone buys some pipe and *one* end cap, I figure he's working on a home repair project."

"Sure," said the manager impatiently.

"But pipe and *two* end caps—there's only one use for that combination."

The manager looked dazed. "Are you saying what I think you're saying?"

"In light of the news this week, it's too big a risk not to think that way, isn't it?"

Josh looked as confused as I did. "What are you talking about?" he asked.

"A bomb," Tim said.

A bomb. The words leaped through the customers.

A pipe and two end caps, I thought, and a bomb made by an amateur.

Evil Ernie, I immediately thought. He was here? I began searching the faces around us. He was such an innocuous little man, he could have been standing right next to me and I'd never have seen him. But of course he was no longer in the store. He'd made his purchases.

"Jake?" I turned to him.

"I heard, sweetheart." He laid his strong hand on my sleeve. "Don't worry. I'm here. Just remember. He doesn't know where you are."

I thought for a minute of the man who had stared at me and immediately threw that idea away. There was no way he was Ernie. Too young. Too tall. Just some curious guy.

Suddenly I breathed more easily. Jake was right. Ernie had no idea where I was.

"We'd better call the police," Tim said.

The manager nodded. "Just in case."

"You want Lem Huber of the Lancaster cops," I said to the manager.

He looked at me like I was an interfering busybody. "Right, lady."

I knew I could argue with him and finally be proved right, but I saw no reason to humiliate myself further. I gave Josh the money for the tree stand and left the store as quickly as I could.

"Come on, Jake. It's time to go home."

Fifteen

JAKE CHARMED MY MOTHER JUST LIKE I KNEW HE WOULD. BY the time Lauren and Davy arrived, Mom was whispering all sorts of romantic encouragement to me, just like Jake was deaf as well as lame.

"He's very handsome, dear, for a man who can't walk. I've always liked them dark and brooding."

"Shush, Mom! He'll hear you."

She just smiled and went to the kitchen to get a Coke.

Later when she thought Jake was reading the paper, she smiled at me and whispered none too softly, "He's the best thing you've ever brought home, Rose. Certainly better than Ben. I bet Jake would never throw away a diamond ring."

I refrained from telling her that neither would Ben.

The pièce de résistance was offered when Mom and

I went into the kitchen to check on the progress of the turkey, "the second one in three days, dear. I didn't want your friends to have to eat leftover meat." Jake remained in the living room with the recently arrived Davy and Lauren.

"Oh, my, Rose," she said, "when he looks at you, the air positively smolders." She sighed, clasping her hands to her heart.

I blinked and shook my head in amusement. "Mom, you've been reading too many romance novels."

"You always were short of imagination, dear. Trust me; I know about these things."

As my critical daughter's eye flashed Mom's sterile life across the screen of my mind, the doorbell rang. I went quickly to see who was there, rolling my eyes as I went. The woman was amazing, but at least I was saved by the bell from making a nasty and thoroughly inappropriate comment, one I'd regret for years.

I froze with my hand on the storm door when I saw who was there. With a blink I recovered myself and opened the door.

"Ben," I said with a stiff smile. "Come in."

Ben followed me into the living room where Mom, Jake, Davy, and Lauren waited. I made introductions.

Ben made a little bowing motion toward Mom, saying, "Mrs. Martin, how good to see you again."

Mom smiled stiffly, offering a carbon copy of my welcoming smile.

"You remember Jake, I'm sure," I concluded.

"Of course he does, Tiger," Jake said with a knowing grin. He stuck out his hand. "Good to see you again, Ben. How's the fiancée?"

Ben looked distinctly uncomfortable.

"Why, Ben," Mom said, "what's this about a fiancée? I take it congratulations are in order." She patted Ben on the back.

Ben flushed and muttered something about thanks and she was a wonderful girl. Mom would like her.

"I'm sure," Mom said. "Pure gold, I don't doubt. Which makes me think, dear Ben. You had to buy another engagement ring, didn't you? What a shame." Trust Mom to stick in the shiv.

"Uh," Ben said, ever quick on his feet. He turned to me. "That's what I wanted to talk to you about."

"You knew I was here?"

He shook his head. "I thought I'd ask your mother for your address. By the way, I was glad to learn that you were still alive."

Suddenly I was struck with a totally inappropriate urge to laugh. "While I was dead," I said, unable to keep the humor out of my voice, "I bet you were relieved. Your little secret was safe."

"Now, Rose," he protested, "how can you think such a thing!"

"Very easily. I've become a skeptic where you're concerned."

"Rose!" Mom said, appalled. "Where are your manners?"

"In the field across the street, Mom." I couldn't resist adding, "With the ring."

"Uh, that's what I wanted to talk to you about." Ben looked acutely uncomfortable.

"The ring?" I said blandly.

"It was quite beautiful," Jake added helpfully.

"When Ben first bought it," I explained to Lauren and Davy, "it was for me. I picked it out. I've always liked the design, the way the diamond was set."

"What are you talking about?" Mom asked. "How would Jake know anything about your old ring?"

"What would you say if I told you Ben never threw the ring away?" I said to Mom as I watched Ben turn a violent crimson.

"He threw away a diamond ring?" Lauren asked, aghast.

"Nope." I looked at Ben, trying to keep my grin from looking smug. "He never did."

"Of course he did," Mom said. "I saw him."

That stopped me. "You saw him?" I turned to her, one eyebrow raised. I had always assumed that the humiliation and ugliness of that night were my private business. Mom only knew about things because I told her later. Apparently that was not the case. "You saw him?"

She cleared her throat and looked uncomfortable. "I just happened to glance out the window."

"Mom, you were spying!"

Mom turned to Lauren to plead her case. "Imagine

if you had a daughter," she began. "Imagine if she was screaming at this man."

"I was not screaming," I protested.

Mom paid no attention. "She was screaming, and he was screaming right back. Wouldn't you look to see what was going on? Wouldn't you? If you loved your daughter and were concerned about her fate?"

Lauren looked wide eyed at me, humor dancing just below the surface, but she wisely kept silent.

"My fate, Mom? You were concerned about my fate? What did you expect him to do? Drag me off by my hair?"

"Well, anyway," Mom said to Lauren, ignoring me again. "I just happened to look out the window and see him toss this diamond ring across the street into the field."

Lauren was struggling not to laugh.

I shook my head. "Mom, the point I'm trying to make here is that he never threw the ring. He just pretended."

"What?"

"He just pretended."

At that point my greatest hope for Ben's survival was that he never face my mother without a room full of witnesses to assure his continued well-being. Her face turned red and her chest swelled three times its normal size. She strode up to Ben and planted her index finger in the middle of his breastbone.

"When I think of all the time I spent in that field

looking for that infernal ring! When I think of what it did to my arthritis! My knees and back will never be the same! Of all the nerve! Ben Abrams, I'm ashamed of you!"

With every word she poked Ben hard, and she had great nails for poking. By the time she was finished, he looked pained and was rubbing his chest.

"But that's not the best part, Mom," I said. "He kept it and gave it to Allie Priestly."

Mom gasped. "That terrible girl who took your place on the cheerleading squad?" She glared at Ben. "Well, you deserve the likes of her, and she—" Mom sniffed significantly. "She deserves a secondhand ring, if you ask me."

I felt really good. My mother was actually standing up for me. I should have known she couldn't let well enough alone.

"Stealing Rose's boyfriend like that," she muttered. "Allie always was untrustworthy."

I rolled my eyes, Ben flushed crimson all over again, and Jake gave a delighted bark of laughter.

"Mom, Ben and I haven't been an item for over two years. And I'm the one who broke up with him."

Mom harrumphed again. Let us not let logic put a crimp in our anger.

Ben turned from Mom and looked at me. "I came to ask…"

His words trailed off and he looked unhappily at all the avid eavesdroppers lining the room. He cleared his throat and squared his shoulders. "I came to ask that you not tell Allie about the ring." He ended up asking the floor.

I looked at his bowed head and wondered at my onetime attraction to him. I guess I'd have to chalk it up to youth. I glanced at Jake and caught him watching me with a grin of pure delight. Whether the delight was with me or the farcical situation, I didn't care. It was just a joy to share it with him.

Ben cleared his throat, and I looked back. "Ben, the last thing I'd ever stoop to is telling Allie about that ring. All that matters is that you two love each other and will be happy together. Honestly, the ring doesn't bother me at all."

He looked at me like he wasn't certain whether to believe me or not.

"If Rose says she won't tell, she won't tell," Mom said so loudly and emphatically that I jumped. "Now let me show you out, Ben. We're having a late Thanksgiving here, and plans are being delayed by this conversation."

Ben looked disconcerted as Mom inexorably led him to the door.

"Good-bye, Ben," she said, all but pushing him down the front steps. "I hope you're more honest with Allie than you were with us." And she shut the door. She walked back into the room dusting her hands as if to say, "Good riddance."

I grinned at her as I heard Ben start up his car, rev the engine, then back out of the drive with a roar.

GAYLE ROPER

"Thanks, Mom. You were great!" And I gave her a big hug. She hugged me in return, then patted me on the back and hurried into the kitchen.

I glanced at Jake, and he smiled at me. I walked over to stand beside him. Absently we watched out the window as Ben squealed his wheels, leaving a totally unnecessary strip of tire behind. He flew down Beaver Dam Road to the stop sign—and drove straight through. He roared across Route 10 without the slightest pause and sped away.

I stepped back like I'd slammed into a brick wall. My hand went to my heart. I was back two years ago when he had roared away into the night in anger, the night someone ran that same stop sign in front of Jake and sent him into the skid that ended with his motorcycle on his back.

The blood roared in my ears and spots danced before my eyes. I was sure I would faint. I bent at the waist, lowering my head with a groan. I was vaguely aware that Jake placed himself between me and the rest of the room where Mom was now talking with Lauren and Davy.

Bands of anguish wrapped about my heart and squeezed the very breath from my body. No matter how much I longed to, I couldn't avoid the truth. I had sent Ben away in anger two years ago. It was my fault he sped into the night. It was my fault he ran the stop sign.

I was responsible for Jake's accident!

"No, Rose." It was Jake, right beside me, his hand

306

making comforting circles on my back. His voice was low and urgent. "You are not responsible. We don't even know that Ben is. No one saw the car or who drove it clearly enough to identify him, not even me."

I stared at him, my eyes wide with horror. "But I—"

"No, Rose. Even if Ben drove away full of anger, stop signs are still the law. Even if he were the one who ran it, it's his fault, not yours."

I listened and tried to believe, yearned to believe.

His eyes were intent and full of emotion. "Think about this, Tiger. Anyone who is cagey enough to pretend to throw away a ring is aware enough to stop at a stop sign."

I stilled as that thought wrapped itself around my trembling heart. "He did pretend, didn't he?" I straightened partway. "He was aware." I felt the pain loosen its claws and the stirrings of something like hope.

"Rose," Jake said softly. "Look at me."

I did so.

"You are life to me, Tiger." He gripped my hand. "You are hope and sunshine and all the good things I could ever think of. You couldn't hurt me if you tried."

I put my arm about his shoulders and laid my cheek on his head for a brief moment. I knew what he said wasn't true. I was hurting him just as he was hurting me even as we spoke, though not willfully. Nor with malice intended. And I knew what he was really saying with his lovely, poetic words. He was saying that he loved me.

"I love you, too," I whispered.

He squeezed my waist and dropped his arm. I straightened and we turned to the room, smiles in place. Amazingly no one seemed aware that my world had stopped for an anguished instant or that Jake, my Jake, had had the understanding and wisdom to restart it. They included us in the conversation like nothing untoward had happened.

"When are you guys going shooting?" I asked a short time later.

"I don't know," Jake said. "Maybe we won't go."

"What?" Davy and I said together.

"You're thinking about the hardware store, aren't you?" I said to Jake.

He nodded.

"Even if Ernie were there, which we don't know for sure, what could he do while I cut down a tree? Bomb the field? You guys go. Just don't stay long."

Jake looked at me, obviously torn between wanting the time with Davy and wanting to be certain I was all right.

"Go," I said. "I'll be upset if you don't."

"Come on," Davy said. "I want to see if that old shotgun of yours is any good. I haven't gone after clay pigeons in a long time."

Jake nodded. "Okay, but we won't be long. We'll meet you at the tree farm."

I nodded. "Sounds good to me."

After Jake left, the house suddenly seemed much emptier. How can that be, I wondered, since he's never been here except today? How could he so quickly imprint himself upon this room, this place?

Dear God, how will I stand it when he leaves my life?

"Come on, Lauren," I said. "Let's go cut the tree."

We pulled on our coats and gloves and I got my father's old bow saw from the basement.

"I'll be waiting," Mom said. "And just think how easy it will be to set up the tree this year with that new stand. Jake was so wise to select one that will make the whole process easier." And she smiled.

I smiled back and thought that the man had already stolen her heart.

It was most convenient having the tree farm just across the road from us. Where as the field Ben hadn't thrown the ring into was directly across Beaver Dam Road from the house, the tree farm was off to the side, across Route 10.

"Hey, look," I called to Lauren as we ran across Route 10. I pointed to her red coat, then to mine. "We're twins!"

"Red coats, green trees," she said. "Christmas colors. How appropriate."

The tree farm was no longer functioning as it once had, but Mom knew the owners and had a standing agreement that she could cut a tree each year for Christmas. Or rather, I could cut a tree each year for Christmas.

"I've never cut a tree before," Lauren said, giving a little skip. "I feel like I'm in a Christmas card, except there's no snow."

"Thank goodness," I said. "I've cut trees in snow, rain, sleet. It's no fun, let me tell you."

"Dare I ask why you don't wait for good weather?" Lauren scooted up the slight bank and into the brier and weed-filled field where evergreens sat, some in solitary splendor, some in clusters.

"Thanksgiving is tree-cutting day, whether I like it or not," I explained. "Some things are not negotiable."

"This is two days after," Lauren pointed out reasonably.

"I was flat on my back with the flu yesterday and caring for Jake the day before," I explained. "Even Mom has to accept illness."

We started looking over the trees, walking among them and around them, trying to decide how big they would actually prove to be when forced into a normal-sized living room. The open spaces and high sky made a true perspective difficult.

"How about this one?" Lauren called. "It's a beauty!"

I walked around a couple of trees and found her admiring a glorious tree about twelve feet tall and six feet around.

"How tall are you?" I asked.

"Five feet, six inches."

"The ceiling is about seven feet. That's a little bit taller than your reach or mine. What do you think?" I stood on tiptoe and stretched. The tree towered above my fingers.

Lauren made a face. "But it's so lovely!"

I recognized the same disappointment a shopper feels when she finds the perfect dress, only to discover it comes in every size but hers. I patted her hand. "There will be others."

We kept looking for that perfect tree, wandering about the field with no pattern in mind. Lauren wandered down one path and I wandered down another. I found a likely candidate and walked around it several times. It looked good every time. There was one hole, but that would be the side that went against the wall. I stretched up on tiptoe and the height looked good. I'd have to clip the top a bit, but that would be all to the good. It was a bit scraggly up there, and the trim would tighten it up just right for the huge red bow Mom insisted on putting at the top.

"Why not an angel like everyone else?" I used to ask before I learned that asking was useless.

"Because everyone else has angels," Mom said with her special logic. "Besides, bows cover up sparse tops very nicely."

I opened my mouth to call Lauren so she wouldn't miss the glorious moment of felling the tree when I heard a garbled sound that froze my blood. It sounded like someone choking.

"Lauren?"

The only answer was the beginnings of a broken-off scream.

My skin crawled and I spun toward the sound.

"Lauren?"

I began to run in the direction I thought the noise had come from. The trees had the effect of dampening the sound and misdirecting it. I ran through a cluster of trees, their branches slapping me in the face, their marvelous, resinous fragrance making a lie of the sudden crackle of danger in the air.

I burst into a little clearing and saw two people struggling, one Lauren, the other the man from the hardware store, the one with the Michigan cap and sunglasses who had stared at me. He held her from behind, an arm about her throat. She was pulling at the arm, trying to loosen it so she could breathe. As I rushed toward them, he raised a piece of pipe above her head.

"No!"

He jerked at my shout and turned toward me as he swung. The pipe hit Lauren a sturdy blow on the back of the head, but it was nowhere near as hard as it would have been if I hadn't called out and distracted him. She crumpled to the ground without a sound.

I felt bile rise as I watched my new friend collapse. I looked at the man in horror.

"Who are you? What are you doing?" My speech was jerky and full of a mixture of fear and anger.

He looked at me, then glanced at the woman at his feet and realized his mistake. From the back he'd seen a woman with short, curly brown hair, and he'd assumed he was seeing me.

He turned to me, swearing. He began walking toward me. He raised the pipe again, waving it angrily, and I saw red on it. Lauren's blood.

I backed up, my heart pounding, talking to him as I went. "You don't want to hurt us." I tried not to sound like I was pleading though, of course, I was. "There's no reason to hurt us. We haven't done anything to you."

"It's your fault!" His face was contorted with fury. "You remember. I know you do!"

"What? What do I remember?"

I kept backing up, drawing him farther and farther from Lauren. I talked as I went, not so much to upset him or to get information from him as because I couldn't keep quiet. It was a nervous reaction to an unprecedented situation.

And suddenly it all came together, the pieces fitting into place as neatly and precisely as cut glass in a Tiffany lamp.

My stunned expression told him the truth.

"You remember! I knew you'd remember!"

"Just this very minute," I said. "If you'd let me alone, I probably would never have."

He came relentlessly at me, and I marveled at the effectiveness of his disguise, the Michigan cap, the wig, the false mustache. No wonder I didn't recognize him at the store.

"I'm going to kill you," he announced. "I'm just sorry the first attempt didn't work. Then you'd never have remembered."

"But I do remember. I remember that you had your sunglasses on when we left the house last Friday," I said.

"You had them on as we helped your mother down the steps and along the walk. You even had them on when I bent over to buckle her in. I remember because I was thinking how Sophie ought to have a pair, driving in the late afternoon like that. The setting sun can be blinding at times."

I backed into a blue spruce and jumped as its sharp needles penetrated my jeans and stabbed my neck. I glanced away from the danger long enough to find a way around the tree. When I looked back, he was much closer. I tried to concentrate on where I was and where either Route 10 or Beaver Dam Road was. I kept on talking.

"Ammon had just climbed into the driver's seat and was ready to insert the key. Suddenly you ran for the house, yelling about needing your sunglasses, the ones you had had on all along." I looked at him with scorn. "You made it safely inside before the bomb exploded, Peter, the bomb that killed your own mother and brother."

"They wouldn't help me," he said, his voice a whine. "I'd borrowed money and they wouldn't help me pay it back."

Somehow I didn't think he'd borrowed from a bank. "Nasty guys, huh? What was it? Gambling? Drugs? Both? And how did you ever manage to get rid of that great fortune your mother told me about? Bad investments? Crackpot get-rich-quick schemes?"

He didn't answer, just pressed closer and closer. I continued to back away as quickly as I could. I felt my heel strike a tree stump, throwing me off balance. I struggled to keep my footing, but I lost my equilibrium and fell on my derriere. The landing jarred my teeth and knocked the breath from me. Peter rushed at me when he saw his opportunity, and I scrambled desperately to my feet.

As he grabbed for me, I put my hands out to protect myself and saw with surprise that I still held my little bow saw. I slashed at the air with it. He ducked, then stilled, then grabbed. Next thing I knew, he and I were having a tug of war over the tool.

He gave a great pull, and I let go. He staggered at the sudden cessation of tension, and I turned and ran. I tore through a cluster of evergreens and wiped at my face as branches and needles slashed across the tender skin. I didn't feel the pain so much as I resented the temporary blocking of my vision.

Dear God, help!

I could hear Peter crashing after me. As I ran through another cluster of trees, I wished my barn jacket were a deep green instead of a bright red. I wished I knew where Route 10 was. I wished I were at home with my mother.

I burst into a clearing and there was Beaver Dam Road. I ran as hard as I could toward the road and the possibility of cars and people and help.

I screamed as a large hand clamped on my shoulder, trying to drag me to a halt and pull me back into the trees. I dug in my heels and struggled against him.

I grabbed at the buttons on the front of my coat, working them with desperation. The gloves made the

GAYLE ROPER

precise movements hard. I jerked a glove off, pushed a
last button through the hole and gave a mighty shrug. At
the same time I forced myself to duck, then run. My coat
slid free from my body, and I was no longer in Peter's
grasp. I heard him curse, and my back prickled as I waited
for another heavy hand to fall on me.

I saw a branch from a blue spruce lying on the
ground in front of me. It was not very long, but it was
sturdy and it had lots of needles. I grabbed the branch,
held it tightly in both hands, and swung around with it
extended as far as I could.

God, give me strength!

The branch caught Peter squarely in the face and
upper body, the impact sending shock waves up my
arms and across my back and neck. He screamed as the
needles raked across his face, scratching and pricking
and gouging. I gritted my teeth and swung again, my
body shuddering when I made contact.

I didn't wait to see what the long-range effect of my
attack was. I'd seen a green van out on the road. I
dropped the branch and ran toward it. I watched as it
turned into the field and bounced toward me. Suddenly
the van swerved and shivered to a stop. The sliding door
flew open and Davy reached for me as Jake yelled out his
window, "Get in!"

I needed no second invitation. I threw myself at
Davy and he hauled me inside. At the same time Jake
leaned out his window, his target pistol extended, and
yelled, "Freeze!"

Davy leaped from the van, a shotgun aimed at Peter who stood bewildered, hands raised, Michigan hat lying on the ground as was the wig he'd been wearing beneath it. His false mustache had been knocked half off by the slash of the branch. The look of disbelief on his face was almost comical, except that nothing about Peter Hostetter and his selfishness was in any way humorous.

Satisfied that Davy had things under control, Jake released his chair and came back to me as I sat on the van floor.

"Are you all right, Tiger?"

I looked at him and nodded. I was afraid to try to talk. I'd probably cry. Now that the crisis was over, my insides were quivering. He touched my cheek gently, then lowered himself to the ground as quickly as he could.

"Get over here," he yelled to Peter, waving his pistol menacingly. "And lie down right there." He pointed and Peter dropped to his knees. "All the way. On your face! Put your hands together in the small of your back."

"Where's Lauren?" Davy asked, his eyes still on Peter. "I thought she was coming with you." He turned to me.

Just then Lauren staggered out of the trees, her hand to her head.

"Lauren!" Davy blanched and dropped the shotgun. He ran to her, catching her as she fell.

Dear God, let her be all right! Let her be all right, please!

"Get the shotgun, Rose," Jake ordered, pulling me

back to our predicament. "Climb out here and hold it on him."

I climbed out of the van, shivering in the cold. I skirted Jake and Peter in a wide arc, moving first to grab my coat from the ground where Peter had dropped it. I shrugged it on, then bent for the gun. When I picked it up, I tried to look like I knew what I was doing. I aimed it at Peter and wondered what he'd think if he knew he was being held captive by guns loaded with blanks, if they were loaded at all, which they probably weren't since the guys would have made certain they weren't loaded when they left the target range.

I looked at Jake in question. "Now what?"

"The police will be here momentarily," he said.

Peter groaned and dared a glance at me. He looked like he expected me to feel sorry for him and help him out. I narrowed my eyes and glared, and he blinked as if surprised.

The guy doesn't get it, I thought. He thinks for some reason that he can disregard the law, and people will understand and make allowances because it's him, even the people he's tried to kill. I thought of Sophie's smiling indulgence and how tragic it was that she had inadvertently contributed to making her son the unprincipled, horrible man he'd become.

"It's cold down here," Peter whined suddenly, putting his hands beside his shoulders preparatory to pushing himself upright. "You could at least let me stand up."

Jake and I didn't bother to answer. Instead Jake released the safety on his handgun and pointed it at Peter's head. With another disbelieving groan, Peter slid his hands down his sides and lowered his cheek to the ground.

All the evil he has done, I thought, and it's brought him nothing but shame and certain incarceration, if not death. He's earned that groan and the many that are certain to follow.

"How do the cops know to come?" I asked Jake.

"Car phone," he explained.

"Ah," I said and smiled at him like he was the wisest man on earth. We waited side by side, our arms touching, our guns trained on the now sobbing Peter while Davy held Lauren, talking quietly to her. That's how Mom found us when she crossed the street to see what was taking us so long.

"I should have known," she said, taking in the scene without any show of surprise. "I can't let you go anywhere alone, Rose."

I refrained from reminding her that I hadn't gone anywhere alone.

She sighed deeply. "My turkey will be ruined before all this is straightened out. I just know it. The second one in three days."

Sixteen

MOM WAS RIGHT. HER DINNER WAS RUINED FOR THE SECOND time this week. First we had to talk with the police. Understandably Davy wanted to take Lauren home immediately.

"When she stumbled out of those trees and collapsed…" His voice trailed away as he was unable to articulate how he felt. He shuddered and gripped his wife's hand.

"Ouch," Lauren said. "You're hurting me worse than my head."

Davy loosened his grip but didn't let go.

I checked Lauren's wound. Though it bled a lot as head wounds do, it wasn't deep enough for stitches. I cleaned it and said, "Keep an eye on her, Davy. If her headache gets worse or if she starts to vomit or has a seizure, get her to a hospital immediately." I smiled at them both. "Otherwise, I think she'll be fine."

Just after Davy and Lauren left, Lem Huber showed up. He danced the jurisdictional waltz with the Honey Brook and West Caln police and the state police. I left them to work out the specifics of incarcerating Peter Hostetter. I truly didn't care where he was jailed just so it was somewhere.

"How did that terrible man know where you were?" Mom asked as we stood by the van. Now that the extent of my danger had dawned on her, she couldn't stop shaking.

"He must have followed us from the hardware store," I said, hugging her. "That's all I can figure. He hid somewhere where he could watch the house. When he saw Lauren and me leave, he stalked us. Because of our matching red coats, he confused us."

Mom hugged herself, looking at me with eyes full of fear. "What if he'd hit you? And hurt you?" Her voice was a whisper.

"He didn't, Mom." I smiled gently.

"Take care of her, Jake," Mom said, grasping his arm. "I couldn't stand to lose her." She hugged me hard, turned, and walked inside, her shoulders slumped.

We followed her in and ate what would have been a marvelous meal if we'd been able to eat it when it was ready. No one had much to say, and I welcomed the silence and solitude. There had been so many lights and sirens, so much static. Just like at Hostetters. Just like with Rhoda and Dad. But I noticed that I wasn't as overwhelmed as I had been before.

I took a deep breath and let it out slowly as I relished another new thought: I felt no guilt. In other times, I would have felt guilty over Lauren's getting hurt. If she hadn't been with me, I'd have reasoned, she wouldn't have been hurt, like being with me was the reason for her injury, not the pursuit of a murderer. I also would have taken back feelings of responsibility for Sophie and Ammon, for Dad and Rhoda. But not anymore. Not anymore. The Great Guilt Bearer bore all my guilt.

"I don't feel guilty." I smiled. "I don't feel guilty!"

"Well, of course not," Mom said. "You're the victim."

But Jake seemed to know what I meant. He looked at me and smiled.

"And you," Mom said, turning to Jake. "You're a hero."

"He is, isn't he?" I grinned at him. "He and Davy."

Jake merely grunted.

When we were in the van, Jake was withdrawn and quiet, but it didn't bother me. I wanted to be silent too. In fact, I napped all the way home.

When we parked in the drive beside the barn, I climbed out of the van and waited for Jake. There were no calls to come sit on his lap tonight, no whispered words, no sweet hugs and kisses. I didn't care. I was too weary for such shenanigans, however pleasant.

I stopped when we reached the stairs to the main house. The house was dark, the family all in bed. The night was crisp and cold, the moon waning. I heard a screech owl shriek, a noise that always sounded too much like someone screaming for my taste. I shivered.

Suddenly Hawk came loping across the lawn and shoved his wet nose into Jake's neck. Jake jumped at the cold touch, then absently petted the animal.

"I want to thank you for being there tonight, Jake," I said softly. "You saved my life. I'm sure of that." I grinned. "You really are a hero. My hero."

He slanted his head to look up at me. I couldn't see his eyes or read his expression in the darkness. He stared without moving for several seconds. Then his hand raised an inch or two from the dog's neck. It hung suspended for another few seconds before he dropped it back down. He sighed as if in pain.

"Jake? What's wrong?"

"G'night," he said abruptly and turned. He rolled off around the corner of the house, Hawk loping after him.

Frowning slightly, I let myself in the front door and went upstairs. I fell into bed before I brushed my teeth and I, Rose of the health police, didn't even care.

Sunday morning was brilliantly sunny, the frost sparkling and the clouds like powder puffs in the crisp blue sky. When I came down for breakfast, I felt light as a feather. All the danger was gone. I could go back to my job, drive my car freely, and resume life as I knew it.

No, I thought. Not as I knew it. Life's better now. There's Jake.

But he wasn't there at the breakfast table. He was already gone for the day, Mary told me.

"Do you know where he was going or when he'll be back?" she asked me just a fraction of a minute before I asked the same questions of her.

I shook my head. I was flattered that she had asked me but saddened that I had no answers. Slightly miffed, too. Not that he was obliged to tell me his plans. It just seemed polite.

I didn't see him all day though I longed to be with him. I smiled somewhat sourly to myself. We would have to talk about what bad form it was to disappear without leaving a message.

At least I wasn't alone in church. I sat with Davy and Lauren and Sam and Becky. It was the first time Becky had been to a service that wasn't Amish, and it was culture shock for her, though in a positive way. Her eyes gleamed and she listened raptly to the message. There was one point during the singing when she teared up, obviously thinking of Trevor. Sam took her hand and held it tightly, and she sang through her tears.

I spent Sunday afternoon in my rooms trying to read while I wondered where Jake was. The family was away visiting on this Sunday, something Jake was well aware of. He knew I was alone in the house, and he left me that way with no word at all.

I was struck by the thought that just two Sundays ago, I would have been delighted to be alone in my apartment with a good book. Now I chaffed at my solitude. I wanted the company of a certain man, and suddenly I wasn't getting it.

By Monday I was more than glad to return to work. I desperately needed activity to occupy my mind. I was fretting far too much and making myself crazy wondering what could possibly be wrong.

I called Mary late in the afternoon to tell her I wouldn't make dinner because I had to work late.

"You're as bad as Jake," she said. "He won't be here for supper either."

Interesting, I thought as I hung up and went back to my paperwork. But what did it mean?

When I pulled into the drive, Jake's van wasn't there. He'd managed to outlast me again.

Tuesday was a repeat of Monday. Jake disappeared after an early breakfast and didn't show until late in the evening. Then he didn't come into his parents' house to greet anyone or seek me out in any way. I began to get truly miffed—and nervous.

Wednesday morning I left the house very early. I had to see a patient and her family before the husband left for work. I was to teach them how to deal with her colostomy bag and all the other sanitary difficulties that went with colon cancer. I also had to check her vital signs and draw blood.

I hurried down my stairs and out the front door at a rush, reviewing what I had to do. I was so preoccupied that I literally ran into Jake at the bottom of the steps and ended up falling over the chair. He reached out and grabbed me to keep me from crashing to the ground.

"Are you all right, Tiger?" he asked, all the remembered warmth and concern evident in his voice. His hands were on my waist.

I staggered, trying to get my feet under me. I put my hands on his shoulders to get better leverage. In seconds I was standing erect, but he kept his hands on me and I kept my hands on his shoulders. We looked at each other.

I saw the concern in his eyes, the affection, and for the first time in days, I started to relax. Nothing was wrong. He was just busy. I was imagining a problem.

Then the shutters closed. Just that quickly, all emotion drained from his eyes, his face became blank, and his hands fell away. I was left standing awkwardly with my hands still on his shoulders.

I flushed and pulled back. "Jake, what—"

He turned his chair abruptly and wheeled toward the drive. "Have a nice day, Rose."

I stared after him. *"Have a nice day, Rose?"* I'd heard him talk to Hawk with ten times the interest as that one sentence to me.

Later that day I decided that the only trouble with being a home health nurse was the time for thinking as I drove from patient to patient, house to house. No matter how high I turned the volume on the radio, no matter which station I put on, no matter which tape I shoved in the slot, I couldn't shut out that cool "Have a nice day, Rose." It repeated itself over and over, with each repetition wrapping itself more tightly like funeral crepe around my heart.

What had happened? What had gone wrong? I asked myself those questions over and over. One minute he was saving my life. The next he was avoiding me. Why? What made such a huge difference in such a short time? I hadn't seen Jake as fickle or feckless. In fact, he was just the opposite.

Maybe he had felt responsible only as long as I was in danger. I understood responsibility like that. I felt it myself for my patients, but I moved on after they were well again. Maybe now that the danger to me was gone, he no longer felt compelled to help me. Now he could let his real feelings show, which is to say, his lack of feelings. By the end of the day, I decided I had to leave the farm if Jake continued as he was. I couldn't deal with the continuing disappointment and hurt.

But, I tried to tell myself, this coolness on his part was a good thing. After all, I couldn't marry him. He wasn't a believer. If he pulled back, then I didn't have to. I might be hurt and upset, but I was being forced to act appropriately.

And there was no reason I should be surprised at his withdrawal. He had told me repeatedly that he wouldn't love me. It wasn't his fault that I didn't believe him.

I should never have declared my feelings. I set myself up for rejection by being too open, too honest. If I'd just kept my mouth shut, we could have at least been friends. Then I'd still have the joy of his company and the warmth of his support.

And that loss of support was what hurt the most. I

had felt a strength flow from him to me time after time, shoring up my flagging spirits. When the Hostetters died, he was there, but it was more than that. He had somehow fortified me and made me stronger than I was. When Trevor died, he had done more than hold me. He had shared my grief. When Ben was revealed as duplicitous, he helped me laugh instead of rage.

As I pulled up to a gas pump, I blinked against the blinding effect of the sun on my watery eyes. I sniffed and cleared my throat. I couldn't have been wrong about the emotional closeness I felt. I just couldn't. I wasn't very experienced with men, but I wasn't an idiot, either. While I loved his kisses and his arms around me, it was the psychological intimacy that I had reveled in most.

I turned the motor off and pulled the keys from the ignition.

Now that intimacy was gone, and I recognized my life as the desert it was. In retrospect, it was amazing to me that I hadn't known just how barren my existence had been before the bombing. Now I knew, and I ached at the thought of a future so bleak.

I climbed out of the car and ran the agency credit card through the slot on the pump. I stuck the nozzle in the car and clamped the handle. The gas started to flow, and I had to blink hard to keep tears from doing the same thing.

Oh, Lord, I need Your help. Paul wrote that when he was weak, then he was strong because of You. I'm weak, Lord. In fact, I feel like I'm dying here. Please, please make me strong.

I give Jake to You. I suspect I'll have to remind myself of this decision every few minutes, so please be patient with me.

The gas clicked off just then, and I returned the nozzle to the pump. I collected the receipt to turn in at the office, knowing Madylyn, the office manager, would be most upset if I forgot it.

The rest of the day passed uneventfully, and I made myself go home in time for dinner. As I drove down the road to the farm, I noticed new construction in the patch of woods beside the cows' pasture. I was surprised since I had assumed that the Zooks owned all the property along the road.

Seeing the beginnings of a new house made me think of a new apartment. I needed to find somewhere else to live. I couldn't spend the rest of my life wondering or worrying about seeing Jake. I'd wither inside.

I just had time to change out of my uniform before we sat down to supper. Jake was conspicuously absent. For once I was glad for the family habit of not talking much at meals. I could barely force myself to swallow, let alone talk. I pushed my food around and drank my sweetened iced tea and pushed my food some more. Finally, Mary reached over my shoulder and took my plate. She patted me gently as she turned away. I blinked back tears of embarrassment that she knew my plight and felt comfort that she cared.

"Rose," Elam said over our dessert of cornstarch pudding, "Esther and I are getting married next Tuesday. We would like it very much if you would come."

"Wow," I said. "You aren't letting much grass grow under your feet."

They both blushed.

"If I can get the time off, I'd love to come to the big event." I was curious to see what an Amish wedding was like.

"Good," Elam said. "Jake knows where. He can bring you."

Sure he can, I thought. He'll love that.

Suddenly I was furious at him for treating me so inconsiderately. I began to simmer and stew. I felt my backbone start to straighten. Who did this man think he was to play havoc with my emotions? How dare he dump me!

I pushed my shoulders back and marched up the stairs, striking each tread with a firm foot. I would not let anyone, least of all Jake, assume control of me or my emotions. I was no one's woman but God's.

I had a full head of steam worked up by the time I reached my rooms. I all but stomped over to the window and stared outside, daring the dark to make me depressed. As I looked, a green van pulled into the drive.

A great wave of grief immediately overwhelmed me. I stood in my darkened room and stared out the window as Jake appeared from the other side of the van and rolled down the sidewalk. I imagined his black eyes laughing into mine. I heard him call me Tiger. I remembered his strong arms holding me. I felt his broad chest beneath my cheek. By the time he disappeared from view under the overhang of the front porch, all my anger had dissipated and I was an emotional wreck once again.

Oh, Lord, I'm dying inside. I imagined myself picking up a valuable gift and handing it to Jesus. *I give Jake back to You. Hold him for me. And hold me, too. Please. Lest I die.*

Sam and Becky got married Saturday afternoon in Pastor Adam's office. It was a bittersweet occasion in many ways.

Becky looked very pretty in a new creamy dress. Her hair hung long down her back, and she wore baby's breath in a circlet on her head. She held a small nosegay of pink rosebuds and baby's breath.

"Aren't they beautiful?" she asked, holding her flowers up for me to smell. "Lauren got them for me."

"You're beautiful, Becky," I said.

She blushed shyly. "Lauren says the baby's breath is for Trevor." Tears suddenly rimmed her eyes and I had to blink too. I hugged her hard.

Jake was Sam's best man.

"After all, you're the first guy I met in Pennsylvania. You even let me sleep on your sofa for most of the past two weeks." He laughed. "But I've got to admit that I like the bed in our new apartment more." Since Wednesday he'd been sleeping in the little furnished apartment they had found over a store on 340.

"We're staying here in Bird-in-Hand for now," Sam said. "Because of Trevor. I'll find work somewhere. God will provide."

The service was short, but the vows given had been sown in love and grown in pain. The radiant looks on both of the young faces made me want to cry, especially since every time I looked at the couple, I saw Jake sitting just beyond Sam.

We ate a celebratory meal at Pastor Adam's home, his wife Mindy serving us with a smile. She had gone out of her way to make the meal special, using her best china and silver, decorating the place with lovely flowers. Becky was delighted, and her smile never dimmed, even when she talked about Trevor, which was often.

Jake did his best to make certain he was never alone with me. He talked animatedly with Davy and Lauren, but with me he was cool and distant and painfully polite.

"Jake," I said, the one time I found myself beside him with no one else close by. "Tell me what's wrong."

He looked at me coolly and with feigned surprise. "What makes you think there's anything wrong? I thought the service went very nicely." And he wheeled away.

"What gives with Jake?" Lauren asked me under cover of the wedding cake being cut.

I shook my head and shrugged. "I don't know," I managed to whisper.

"I'm sorry." She squeezed my hand. "We had great hopes for you two."

It was all I could do not to say, "Me, too."

Amid hugs and best wishes, Sam and Becky left for two nights at the lovely Hershey Hotel up in Hershey,

Pennsylvania, a gift from the couple who had brought them both to Christ.

"Enjoy it, Becky," I whispered as I hugged her. "It's so elegant and beautiful. That is, if you can take your eyes off Sam long enough to look around."

"I'll look," she promised. "Just for you. And thank you for all you did for Trevor and me, Rose. You'll never know what your friendship means to me."

I left soon after the newlyweds, climbing into my car alone and going back to the farm. I spent the evening trying to read, trying to watch TV, trying to do some needlepoint. The only thing I seemed capable of doing effectively was pitying myself.

My beeper sounded at 2 A.M. I fell out of bed and scrambled into some clothes. I sped to the fire hall, being careful to watch for Amishmen on scooters also responding. I slotted my car into a parking spot behind the fire hall at the same time as Harry. We climbed into the ambulance and went to the nightmare.

By the time I returned to the farm, I was numb. I climbed wearily out of the car and walked to the house. The quiet and peace of this place were exactly what I needed to restore my spirit. I leaned against the wall at the bottom of my stairs, trying to get the energy to climb them. I laid my head against the wall and closed my eyes.

Lord, I have no resources left. You have to be there for me. You have to.

"Rose?"

I opened my eyes and saw Jake coming through his doorway. I didn't even have the energy to react.

"Are you okay?" His voice was soft and rich with the concern I used to hear in it.

I shook my head. "It was terrible. Everything I hate in a call. Kids drinking. Innocent people killed. Waste." I slid down until I sat on my third step. I rested my head on my knees. "Terrible, terrible waste."

Jake wheeled up until his chair made a *T* with my knees. "Tell me about it, Tiger."

"Some kids were drinking and weaving all over the roads. A local cop saw them and drove up behind them with his lights flashing. The kids took off. The cop wisely did not pursue them. He didn't want to cause an accident. There was one anyway. The kids came around a curve at high speed and there was a buggy. They ran into it and then into the tree just beyond it. The couple in the buggy was killed and so were three of the four kids in the car. So was the horse. The only survivor was a boy who panicked and ran. They found him about a mile from the scene, curled in a ball beside the road, crying like a baby."

"Rose!" Jake looked at me, appalled.

I smiled wearily back. "Things aren't usually this bad. Tonight's an exception. It was a job for the coroner, not us."

We sat in silence for several minutes, not touching physically, but I felt the emotional strength and warmth, the oneness, the passing of energy from him to me.

"Thanks, Jake," I whispered. "You're a special guy." And I laid a hand on his forearm.

He started to raise his other hand like he would cover mine, but he stopped after moving mere inches. His hand fell, and in an instant I felt that barrier rise between us again. Gone was the man who had cared enough to wait up until I came back, and the distant stranger of the past week was back.

"I'm glad you're fine," he said in a chilly voice. With a curt nod, he turned and wheeled into his rooms, his door snapping shut with a finality that congealed my blood.

Seventeen

I ended up not attending Elam and Esther's wedding. My supervisor, understandably but disappointingly, wasn't willing to give me any time off after my recent hiatus. I had mixed feelings about missing the great event. Much as I wanted to be there for Esther, I was just as glad to avoid Jake. That click of the door early Sunday morning had shattered something inside me.

Tuesday morning while everyone else was at the wedding, I had a patient to visit not too far from the farm. I drove down our road past the new construction in the woods. I glanced at it, thinking that the builders were making astonishing progress. It was like watching a barn raising, given the speed with which the project was developing.

As I looked, a familiar figure with light hair walked

across what would someday be a front yard. I stared, surprised and pleased, as Sam disappeared around the far side of the rapidly appearing house. I smiled to myself as I drove on. Someone's story was ending well, I thought, even if mine wasn't.

It was late in the day when I stopped at the supermarket at the junction of 340 and Business Route 30 for some sodas and snack crackers to replenish the stash I kept in my room. I turned down one aisle and bumped into a dusty, work-weary Sam.

"Hey, guy," I said, "I saw you on the job site today. Congratulations!"

He pumped his fist in the air and grinned. "Isn't it great? And Becky got a job at the outlet mall." He grabbed at the loaf of bread that was sliding off his load of purchases. "Soon we'll be able to get a car for her." He leaned in close. "Then I won't have to stop at the store anymore. I hate the store, any store."

"Spoken like a man." I grabbed the frozen orange juice that was sliding from beneath his arm. I slipped it into his jacket pocket. "They have carts here, you know."

He grinned sheepishly. I shook my head at him and said in mock disgust, "Guys! Just don't forget this juice at the checkout or they'll take us both away."

Sam nodded his thanks. "I hear they took your guy away and that he's now in jail."

"And what a relief that is!"

"I'll just bet." Suddenly Sam looked shy, even blushing slightly. "The Hershey Hotel is really nice."

I was delighted at his embarrassment. "Isn't it beautiful?"

"Almost too beautiful for us," he said. "We felt funny just walking around, let alone eating in the dining room and all."

I could imagine how the opulence affected a pair of country kids. "But it was fun for a special time, wasn't it?"

He grinned. "It was great." I didn't think he meant just the hotel.

He started for the checkout counter, then turned and called over his shoulder, "Stop at the house sometime. I know you drive by it a lot." I thought he meant his apartment at first. "It's going to be a big rancher with wide halls and specific-height counters and stuff, all designed just for Jake." He shook his head. "It's going to be something special."

I stared at his retreating back as my new heart wound bled fresh blood.

The new house was Jake's.

And he'd never told me about it. He'd never once indicated he had something as momentous as a specially designed house breaking ground. He'd always sounded as if he meant to live forever in the grossdawdy haus.

Of course I was glad he was moving out on his own. After all, I'd lectured him about being dependent often enough.

But a house with never even a whisper? Nothing could have told me more clearly where I stood with him.

At the checkout I picked up all the local newspapers I could find regardless of date. I grabbed a *New Era*, an *Intelligencer Journal*, and a *Pennysaver*. Tonight I would read all the rental ads and begin searching for that new apartment.

As I struggled against a breeze and full arms to open my passenger side car door, Pastor Adam and Mindy pulled in next to me.

"Here, let me," Pastor Adam said as he scrambled to help. He pulled the door open and I dumped my newspapers and bag onto the seat.

"Thanks. I had visions of the papers slipping free and carpeting the parking lot."

"You look tired," he said. "Hard day?"

More than he knew. "Every day is tiring, I guess. I think I need to get a heavier concealer stick for the circles under my eyes." I smiled to show I was all right.

"One good thing," Pastor Adam said. "Your friend Jake is a wonder."

"He is," I said, not quite a statement, not quite a question.

"He hasn't missed a morning since we began our Bible study over a week ago. Six-thirty comes and there's Jake. He is hungry for the things of God."

If Sam's revelation about the house had jarred me, this news knocked me to the canvas.

"Jake's meeting with you?" My voice squeaked.

"Whoops," Pastor Adam said. "I hope I'm not giving away a secret."

"No, no," I hurried to say. "I just didn't realize it was every day." Or any day.

"I love it when a man comes to Christ and then wants desperately to grow. He's been a true pleasure."

"Excuse me, you two," called Mindy apologetically. "I hate to interrupt, but we're going to be late, Adam, if we don't get a move on."

"Yes, dear," he said like a henpecked husband, but he smiled at his wife with that you're-something-special look Jake used to give me. With a nod in my direction, he and Mindy disappeared into the store, his arm casually draped around her waist.

I slowly drove home in the dark of the early winter evening feeling very alone, more alone than I'd ever felt in my whole lonely life. It seemed that every time I thought I couldn't feel worse, something happened and I felt worse.

As I went down the road, I was drawn to Jake's new house. I slowed as I passed it, peering through the darkness, trying to assess the day's progress. I noticed a crushed-stone drive, and on impulse I turned in. The beams of my car lights illuminated the wooden frame of the house. It sprawled in a great *U* with interesting roof angles and lots of windows.

With a deep sigh I imagined waking up and looking out those windows at the trees with their summer canopies in place, planting a garden and filling the house with flowers clipped fresh each morning, swinging on one of those wooden swings hanging from a great tree. I imagined having a breakfast picnic on the back deck and sitting in the living room in winter before a roaring fire. And I imagined it all with Jake beside me, cheering me on, holding me tight, loving me.

Lord, I love him. I know he doesn't love me, but I love him. I do. I'm glad he'll have this beautiful house, but, oh, Lord, help me deal with the fact that I won't live in it with him.

Since the family was still at the wedding celebration, I went home to an empty house. I raided the refrigerator and carried my food up to my rooms. I ate watching the evening news and *Jeopardy.* The hours until bedtime stretched endlessly before me. I pulled out the newspapers I'd gotten and studied them for possible rentals.

It's hard to find a place in a town with no apartment complexes, and I wanted to stay here because of the proximity to the ambulance. I wanted to stay with Harry and Alice and all the others. It looked like they were going to continue to be the closest thing I had to family. Except for Mom, of course.

I ran my hands through my hair. There had to be someplace I could live. I wasn't fussy. Look where I'd lived before the farm. I could live in a place like that again. Couldn't I?

I was feeling almost desperate when I heard Jake drive in. I resisted the urge to look out my window and watch him from afar, but I listened closely until I heard the door downstairs open and close. He was home.

I wanted to talk to him so much I could taste the

words, to ask him about the house and his secretiveness. I wanted to know what had led him to visit Pastor Adam every morning, to know why he hadn't told me he'd become a believer.

I wanted to punch him out and hug him hard.

First my fingers tapped restlessly on my thighs. Then my foot started bouncing up and down. Soon both feet were twitching and I could hardly stay in my chair. When I began pacing, my strides were long, fueled by anger and anxiety. I marched to the top of the steps and stared down into the darkened house. I marched back into my living room and told myself to stay there. I was going to make a fool of myself.

"So what else is new?"

Finally I just shrugged, stalked downstairs, and knocked on Jake's inside door.

"Come in."

I opened the door and walked to the living room. He was sitting on his leather sofa, the one that was so deep my feet didn't touch the ground. He was leaning against the arm, a pillow behind him, his legs stretched out along the cushions.

"Hello, Jake." I said uncertainly from the doorway.

He looked at me without speaking for a minute. "Hello, Rose."

I felt foolish. I shouldn't have come down. I should just leave. He didn't want me here. I walked over and sat in the rocker by the sofa. That way he wouldn't have to look up to talk to me.

I wanted to kick myself for that move. I was being *nice* even in extremity.

"I wanted to tell you that I'm looking for an apartment." I made my voice as cool as I could as I looked at a spot on the wall beyond his head. "The rooms will be vacant soon."

He said nothing, just continued to look at me.

I rubbed my sweating hands over my jeans and raised my chin to show I wasn't affected by him. "I thought you ought to know."

He nodded. "Thank you. That was kind of you."

So formal. You'd have thought we were practicing to make Miss Manners proud. How did this happen to us? How did we go from understanding each other's minds to not even speaking naturally?

"I understand you'll be moving soon too." Now I looked at my lap as I spoke, trying to hide my hurt.

"Yes." He cleared his throat. Nerves? I hoped so. Why should I be the only one uncomfortable here? "Elam and Esther will live in the addition." He swept an arm to indicate the rooms. "We'll make it one apartment again instead of two like it is now."

"Oh. That makes sense."

"Um. The plans have been in the works for a long time, really since soon after my accident. It's Father's idea. He says Elam will get the farm, but I'll get this special house." He looked at me, one side of his mouth quirked. "But don't worry. I won't stay dependent. I plan to pay him back as soon as I'm finished with school, as

344

soon as I'm working."

I managed a small smile in return. "Will he let you?"

Jake shrugged. "Who knows? But that's not the issue, is it?"

I shook my head. "No, it's not."

We were silent a minute. Then Jake said, "The wedding suddenly made it urgent to carry out the building project immediately."

"When will your house be ready?"

"In a month or so. They have extra men working on the project now that these rooms are needed."

I thought for a moment. "So I would have had to move even if I hadn't decided to on my own," I said, angry that my voice quivered, then just angry.

"Yes."

"I suppose someone would have gotten around to telling me before I found myself on the street?"

He looked at me, startled by the sudden tartness of my voice. "Of course."

I stood up and stared down at him. "When, Jake?" I was furious at him. "The day before I had to go? Or would you have kept on avoiding me up until Elam and Esther started moving their furniture in?"

"Now, Rose." He held up a placating hand.

"Don't *now Rose* me! Even Ben was more considerate than you! He screamed and shouted, but at least he talked!" I pointed a finger at him. "You, on the other hand, are an inconsiderate ingrate! Why, you've even come to Christ and you never told me! How could you!

You know what that meant to me!" By now I was pacing in my agitation.

Jake looked at me with a wry smile. "I bet you're the only Christian to become mad at someone because he's become a believer, too."

I looked at him, appalled that he would joke while I was dying. "How dare you mock me!"

He blinked, startled. "Rose, I'd never mock you. Never in a million years."

"How would I know that?" My voice was shaking again. "You've made a mockery of what I thought was a special friendship. Why not mock me too? Good old Rose the Evangelist. Who cares about her?"

He closed his eyes and lowered his head as if in pain. "Rose, don't do this to me." He spoke in a whisper.

"Don't do what to you?" I yelled. "Who's doing what to you? I'm the one." I punched him in the arm. "I'm the one!" I punched him again. "I'm dying here, and you say don't do it to you?" I raised my fist again though I was having trouble seeing my target through my tears. I struck out feebly.

He grabbed my fist and pulled. Suddenly I was trapped against his chest by the steel bands of his arms.

"Stop it, Rose." His voice was soft and full of that enveloping warmth.

"Stop what?" I raised hot eyes to his face. "Stop beating on you? Stop yelling at you? Or stop loving you?"

Jake groaned from deep in his soul. "Oh, God, I can't do it."

"Are you praying or blaspheming?" I demanded. "If you're swearing, I'm telling Pastor Adam."

I felt a laugh rumble deep in his chest. I glared at him. "Don't you dare laugh at me, Jake Zook. Don't you dare!" Unfortunately, the last came out in a wobbly whisper.

"Oh, Rosie," Jake said in a soft voice. He reached out and took my glasses from my nose. He dropped them on the floor.

"Jake?"

His kiss was that of a man who had been without water for too long and I was the refreshing spring. I melted against him and let him drink.

When we broke free, I lay my head on his chest in utter despair. Now I'd have to go through all that agony of separation all over again. I felt his hand beneath my chin lifting my face toward his.

"Don't, Jake," I pleaded. "I can't stand the pain."

"Kissing me's that bad?"

I pushed myself away from him, dropping to my knees beside the sofa. "You know what I mean."

He looked at me with an intensity that took my breath. "When I saw Peter Hostetter chasing you with that pipe raised, my heart stopped beating," he said. "I knew I'd put myself in your place if I could. I knew I'd die if you did."

This time it was my heart that stopped beating.

He put his hand over mine and held tightly. "All I kept thinking was, 'God, save her! God, save her!' And then I thought, why should He? I'd been pushing Him away for years, and suddenly I'm screaming for Him, and He should come? I was shoving my gun out the window when it struck me that you can't pick the parts of God you like and discard the others. I couldn't reject His free forgiveness and accept His help in need. God is a whole."

My spirit leaped to hear him talk in this manner. "I've always thought God is like a string of pearls," I said.

He looked at me, eyebrow raised.

"Now think about it before you scoff," I said. "God is a whole, like you said, like the string of pearls. We try to break Him down so we can understand Him. It's like each pearl is an attribute of God. One is His love, one is His grace, one is His holiness, one is His forgiveness. While there's value in the individual pearl, the individual attribute, it's the whole string that's invaluable. It's the entirety of God that is the wonder."

Jake nodded. "Yes, the entirety! As I was thinking about this new idea, at least new to me, I looked at Peter Hostetter, by now lying on the ground. Here was a man who tried to take a part of something precious and in doing so lost the real value. He wanted not the people of his family, but the family wealth. He wanted to pick and choose when he had no right to make the choice. Suddenly I saw myself in him."

I made an automatic move of disclaimer.

He held up a hand. "I wanted to pick and choose where I had no right to do so either. I wanted to take the parts of God I liked, and then only when I needed them. That's when I knew I had to talk to Pastor Adam."

He became quiet, so I prompted him. "So you called him?"

He nodded. "By the time I went to see him, I'd already told God that I accepted his free forgiveness in Christ." He looked at me. "It was amazing to me the peace that came with my decision."

I grinned at him, joy bubbling from my heart. "Oh, Jake!" I gave him a quick, fierce hug. "You have no idea what it means to me that you're a believer." I looked up at the ceiling. "Thank You, God," I breathed. "Thank You!"

"I should have told you sooner, back when it happened," Jake said. "I'm sorry."

"How could you tell me? You weren't speaking to me." I took a deep breath and looked at him, the turmoil of my emotions flashing across my face. "Which brings us to our next point of discussion. Why, Jake? Why weren't you speaking to me?"

He didn't answer. He just reached out and brushed at a strand of my hair, then rested his hand briefly on my cheek. "I never knew," he said, "that one person could cause such unbelievable pleasure and pain."

When he went to move his hand, I grabbed and held it in place. The feel of his palm on my skin made me weepy.

"What do you mean, pleasure and pain?" I asked, though I knew. I knew full well.

He smiled and rubbed his thumb back and forth across my jaw. "The pleasure's easy. I've never enjoyed being with anyone as I enjoy being with you. You are my light and my joy." His eyes were dark and luminous, and I saw in them a yearning that I knew was reflected in mine.

"And the pain?"

He didn't answer. Instead he said, "What am I to do with you, Rosie?"

I didn't hesitate for a second. "Marry me, Jake." I leaned forward and stared into his eyes. "Marry me."

I felt him jerk as though shot and begin to pull his hand away.

"Rosie, please," he whispered, looking at me with anguish.

I wrapped both my hands about his and held it to my heart. "Jake, I love you."

He made a sound deep in his throat, a wounded groan, but he said nothing.

"And you love me," I informed him, staring at him, willing him to agree. He just looked at me. "I know you do. I know it! I can see it in the way you look at me, the way you talk to me, the way you touch me, and even," I said with sudden insight, "in the way you've avoided me." I lay my head on his chest and whispered, "Jake, you love me."

Again he groaned, and his other hand threaded itself through my hair, pressing me against him.

"Marry me, Jake," I whispered to his heart. "Please.

I shall die if you won't."

When he said nothing, I raised up and looked at him. Tears sat in his eyes.

"Rosie," he whispered. "Look at me!" He stared at his inert legs.

"So?" I said, and he closed his eyes against my foolishness. "Jake, you're not legs and bladder and spinal cord. You're heart and mind and spirit. You're creativity and curiosity and German stubbornness. And I love you, Jake, with all my heart. I always will, no matter what you think is best for me, for us, no matter how noble you want to be. I don't want to be just your friend, just your sister in Christ. I want to be your wife, to love you wholly, to struggle with you and rejoice with you and be loved by you."

I looked at his closed eyes, the tear running down his cheek. I leaned over and kissed the tear away. He jumped as though burned.

"I'm not going away," I said. "I'm not."

He opened his eyes and looked at me. "Tiger, you're killing me here."

I shut my eyes briefly as protection against the pain and emotion I saw there, then forced them open to look at him. "I know."

Suddenly he moved, lifting himself against the back of the sofa, opening up an area of the cushion. He patted it. "Sit here. Get off your knees."

I got up and sat facing him, hip to hip. I was momentarily distracted by the feel of him pressed against me; he couldn't feel me.

"What's wrong with my being on my knees?" I asked. "I don't mind begging, you know."

"Woman, you appall me," he said, looking genuinely aggrieved. "Where's your self-respect?"

I slipped to my knees again, my hands folded in supplication. "I have none where you're concerned."

He winced, closed his eyes, and turned away. I reached out and smoothed the frown lines between his eyes, lines he refused to let be soothed. I rested my head on his chest again and was moved to the point of tears when his hand came once again to lace itself in my hair.

Father, give me courage! And give him grace!

I took my seat on the sofa again and said, my tone tart, "Besides, you have more than enough pride for both of us."

He looked surprised, then grinned crookedly and didn't deny the charge.

"Jake, look at me."

His eyes played hide-and-seek with mine before they settled down. I looked straight into him.

"Tell me you don't love me," I whispered. "Look me in the eyes and tell me."

"I have nothing to give you," he said, his voice cracking. "Only brokenness."

I smiled. "But, my love, you've already given me wholeness. You've made me laugh and cry and feel more alive than ever in my life. So we'll never play tennis together or go skiing. Big deal. But we're good together,

Jake. You know it and so do I. The more I pray about us, the more my heart's drawn to you. The whole time you weren't speaking to me, I prayed and prayed and wanted you more than ever. God and I know you're the man for me. We're just waiting for you to agree."

Suddenly he reached for me, wrapping both his strong arms about me, pressing me to his chest. "Rosie, Rosie, you win. You're right. I love you so much my teeth ache. I think of you all day and dream of you all night, and how can I ask you to take less than you deserve?"

I pulled back and looked at him. "How about asking me to take what I *want?*"

"And you want me?" His voice was incredulous.

"With all my heart."

He pulled me to him again, and this time he kissed me as I'd dreamed he would, with enough passion to leave me weak all over.

When I'd finally gotten my breath back, I rested with my cheek against his chest, my head in the hollow of his shoulder. "Tell me," I said. "Say it again. I want to hear it. I need to hear it."

I felt as much as heard the rumble of laughter and smiled too.

"I love you, Tiger. I love you with all my heart. Marry me?"

I lifted my head, looked at him, and said, "How soon?"

Epilogue

Three years later

IT WAS A LOVELY MAY MORNING AS I SAT OUT ON THE BACK deck with a cup of tea in my hand and a forbidden doughnut on the table tempting me.

"Jake, come take that away before I eat it," I called to my husband. "I weigh enough to sink the *Titanic* as it is."

Laughing, Jake wheeled to the table and moved the doughnut out of my reach. He continued around the table to me.

"You look beautiful, Tiger," he said, resting his hand on my very pregnant middle. His compliment was rewarded with a swift kick from his gestating offspring.

I leaned my head back and smiled up at the trees with their summer canopies growing fuller daily. "Did you know I dreamed of sitting here with you?" I looked at him, dressed today in a white shirt and tie, dress pants and shoes. "When I found out this was your house being built, I stopped in the driveway one night on the way home from work and dreamed of sitting on the deck with you for a breakfast picnic just like this."

"Was that before or after you proposed?" His black eyes gleamed, and the sun struck glints on his dark hair.

"You can tease me all you want about proposing," I said with a grin, "but one of us had to have some common sense."

He picked up my hand and kissed it. "I'm glad you were so smart. I wouldn't have missed this ride for the world."

We had waited six months from the night I proposed before we married. During that time, Jake lived in this wonderful house, Elam and Esther moved into the grossdawdy haus, and I roomed with Annie Stoltzfus in what proved to be a mutually beneficial arrangement. To this day I love Annie like my own mother, and I mourned deeply when she went to be with the Lord several months ago.

Elam and Esther and their two babies still lived in the grossdawdy haus, but it wouldn't be long before they moved into the main house, and John and Mary moved into the addition. Esther was pregnant again, and needed living space would be the deciding factor.

Becky and Sam had sought us out last Sunday at church, and I guessed from the electric joy pulsing from them what they wanted to tell us. They would be having a wonderful Christmas present, and Becky glowed at the prospect of being a mother again. I had been so pleased that they waited to have a baby. Now their marriage was stable, Sam was foreman on a construction crew and their faith was more vibrant than ever.

We had gone to Texas twice to visit Davy and Lauren. I wanted them to move to Pennsylvania, but some wishes just don't get granted. Their year-old daughter Carrie was the image of Lauren and as sweet as she could be.

If there was any difficulty in Jake's and my marriage, it would be my occasional resentment of The Chair. When I was feeling its limitations, it became uppermost in my mind. I realized that Jake hadn't been completely wrong when he hesitated to marry me.

"How am I supposed to hug someone in a chair?" I asked through tears one day. "Just answer me that!"

Jake looked at me with sad eyes, and I immediately felt terrible, just as I did anytime I raged against the chair. If it was terrible to me, I knew it was many times worse for him.

I fell on my knees and leaned into him. "I'm sorry." I wrapped my arms around his middle and put my head on his chest. I straightened immediately and sighed. "See? I've got your belt buckle in my chin!"

"I guess the great blessing of the chair is that dealing with it keeps both of us in prayer," Jake said as he rubbed my chin. "Just don't let it come between us,

Tiger. I couldn't stand that."

He wheeled himself to the sofa and, using his board, slid himself onto it. He lay down and held out his arms.

I fell into them, and he hugged me quietly.

Finally I levered myself up on an elbow. "I have no regrets, Jake. You need to know that. I'd marry you all over again in an instant. All that the chair is is frustration. You, on the other hand, are my life."

But today as I sat at the table on the deck with the warm spring sun shining on us, I had only happy thoughts. I absently patted the little fiend who was kicking me to death internally and with impunity as contentment flooded through me.

"It's time, Tiger."

I nodded and pulled myself upright. It was not an easy feat. I straightened my voluminous dress and picked up my purse, then I walked to my husband.

"I'm so proud of you, sweetheart. This is a big day for a little Amish boy."

He swept his arm around my waist and pulled me to his lap.

"You'll be sorry," I said. "Especially when I try to get up."

He nuzzled my neck. "Never will I be sorry about you."

The front doorbell rang and a voice called, "Anybody home?"

"On the back deck, Mom," called Jake as I struggled to get to my feet. He held me tight. "Stay put, Tiger. It's okay if she sees you in my lap. She knows I love you."

I glanced at my belly. "It'd be hard to miss."

My mother walked onto the deck and groaned. "Look at you two. Smoldering looks at nine o'clock in the morning." Then her face brightened. "Oh, good. A doughnut."

"I saved it for you," Jake said as he helped me to my feet. "Now we've got to get a move on or we'll be late. I don't want to miss my first graduation ceremony."

Wiping powdered sugar from her chin, Mom said, "I'm proud of you, Jake. Just think: a college graduate and a schoolteacher. And someday maybe a principal."

Jake and I looked at each other and grinned. Mom's dreams might come true, but right now graduating and teaching were enough.

"And you," she said, pointing her finger at me. I looked at the lethal nail and hoped she wouldn't start poking me. I didn't think either the baby or I could survive. "At least you're not chasing ambulances all over the place anymore."

"I don't chase ambulances, Mom. Lawyers do that. I ride in them. And I'll be back riding in a couple of months. I may have given up my day job to stay home with the baby, but I'm not giving up the ambulance. I'd miss Harry too much."

"Ah yes, Harry," Mom said. "Such a nice man. Maybe you should stay with the ambulance after all. Those poor hurting people will need you."

Jake and I looked at each other and rolled our eyes.

Harry had been a widower for a year and a half, and recently Mom had become very curious about him. Harry didn't seem to return the favor, not that that stopped Mom.

"Into the van, girls," Jake said, shooing us toward the garage. He patted my tummy. "All three of you."

I looked at Jake and my heart swelled with love and pride. My graduate. My friend. My husband.

Dear Reader,

When Jake and Rose struggle with various aspects of forgiveness, I think they struggle with a concept that gives
many of us trouble.

For those considering the claims of Christ, the idea
that forgiveness is free, that salvation can't be earned,
seems almost un-American. We are a nation of folks who
historically have made their own way. We are especially
proud of those who pull themselves up by their own
bootstraps.

But the Bible says clearly that God's forgiveness is a
gift. No bootstraps wanted or allowed here.

And often those of us who believe have just as much
trouble accepting forgiveness. We get caught, like Rose,
in feeling we must forgive ourselves.

I received a note one time from a young woman
who had come to hear me speak.

"I believe God forgave me for the terrible thing I did,
but I can't forgive myself," she wrote. "Help me please.
Give me some hope."

"Oh, God," I prayed. "What in the world do I say to
her?"

As I thought and prayed, I came to three conclu-
sions:

1. God doesn't ever ask us to forgive ourselves. God
will forgive us and we are asked to forgive each other,
but never does the Bible ask us to forgive ourselves. I'm
not sure what that means, but if forgiving ourselves were

something we had to do, wouldn't God have told us?

2. All sin is an offense to God. We tend to think that the things we have done that have been blatantly wrong or that have caused others hurt are the worst anyone has ever done. Not true. And even if it were true, *all* sin—big stuff and little stuff—is offensive to a perfect God.

3. If we say we have to forgive ourselves, are we saying Jesus didn't do enough when He died for us? We need to add to it? What a scary idea that we can elevate ourselves to the level of Christ. Salvation and the forgiveness that comes with it are "not a reward for the good things we have done, so none of us can boast about it."

God chooses to give forgiveness as a gift. All we need to choose to do is accept that God's great gift is enough.

Gayle Roper

You can write to Gayle:
c/o Palisades•P.O. Box 1720•Sisters, Oregon 97759

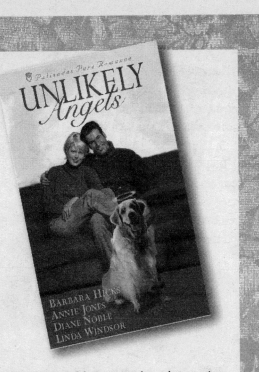

This anthology of four stories shows love getting
an unexpected hand. In *Cupid's Chase*, Reid and
Carina try to sabotage the romance between his
mother and her father. A greyhound helps a pro-
fessor decide if love deserves a second chance in
Fool Me Twice. Two retirees take on more than
they bargained for in *Birds of a Feather*. And in *A
Season for Love*, a woman returns to her childhood
home to find a surprising love.

Available in October! At a bookstore near you.
ISBN 1-57673-589-3

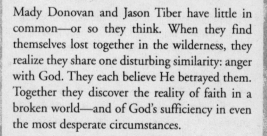